DATE DUE

A Guide to Pseudonyms on American Records, 1892–1942

A Guide to Pseudonyms on American Records, 1892–1942

Compiled by
Allan Sutton

Greenwood Press
Westport, Connecticut • London

Library of Congress Cataloging-in-Publication Data

Sutton, Allan.
A Guide to pseudonyms on American records, 1892-1942 / Allan
Sutton.
p. cm.
Includes bibliographical references and index.
ISBN 0-313-29060-1
1. Sound recordings—United States. 2. Anonyms and pseudonyms.
I. Title.
ML158.S9   1993
780'.92'2—dc20   93-4768

British Library Cataloguing in Publication Data is available.

Library of Congress Catalog Card Number: 93-4768
ISBN: 0-313-29060-1

First published in 1993

Greenwood Press, 88 Post Road West, Westport, CT 06881
An imprint of Greenwood Publishing Group, Inc.

Printed in the United States of America

The paper used in this book complies with the
Permanent Paper Standard issued by the National
Information Standards Organization (Z39.48-1984).

10 9 8 7 6 5 4 3 2 1

To Jill,
for making this
(and so many other
good things) possible.

Contents

Preface

This project began several years ago in response to the need for a single easily accessible listing of artist pseudonyms employed during the early years of the American recording industry. Many researchers have worked to unmask fictitious names on early recordings, but their efforts have been widely scattered, often in difficult-to-obtain specialist publications.

In the course of compiling this work, I began to build a database correlating matrix numbers of pseudonymous with non-pseudonymous issues. Eventually, this database revealed a substantial number of previously unknown pseudonyms, as well as revealing errors in earlier works. I first made some of this material available in 1991 through a self-published pamphlet entitled *A.K.A.: Pseudonyms on American Records*. Response was very positive, resulting in many of the additions and corrections incorporated within the present work.

I have expanded my initial effort to include jazz, blues, gospel, and country music performers in addition to mainstream popular and classical artists. New listings of private recordings, radio transcriptions, and foreign issues from domestic masters reveal exactly how widespread the use of fictitious names became in the early years of the recording industry.

As in any compilation of this type, errors and omissions are inevitable. Documented additions and corrections are invited and will be duly acknowledged in future editions.

Acknowledgments

I offer special thanks to Gilbert Louey (Hanover, PA) for allowing access to his personal collection and sales stock and for his generous donation of reconstructed catalog listings. Gil's interest and support had much to do with my decision to pursue this and other projects.

Thanks are also due to the following individuals who supplied additions and corrections to the earlier work:

Peter Burgis (Sound Archivist, National Library, Canberra, Australia) for information on Australian-born performers; Frederick Crane (Iowa City, IA) for his investigation of New York Recording Laboratories products; Daniel Langan (New York) for updating and correcting many of the 1920's minor-label listings; and William Shaman (Bemidji, MN) for sharing his research of concert performers on minor labels, as well as his encouragement and advice.

The late George Blacker supplied partial copies of the original Starr Piano Company (Gennett) and Plaza Music Company/American Record Corporation (Banner) ledgers. Much of the material on early group personnels was provided by the late Jim Walsh, who generously shared material from his early articles and engaged in ongoing correspondence through the mid-1970's.

Thanks also to the staffs of the Columbia Broadcasting System (New York), Radio Corporation of America (New York), Edison National Historic Site (Orange, NJ), Library of Congress (Washington, DC), and Enoch Pratt Free Library (Baltimore, MD), for their assistance in the earliest stages of this project.

Introduction

Historical Perspective

When Emilio de Gogorza's first records appeared late in the last century, the phonograph was still viewed as a crude toy scarcely suited to capture the art of a serious vocalist. De Gogorza may have concurred, for many of his early efforts (and those of his contemporary, de Bassini) appeared not under his own name, but rather under an imaginative group of pseudonyms. It was the beginning of a practice that would become widespread in the recording industry.

Artist pseudonym use was fairly limited before 1910. Anonymous releases were the norm when a performer or manufacturer felt the need to mask identity. Thousands of department store, mail order, and private-label issues bearing only generic artist descriptions were produced by Columbia, the International Record Company, Leeds & Catlin, Zon-O-Phone, and other early manufacturers. To further guarantee anonymity, Columbia devised a method of effacing spoken introductions from its off-brand pressings, and the American Record Company recorded alternate masters for off-brand release which retained the spoken announcements but omitted any mention of performer.

By 1910-1912, new manufacturers were entering the American record market. Prevented from producing laterally cut discs by the Victor-Columbia patent pool, Phono-Cut, Keen-O-Phone, and Edison slowly created a market for vertically cut discs, paving the way for the later success of Aeolian-Vocalion, Okeh, Pathé, Starr, and other hill-and-dale brands. With the growth of new record companies came a corresponding increase in the use of fictitious artist credits. The market for vertically cut discs was small, and the newcomers, often lacking resources to attract exclusive artists, instead created a fanciful array of pseudonyms to lend an air of exclusiveness to the studio free-lance performers on whom they relied. Ernest L. Stevens, a prolific studio pianist who recorded in the early 1920's as Harry Osborne and Franz Falkenburg, recalled ''I had already made so many piano solos that the Edison Company didn't want people to start thinking I was the only pianist they had...so this is the main reason for the use of fictitious names.'' Harry Pace found the use of fictitious names an easy way to disguise the fact that he had broken his pledge to feature only black talent and was issuing material from the all-white Olympic catalog on his Black Swan label. The aptly named Phantasie Concert Records went so far as to proclaim, in bold type on their labels, that their pseudonymous performers performed ''Exclusively For Phantasie Records;'' peeling away Phantasie's pasted-on labels reveals the Lyric originals (and, in many cases, the true performers' identity) below.

''Name'' artists, under exclusive contract to major labels, occasionally made clandestine visits to competing studios provided that the results were issued under names other than their own, but this was not a common practice and seems to have been avoided entirely by the major labels' highest-paid stars. In several cases, however, well-known concert performers took assumed names when recording popular material on lower-priced series. Red Seal artists de Gogorza, Werrenrath, and Williams can all be found in Victor's black-label popular listings under names other than their own, and Victor even went so far as to print a fictitious photograph of one ''Harry Evans'' to mislead any listener who might notice a striking similarity to Evan Williams' voice. Columbia's Charles Hackett enjoyed limited success as pop singer Edwin Dale in the early 1920's, and Jan Peerce, just embarking on a career as a concert artist, moonlighted as a dance band vocalist under several assumed names in the early 1930's.

Before the early 1920's, pseudonym assignment had been fairly orderly, to the extent that performers like Walter Van Brunt (who was equally popular as Walter Scanlan) or Charles Harrison (who frequently recorded as Hugh Donovan) were nearly as well-known by their pseudonyms as by their own names. That state of affairs came to an end in the early 1920's. Basic patents on lateral-cut disc recording had expired, and new manufacturers flooded the record market. Many brands introduced between 1919 and

1922 were premium-priced lines intended to compete with Victor and Columbia, and many failed during the economic crash of 1921-1922. The success of 50¢ Regal records (introduced by an Emerson subsidiary in 1921) revealed the market for cheaper labels. 50¢ Cameo records appeared in early 1922; Grey Gull, having failed to convince the public that it was a premium brand, cut both price and quality drastically at about the same time. Pathé also introduced its inexpensive Perfect side-line in 1922, and cheap mail-order sets, sold under the National Music Lovers label, appeared in October of that year. By 1924 the market was flooded with dozens of inexpensive dime-store and mail-order brands.

These cheap new labels were often manufactured by the Scranton Button Company, Bridgeport Die & Machine Company, and other independent pressing plants that maintained no studios of their own, drawing instead on masters leased from other producers who were quick to realize the problems that would ensue were the record-buying public to discover, for example, that a 75¢ Paramount record could be had on Oriole or Grey Gull for less than half of that price. Pseudonym use on the cheapest labels, notably National Music Lovers and the Grey Gull-chain brands, became such a chaotic affair that we will probably never know who performed on many releases. It was not uncommon for a single pseudonym to be assigned to four or more performers, and in rare cases the pseudonym did not even accurately reflect the sex of the performer. A further complication is encountered in jazz and dance band releases of the 1920's and early 1930's. Band leaders and contractors often sent hastily recruited pickup units or, in rare instances, competing bands to fulfill their contractual obligations. Even Paul Whiteman, normally a model of respectability, had at least three Ben Selvin sides issued under the Whiteman Orchestra name.

The major manufacturers were slow to realize the appeal of inexpensive labels. Columbia's fifty-cent Harmony and Velvet Tone labels, and the Starr Piano Company's low-priced Champion label appeared in 1925. The Victor Talking Machine Company remained aloof; by the time the company finally introduced its cheaper Bluebird, Electradisk, Sunrise, and Timely Tunes lines in the early 1930's, it had been acquired by the Radio Corporation of America. Fortunately, original recording files still exist for these companies, revealing a wealth of pseudonyms.

The early Depression years saw the demise of many of the cheapest labels and the consolidation of others under a handful of major manufacturers. The success of the inexpensive Bluebird and Decca labels, introduced in 1933 and 1934, respectively, proved that it was possible to feature name-brand talent on bargain-priced records, and the later 1930's saw a dramatic decrease in the use of pseudonyms on commercial releases. Pseudonym use did enjoy a brief revival on radio and private-use transcriptions in the mid-to-late 1930's as early independent transcription producers drew on talent already under exclusive network and record company contracts. By the time of the Petrillo ban in 1942, pseudonym use was relatively rare.

Research Methods

In 1944, pioneer record researcher Jim Walsh published the first major listing of assumed names used on popular discs and cylinders of the pre-Depression era in *Hobbies* magazine. A revised version, published in *Hobbies* in 1962, was expanded to a few hundred listings. Unfortunately, Walsh relied largely on aural identification and anecdotal evidence. Nevertheless, his investigation sparked interest in the subject and provided a firm foundation for the present work. Later researchers, including (but by no means limited to) Tim Brooks, Martin Bryan, Bill Bryant, Dave Cotter, Robert Dixon, John Godrich, Brian Rust, and the late George Blacker have employed more methodical methods in researching pseudonym use. Hundreds of additional pseudonyms have been uncovered while researching this guide; countless others remain to be revealed.

Entries have been carefully verified, and speculative listings are identified as such. A summary of research methods follows.

Original Documentation — Original company documentation still exists for Columbia, Edison, and Victor recording sessions and was consulted during the earliest stages of the project. In addition, partial original documentation remains from the Starr Piano Company (Champion, Gennett, *et al.*) and the Plaza Music Company/American Record Corporation/Brunswick Record Corporation conglomerate (Banner, latter-day Brunswick, Perfect, *et al.*). Although Edison, Starr, and Plaza/ARC/BRC occasionally logged sessions pseudonymously, their original documentation can generally be considered irrefutable.

Master- and Issue-Number Correlation — In the absence of original documentation, listings have been verified by correlating master and/or issue numbers of pseudonymous issues with those of the original non-pseudonymous issues from which they derive. This method has proven indispensable in researching material issued by Federal, Grey Gull, Olympic, the New York Recording Laboratories, Pathé, and other companies for which original files no longer exist. In the final stages of this project, a computerized database was created, allowing quick and positive master-number correlation. As this database expands, it will add greatly to our knowledge of pseudonyms.

Aural Identification — Where ledgers or other source materials no longer exist and master- or catalog-number correlation is impossible, careful comparison by ear (aural identification) has been made. Many early free-lance performers (Arthur Fields, Irving Kaufman, and Jones & Hare among them) possessed such distinctive voices and styles that a single playing is often sufficient to reveal the voice behind the pseudonym. Unfortunately, this method is not reliable for identifying instrumentalists or less-distinctive vocalists, and therefore has been used very cautiously and only as a last resort. However, it is the only method applicable to several manufacturers (notably Grey Gull, Lyraphone, and Pathé) that used pseudonyms freely on their original as well as off-brand releases.

Compilation from Previous Works — A substantial body of research already exists in the jazz, blues, and gospel fields, and it is not my intent to simply republish existing data. Nevertheless, it was felt that the inclusion of performers from those fields was essential to a comprehensive investigation of pseudonym use. A large portion of the jazz and blues listings are based on the work of Rust and Dixon & Godrich, respectively (see *References*). Whenever possible, previously published identifications have been cross-checked against original source material, questionable attributions have been deleted, and corrections or qualifications have been added. Because many older editions of both *Jazz Records* and *Blues and Gospel Records* are still in circulation, errors in those works have been pointed out even though corrections may have been made in subsequent editions. Listings for which no labels are cited are primarily from Walsh's original work and other early research, much of which was based on anecdotal evidence. Because many errors have become apparent in these earlier works, such entries should be considered speculative.

Limitations — Research has been limited to pseudonym use on recordings made in the United States (including foreign issues pressed from American masters) from 1892 until the Petrillo recording ban of August 1, 1942.

ALPHABETICAL LISTINGS
BY PSEUDONYM

Vocalists and Vocal Groups: Domestic Issues

*Pseudonyms appear in **bold type**, followed by artist indentification. Artists who performed under stage names (e.g., Abe Finkelstein, who performed as Arthur Fields) are identified by stage name rather than given name. A list of legal names appears in Appendix I.*

Entries for which no label is given are taken from Walsh's lists and other reasonably reliable sources, but have not been verified and should be considered speculative.

Pseudonyms followed by an asterisk (*) also appear in the foreign-issue listing.

ACME MALE QUARTET = Shannon Four (Pathé and related labels)

ADAMS & CLARK = Frank Luther and Carson Robison; possibly Bob Miller and Barney Burnett (Madison)

ADAMS & CONWAY = Bob Miller and Barney Burnett (Van Dyke)

ADAMS, JOE = Frank Luther (Madison, possibly others)

AEOLIAN MALE QUARTET = Criterion Quartet (Aeolian-Vocalion)

AHERN, JAMES = Vernon Dalhart

ALEXANDER, ALFRED = Henry Burr (Pathé and related labels)

ALIX, MAY = Edmonia Henderson (Silvertone 3521); Edna Hicks (Silvertone 3520); Alberta Hunter (Famous, Harmograph, Paramount, Puritone). Another performer (definitely not Hunter) recorded as May Alix with the Louis Armstrong and Jimmie Noone Orchestras in the late 1920's and early 1930's, but it is not known if this was an actual performer or simply another pseudonym.

ALLEN, EDWARD = Arthur Middleton

ALLEN, GARY = Len Spencer

ALLEN, MACK = Vernon Dalhart (Harmony and related labels)

ALLEN, MARK = Vernon Dalhart (Regal)

ALLEN, MAYBELLE = Edith Johnson (Broadway)

AMERICAN QUARTET (I) = Haydn (Edison Male) Quartet (Berliner, Improved Gram-O-Phone, Lambert cylinders, Victor [including Monarch and other variations], and probably others, 1898-1904)

AMERICAN QUARTET (II) – Original 1909 personnel included John Bieling (tenor), Billy Murray (lead tenor), Steve Porter (baritone), and William F. Hooley (bass). Walter Van Brunt replaced Murray on at least one occasion. John Young replaced Bieling in 1914, and Donald Chalmers replaced Hooley in 1918. When Murray became exclusive to Victor in November 1920, the quartet was reorganzied as Albert Campbell (tenor), Murray (lead tenor), John H. Meyer (baritone), and Frank Croxton (bass). At the Quartet's last session (11/10/25), personnel was John Ryan (tenor), Murray (lead tenor), Steve Porter (baritone), Donald Chalmers (bass).

AMERICAN SINGERS – Original 1927 personnel included Charles Harrison, Redferne Hollinshead (tenors), Vernon Archibald (baritone), Frank Croxton (bass). Lambert Murphy replaced Hollinshead in or around 1929.

AMES, MOLLY = Beaulah Gaylord Young (Columbia)

AMES, TESSIE = Trixie Smith (Silvertone)

AMPHION QUARTET = The Harmonizers (Brunswick)

ANDERSON, CHARLES = Elliott Shaw (Puretone and related labels)

ANDERSON, JELLY ROLL = Blind Richard Yates (Champion)

ANDERSON, MAYBELLE = Ruby Gowdy (Supertone)

ANDREWS, BARNEY = Ozzie Nelson (Associated transcriptions, late 1930's)

ANDREWS, JACK = Irving Kaufman

ANDREWS, JIM = Arthur Fields (usually); Irving Kaufman (infrequently) (Harmony and related labels)

ANDREWS, JOHN = Irving Kaufman (Banner, Melotone, Oriole, Perfect and other American Record Corporation labels, late 1920's); Smith Ballew (occasionally, early 1930's ARC labels)

ANNETTE, MISS = Annette Hanshaw (Pathé, Perfect and related labels)

ANTHONY & HARRISON = John Young and Frederick J. Wheeler (Victor and others)

ANTHONY, HARRY = John Young (Victor, possibly others)

APOLLO (MALE) TRIO = Crescent Trio (Pathé and related labels)

APOLLO VOCAL TRIO = Sterling Trio (Crescent)

APOLLO QUARTET OF BOSTON = William Whittaker, Lyman Hemenway, John Smallman, Alexander Logan (per Edison supplement; voices not given)

ARKANSAS TRIO = Vernon Dalhart (lead tenor/harmonica) and Ed Smalle (tenor), with banjo accompaniment by John Cali (Edison)

ARMSTRONG, SHELLEY = Amos Easton (Champion)

ASPARAGUS JOE = Pie Plant Pete (Champion)

AUDREY, IRENE = Irene Williams (Brunswick)

AUNT JEMIMA = Tess Gardella (Columbia)

AVON COMEDY FOUR = Irving Kaufman (lead tenor) with Harry Goodwin, Joe Smith and Charles Dale. Eddie Miller replaced Kaufman after the group stopped recording in 1918. According to Walsh, Arthur Fields was a member for a short time, but he is not evident on any issued recordings. (Columbia, Emerson, Victor).

BABS & HER BROTHERS = The Smoothies (Decca)

BABY BENBOW = possibly Benbow Hicks (identification per Rust) (Okeh)

BABY BONNIE = Ernestine Bomburyero (Buddy, Gennett, Silvertone)

BAIRD, JIM = Bill Elliott (Victor)

BAKER, DONALD = Arthur Fields (Regal). This name is also reported as a pseudonym for Irving Kaufman, but no examples have yet been verified.

BAKER, FANNY = Lillyn Brown (Oriole, from Emerson masters); Lucille Hegamin (Muse and Tremont, from Cameo masters)

BAKER, JOSEPHINE = Dorothy Dodd (Phantasie Concert Record only). Identification per Brian Rust; all other similarly credited issues are actual Josephine Baker recordings.

BALDWIN, ARTHUR = Arthur Fields (Cameo)

BALDWIN, LUKE = Bill Cox (Champion)

BALL, RAY = Frankie Marvin (Jewel, Oriole and related labels)

BALLARD & SAMUELS = Vernon Dalhart and Carson Robison (Broadway)

BALLARD, WOLFE = Vernon Dalhart (Broadway, Paramount, Herwin; probably other New York Recording Laboratories products)

BANCROFT, TED = Smith Ballew, Irving Kaufman (Pathé, Perfect); Ben Pollack, as a vocalist with his orchestra (identification per Rust; Banner 32074, Conqueror 7772, Jewel 6193, Oriole 2193, Perfect 15424, Regal 10250, Romeo 1561); other unidentified vocalists with Pollack's Orchestra (and derivative groups) on the American Record Corporation chain of dime-store labels (Banner, Regal, *et al.*).

BANJO JOE = Gus Cannon (Paramount only); William Hodgin (Columbia 15000-D series only)

BANJO-KER & THE SONGSTER = Bailey and Barnum (entered as such in the Gennett ledger, but probably a pseudonym itself) (Champion)

BARBECUE BOB = Robert Hicks (Columbia)

BARNES & LANE = Bob Miller and Barney Burnett (Grey Gull, Radiex and related labels)

BARNES & RAY = Bob Miller and Barney Burnett (Grey Gull, Radiex and related labels)

BARNES, BILL = Bob Miller (Grey Gull, Radiex and related labels)

BARNES, BILL & CHARLOTTE = Bob & Charlotte Miller (Grey Gull, Radiex and related labels)

BARNES, FAE = Maggie Jones (Black Swan, Paramount)

BARNES, WILLIAM = John Barnes Wells

BARR, HARRY = Henry Burr (Harmony and related labels)

BARRETT, BETTY = Marie Tiffany (Edison)

BARTON, TIPPY = Josh White (Vocalion)

BATES, DEACON L.J. = Blind Lemon Jefferson (Paramount)

BAXTER, CLYDE = Charles Kaley (Oriole)

BEALE STREET SHEIKS = Frank Stokes and Dan Sane (Paramount)

BEAMAN, LOTTIE = Lottie Kimbrough (Brunswick, Paramount)

BEASON, KITTY = Delores Valesco (Champion)

BEATTY, JOSEPHINE = Alberta Hunter (who borrowed the name from her sister-in-law) (Buddy, Gennett, Silvertone)

BEAUMONT, REV. & CONGREGATION = Rev. Johnson & Congregation (Oriole)

BEAVER, GEORGE = Irving Kaufman (numerous minor labels)

BEAVER, HARRY = Irving Kaufman (minor labels)

BEAVER, HENRY = Irving Kaufman (Cameo, Jewel, Oriole, Pathé, Perfect and probably many other minor labels)

BECKNER, FREDERICK = Jerry White (*q.v.*) (Champion)

BELL, EDDIE = Frank Luther (Bluebird, Timely Tunes, Victor)

BENBOW, BABY = possibly Benbow Hicks (identification per Rust) (Okeh)

BENNETT, JOHN = Al Bernard; possibly others (Madison)

BENNETT, PHIL = Ben Pollack (as a vocalist with his orchestra) (Broadway)

BERGERE, BETTINA = Gladys Rice

BERINI, STANISLAU = Max Bloch (Banner, Regal)

BERINI, STASSIO = Max Bloch (Muse, from Emerson masters). An Emerson issue listed under this name is presumably by Bloch also, but has not been verified.)

BERNARD & BEARD = Al Bernard and Billy Beard (Okeh)

BERNIE, D. BUD = Arthur Fields (Emerson and related labels)

BERT, FLO – Bert was an actual vaudeville headliner, one-half of the team of Brendler & Bert, as verified in various issues of *Variety*. Rust's theory that Bert was a pseudonym for concert performer Florence Cole-Talbert is totally unfounded. (Gennett and related labels)

BETHEL JUBILEE QUARTET = Rev. T.H. Wiseman (director/vocal) with A.C. Brogdon, H.S. Allen, and J.C. Eubanks (vocals) (Victor). Aural evidence suggests that this may be the same group that recorded as the Wiseman Quartet (*q.v.*) for Gennett, Rainbow, and other minor labels in the early 1920's.

BIEHLING = John Bieling (Lambert cylinders)

BIG BILL = Big Bill Broonzy (Columbia, Oriole, Perfect, many others)

BIG BOY & SHORTY = Phil Cook and Victor Fleming (Oriole)

BIG FOUR (I) = Byron G. Harlan, Joe Natus (tenors), Arthur Collins (baritone), A.D. Madeira (bass) (Edison cylinders, 1901)

BIG FOUR (II) = Peerless Entertainers (Champion, 1920's)

BIG SISTER = Mae Glover (Varsity 6063, dubbed from Gennett)

BILL & SLIM = Hokum Boys (Champion)

BILLINGS & ROBISON = Frank Luther and Carson Robison (Victor)

BILLINGS BROTHERS = Frank Luther and Carson Robison (Victor)

BILLINGS, BUD = Frank Luther (Victor)

BILLINGS, JOE = Carson Robison (Victor)

BILTMORE TRIO = Elmer Feldkamp (tenor) with unknown others (minor labels, early 1930's)

BIRMINGHAM BLUE BUGLERS = Vernon Dalhart and Ed Smalle with banjo accompaniment by John Cali (Gennett)

BIRMINGHAM BUD & HIS UKE = Frank Luther (?) (Edison)

BISON CITY QUARTET = Charles C. Miller, Ben R. Cook, Harry C. West, and Lester L. Pike (reported by Walsh; no examples are known to exist) (New Jersey cylinders, 1892)

BJOERLING TRIO = Jussi, Olle and Gösta Bjoerling ("Juvenile Trio" per label) (Columbia E- series). These are Jussi Bjoerling's first commercial recordings, made in the United States *c.* 1920-1921.

BLACK & WHITE = Billy Jones and Ernest Hare (Champion)

BLACK BROTHERS = Frank Luther and Carson Robison; Carson Robison Trio (both on Okeh)

BLACK, HERBERT = Greek Evans (Black Swan); Charles Harrison (Black Swan 2092-B only); Charles Hart and Elliott Shaw (Black Swan 2030 only); Howard Shelly (Black Swan 18048-B only) (all from Olympic masters); possibly others.

BLACK, WILLIE = Noble Sissle (Medallion)

BLACKBURN, MAMIE = Ardelle Bragg (Herwin)

BLAKE & JUDSON = Billy Jones and Ernest Hare (Actuelle, Pathé, Perfect and related labels)

BLAKE, HARRY = Ernest Hare (Crescent and possibly other Pathé-derived labels, *c.* 1917); Billy Jones (Actuelle, Pathé, Perfect and related labels, 1920's)

BLANCHARD, DAN = Frank Luther (Champion)

BLIND AMOS = Blind Joe Taggart (Vocalion)

BLIND ANDY = Andrew Jenkins (Okeh)

BLIND SAMMIE = Blind Willie McTell (Columbia)

BLUEBIRD TRIO = Billy Jones and Ernest Hare with unidentified piano accompaniment; possibly others (Romeo and related labels)

BLUE, BOB = Smith Ballew (minor labels)

BLUE, BUDDY* = Smith Ballew (nearly always, on Banner, Crown, Oriole and other minor labels); Scrappy Lambert (Oriole 1844); there may be other exceptions as well. This name was also used for various dance orchestras in the early 1930's, usually featuring Ballew's vocals.

BLUE RIDGE DUO = Gene Austin (vocal/guitar) and George Reneau (vocal/harmonica). Austin (a pop performer) is featured on some sides, Reneau (an authentic country performer) is featured on others, and their voices are easily distinguished. (Edison, Vocalion)

BON BON = George ("Bon Bon") Tunnell (minor labels, 1930's-1940's)

BONNER, WILLIAM = possibly William A. Kennedy (conjecture per Walsh; no verification yet found in Edison documentation) (Edison)

BONNIE, BABY = Ernestine Bomburyero (Buddy, Gennett, Silvertone)

BOSWELL SISTERS = Martha (vocal/piano), Connie (vocal/saxophone/cello), and Helvetia ("Vet") (vocal/violin) (Brunswick, Decca, Harmony and related labels, Okeh, Victor)

BOYS FROM WILDCAT HOLLOW = Monroe County Bottle Tippers (Champion)

BRACKEN, JIMMY = Ben Pollack (as a vocalist with his orchestra) (Brunswick)

BRADFORD, AUNTIE MARY = Mary H. Bradford (Paramount)

BRADY, ART/ARTHUR = Al Bowlly (Associated transcriptions, late 1930's)

BRADLEY, VELMA = Ida Cox (Broadway)

BRASLAU, MARCEL = Charles Laird (possibly a pseudonym itself) (Grey Gull and related labels, Oriole; from Olympic masters)

BREFELLI, MARIO = Max Bloch (National Music Lovers)

BREFELLI, MARTINO = Max Bloch (Emerson)

BREWER, LOUIS = John Ryan (Van Dyke)

BRIGGS, ARNOLD = Ozzie Nelson (Associated transcriptions, late 1930's)

BRITT, ADDY – Some confusion surrounds Cameo issues under this name. Although Britt was a popular songwriter and performer in the mid-1920's, the voice on some Cameo releases is almost certainly that of Arthur Fields.

BRITTEN, FORD = Arthur Fields; unidentified others (Columbia)

BRITTEN, PEGGY = Peggy English (Cameo)

BROADWAY QUARTET = Columbia Stellar Quartet (Columbia); Criterion Quartet (Vocalion and others)

BRONSON, GEORGE – Originally used indiscriminately on Oriole for concert and sacred material by Ernest Davis (*q.v.*), Reed Miller, Lane Rogers, and possibly others, generally drawing on Emerson masters. After 1923, the name is associated almost exclusively with pop material by Irving Kaufman on the Plaza Music Company (Banner, Oriole, *et al.*) and Consolidated Record Corporation/Grey Gull labels. Isolated issues by Arthur Fields and Lewis James have also been reported.

BROOKS, REV. GEORGE M. = Rev. Joseph Callender (Champion)

BROWN, AMANDA = Viola McCoy (Columbia, Pathé, Perfect)

BROWN, ARTHUR = Irving Kaufman (Vocalion)

BROWN, BESSIE – There were two Bessie Browns, neither apparently pseudonymous. One recorded for Columbia in 1924; the other (sometimes billed on labels as *Original Bessie Brown*), recorded for Brunswick, Pathé, and the Plaza Music Company (Banner) chain in 1925-1929.

BROWN, BETTY = Vaughn De Leath (?) (Grey Gull and related labels)

BROWN, BILL = Horace Smith (Varsity, dubbed from Gennett originals)

BROWN, CHOCOLATE = Irene Scruggs (Paramount)

BROWN, EDNA = Elsie Baker (Victor)

BROWN, FLOSSIE & DUKE = Mae Glover and John Byrd (Champion)

BROWN, KITTY = Viola McCoy (?) (Domino)

BROWN, LIL & WILL = Trixie Williams with piano accompaniment by Will Brown (Black Patti)

BROWN, LINDY = Vaughn De Leath (?) (Cardinal, from Gennett masters credited to "Mandy Lee" [*q.v.*])

BROWN, LOTTIE = Lottie Kimbrough (Supertone)

BROWN, RUTH = Kate Smith (Harmony)

BROWN, TOM = William Robyn (Lincoln)

BROWN, WILLIAM = Scrappy Lambert (National Music Lovers 1234; New Phonic)

BROWN, WILLIE = Noble Sissle (Medallion)

BROWNING & HUGHES = W.E. Browning and Joe Hughes (Emerson)

BROX SISTERS = Kathlyn, Dagmar and Lorraine Brox (vocals, occasionally self-accompanied on various instruments) (Brunswick, Victor)

BRUCE, ROBERT = Lewis James (Emerson, Pathé and related labels)

BRUNN, EWART = William Wheeler (Pathé)

BRUNO, ANTONIO = Millo Picco (?) (National Music Lovers, from Olympic masters)

BRUNSWICK MALE QUARTET = Audrey Hackett, Arthur Clough (tenors), Harry Wieting (baritone), A. Duncan Cornwall (bass) (Columbia)

BRYCE, FANNIE = Fanny Brice (misspelling on Columbia)

BUCKLEY, EUGENE = Arthur Fields (Columbia)

BUCK & BUBBLES* = Buck Washington and John "Bubbles" Sublett (Columbia)

BULLUM, JOE = Jimmie Gordon (Decca 7043, later reissued under Gordon's name)

BURKE, EDWARD = Elliot Shaw (Regal)

BURKE & COAT = Doc Roberts and Asa Martin (Champion)

BURKE, FIDDLIN' JIM = Doc Roberts (sometimes with Asa Martin) (Champion)

BURNETT BROTHERS = Bob Miller and Barney Burnett (Bluebird, Victor)

BURNETT, DICK = Irving Kaufman (Harmony and related labels)

BURNS, JOHN = Walter Van Brunt; possibly others (Oriole)

BURNSIDE, GEORGE = Louis Winsch (Crescent, Pathé and related labels)

BURRELL & BRONSON = Reed Miller and Lane Rogers (Oriole)

BURT, VIRGINIA — Some confusion surrounds this name. Aural comparison of her *Dreamy Hawaiian Shore* on Edison and Okeh reveals two apparently different voices, and several researchers have suggested that Vaughn De Leath was responsible for the Edison issue, Helen Clark for the Okeh. However, Burt is credited as composer on these sides and was probably an actual performer.

BURTON & SIMS = Frank Bessinger and Frank Wright (Champion)

BURTON & WILSON = Frank Bessinger and Frank Wright (Champion)

BURTON, BILLY = Vernon Dalhart (Oriole); Charles Harrison (Domino, Regal and related labels)

BURTON, DICK = Ozzie Nelson (World Program Service transcriptions, mid-1930's)

BURTON, HOWARD = Arthur Hall (Champion)

BUSTER & JACK = Buster Elmore and Jack Cawley (Montgomery Ward, Victor)

BUTTERBEANS & SUSIE = Joe and Susie Edwards. One "Grasshopper," (possibly be Eddie Heywood, per Rust) replaced Susie on mx. 74069. (Okeh)

BYRD & GLOVER = John Byrd and Mae Glover (Champion 50037)

CALHOUN & ANDREWS = Vernon Dalhart and Carson Robison (Grey Gull and related labels)

CALHOUN & LEAVITT = Frank Luther and Carson Robison (Van Dyke)

CALHOUN, JEFF – Usually Vernon Dalhart on Grey Gull, Radiex and related labels, through mid-1927. Beginning in late 1927, the name is most often associated with Frank Luther (confirmed on, but not limited to, Grey Gull mx's. 2342-E, 2343-, 2360-E, 2396-, 3017-B, 3031-A,-B,-C, and 3032-A,-B, 3378-A, 3443-A, 3445-A, 3628-A, 3629-A, some of which are remakes of earlier Dalhart masters). Most Van Dyke issues under this name are by Luther. Arthur Fields is confirmed on Grey Gull mx. 2511-B, and there are undoubtedly other occasional exceptions on Grey Gull, Madison, Radiex, Van Dyke and related labels.

CALHOUN, JESS = Vernon Dalhart; probably others on occasion (Grey Gull and related labels)

CAMPBELL, ORAN = David Miller (Champion)

CAMPUS GLEE CLUB = Shannon Four (Cameo)

CANNON, JIMMY = Vernon Dalhart

CAREAU, FRANKLIN = Frank Croxton

CAROLINA TWINS = Gwen Foster and Dave Fletcher (Victor)

CARROLL, BOB = Irving Kaufman (Columbia)

CARROLL, JOE = Red McKenzie (World Program Service transcriptions, 1933)

CARROLL, ROY = Dick Robertson (Harmony and related labels, Okeh)

CARTER, ALICE / CARTER, ALICE LESLIE – These are not the same performer, and neither is known to be a pseudonym.

CARY, CLARA = Clara Herring (Varsity, dubbed from Gennett)

CARSON, CAL = Carson Robison or Frank Luther (Durium Junior [4″])

CARSON, CAL & GID = Frank Luther and Carson Robison (Durium Junior [4″])

CARTER, FLOYD = Bob Miller (Perfect)

CASEY BILL = Will Weldon (of the Memphis Jug Band) (Bluebird, Vocalion)

CASEY, MICHAEL = Russell Hunting (Columbia, Pathé and others, often from British masters); Len Spencer (infrequently, and only from domestic masters). Several other performers recorded *Casey* routines in the late 1890's and early 1900's (including Joseph R. Gannon for Concert Phonograph Company cylinders in 1899 and John Kaiser for Edison beginning in 1899), but usually are credited under their own names in the spoken announcements.

CATHEDRAL (MALE) QUARTET = Shannon Four (Emerson and related labels); Revelers (Pathé, Perfect)

CHAMLEE, ARCHER = Mario Chamlee (Brunswick)

CHAMPION QUARTETTE = Criterion Quartet (Champion)

CHAPPELL, MISS = Edith Chapman (Edison)

CHARLES, HAROLD = Irving Kaufman (Challenge, Silvertone, probably others)

CHAUTAUQUA PREACHERS QUARTET = John Wesley Holland, Fay Arnold Moon, Charles A. Gage, Charles Alfred Briggs (Columbia)

CHEERIO = C.K. Field (recording under his radio pseudonym) (Roycroft)

CHICK & ANDY = Chick Ciccone and Andy Albane (Perfect and related labels)

CHOCOLATE BROWN = Irene Scruggs (Paramount)

CHRISTY BROTHERS = Irving and Jack Kaufman; Arthur Fields and Charles Harrison (various minor labels)

CHRISTY, FRANK = Irving Kaufman

CINWAY, CHARLES = Lewis James (Pathé and related labels)

CLARE & MANN = Al Bernard and Ernest Hare (Pathé and related labels)

CLARE, JACK = Al Bernard (Pathé and related labels)

CLARK BROTHERS = Sweet Brothers (Champion)

CLARK, FRANK = J.P. (Joe) Ryan (Champion)

CLARK, ETHEL − Edmonia Henderson (Silvertone)

CLARK, JACK = Al Bernard

CLARK, JAMES = Carson Robison

CLARK, JOHN = Herbert Sweet (Champion)

CLARK, ROY = Jack Kaufman (Broadway)

CLARKE & THOMAS = Billy Jones and Ernest Hare (Grey Gull, Radiex and related labels)

CLARKE, BILLY = Irving Kaufman; Arthur Fields (Clover, Dandy, Grey Gull, New Emerson and related labels, all from Consolidated Record Corporation masters)

CLARKE, CATHERINE = Grace Kerns

CLARKE, GLORY = Vaughn De Leath (Van Dyke)

CLARKE, HAROLD = Scrappy Lambert (minor labels)

CLARKE, JANE = Grace Kerns

CLAYTON, BOB = Gene Autry (Broadway and related labels)

CLAYTON, BOBBY = Buddy Clark (Associated transcriptions, late 1930's)

CLEMENTS, GEORGE = Reed Miller (Grey Gull, Oriole and related labels)

CLEMON, JAMES = Walter Van Brunt (Oriole)

CLIFFORD, ARTHUR = George Alexander (Edison cylinders)

CLIFFORD, BOB = Buddy Clark (Associated transcriptions, late 1930's)

CLIFFORD, ED = Cliff Edwards (Bell). Walsh identified Clifford as Vernon Dalhart, but no label was cited, nor have examples been found.

CLIFFORD, FRANCES = Mazie Green (a pseudonym itself; true artist identity has never been established) (Oriole 420)

CLIFTON BEACH SERENADERS = Sybil Sanderson Fagan Ensemble (Champion)

CLIFTON, EDWARD = Cliff Edwards (Regal, possibly others)

CLIMAX MALE QUARTETTE = Columbia Male Quartet (early Columbia products)

CLINCH VALLEY BOYS = Marion Underwood & Sam Harris (Champion)

C.M.A. (COLORED) GOSPEL QUINTET = F.H. Lacy (1st tenor), S.R. Jones (2nd tenor), J.W. Parker (3rd tenor/director), H.D. Hodges (1st bass), A.E. Talbert (2nd bass) (Columbia Personal Records)

COAT, JESSE = Asa Martin (Champion)

CODY, BILL = Bill Coty (Crown)

COLE, LUCY = Billie Wilson (Champion, Supertone)

COLE, REX = Arthur Fields (Perfect, Polk, possibly others)

COLE, SAM = Arthur Fields (Conqueror, Perfect)

COLEMAN, ELLEN — Coleman has traditionally been identified as Helen Baxter. However, Raymond Wile reports the existence of an Edison paycheck made payable to, and endorsed by, *Helen* Coleman for the *Ellen* Coleman session, raising the possibility that Helen Coleman was Baxter's legal name or (less likely) that the Baxter attribution is incorrect and that Coleman was a performer in her own right. (Edison discs and cylinders)

COLLINS & REYNOLDS = Albert Campbell and Jack Kaufman (Madison)

COLLINS, BILL = Gene Austin (Victor)

COLLINS, JANE = Helen Clark (1920's minor labels)

COLLINS, SALLIE = Helen Clark (Edison)

COLLINS, VIE = Sodarisa Miller (Silvertone)

COLONIAL QUARTET = Rambler Minstrel Company (Zon-O-Phone)

COLUMBIA DOUBLE QUARTET — No personnel is listed in the Columbia files or catalogs. Walsh suggested that the group combined members of the Columbia Stellar and Peerless Quartets (*q.v.*).

COLUMBIA LADIES' QUARTET = Grace Kerns, Louise McMahon (sopranos), Mildred Potter, Clara Moister (contraltos)

COLUMBIA MALE QUARTET — Original late 1890's personnel included Albert Campbell (tenor), J.K. Reynard (lead tenor), Joe Belmont (baritone), Joe Majors (bass). Henry Burr replaced Reynard *c.* 1903. By 1904, usual personnel was Campbell, Burr, Steve Porter (baritone), "Big Tom" Daniels (bass), although membership varied. In 1906 Frank C. Stanley replaced Daniels and reorganized the group as the Peerless Quartet (*q.v.*), although Columbia continued to issue Peerless material under the Columbia Quartet name exclusively through 1911, and occasionally after that.

COLUMBIA OCTET – No personnel is listed in Columbia files or catalogs. Walsh suggested that the group combined members of the Columbia Stellar and Peerless Quartets.

COLUMBIA SEXTET = Byron G. Harlan, Joe Belmont (tenors), Frank C. Stanley (baritone), and (allegedly) three unidentified female members of the original *Floradora* cast. (Columbia)

COLUMBIA STELLAR QUARTET – Original 1914 personnel included Charles Harrison, John Barnes Wells (tenors), Andrea Sarto (baritone), Frank Croxton (bass). Henry Burr replaced Wells almost immediately. By 1916, personnel was Harrison, Reed Miller (tenors), Sarto, and Croxton, although Lewis James occasionally replaced Miller. Walsh notes that Billy Jones sang lead on one unspecified 1922 issue. In addition to their work for Columbia, this group recorded extensively for minor labels under several pseudonyms.

COMBS, IRVING = Irving Kaufman; possibly others (Silvertone)

CONFIDENTIAL CHARLEY = Ernest Hare (Oriole and related labels); Irving Kaufman, possibly others (Harmony and related labels)

CONROY, FRANK = William Robyn (Variety)

CONROY, FRED = William Robyn (Variety)

CONSOLIDATED MALE QUARTETTE –Columbia Male Quartet (through 1906); Peerless Quartet (after 1906) (Consolidated)

COOK & MITCHELL = Phil Cook and (?) Mitchell (first name unknown) (Banner and related labels)

COOK, TOM = Frank Luther (Grey Gull, Van Dyke and related labels)

COOMBS, IRVING = Irving Kaufman (Silvertone)

CORTES, LESTER = Irving Kaufman (Harmony, Velvet Tone and related labels)

COTTON & MORPHEUS = Phil Cook and an unknown partner (Brunswick)

COUERT, RAY = Jack Kaufman (Oriole)

COUNTRY HARMONIZERS = The Harmonizers (Pathé and related labels)

COWBOY ROGERS = Frankie Marvin (Varsity)

COX, WALLACE = Ernest Hare (Crescent, Pathé and related labels)

CRAIG, AL = Arthur Hall; possibly others (Domino and related labels)

CRAIG, ALLEN = Arthur Fields (Domino); Irving Kaufman (Oriole)

CRAMER, AL = Vernon Dalhart (Broadway)

CRAMER BROTHERS = Vernon Dalhart and Carson Robison; possibly others (Broadway)

CRANE, GEORGE = Irving Kaufman (Oriole, Pathé, Perfect and related labels)

CRANE, HARRY = Arthur Fields (Oriole and related labels)

CRANE, MARY = Maude Mills (Oriole)

CRANE, RALPH = Royal Dadmun (Victor)

CRANE, THORNELY = William Robyn (Brunswick)

CRAVER & WELLS = Vernon Dalhart and Carson Robison (Columbia)

CRAVER, AL = Vernon Dalhart (Columbia)

CRAWFORD, MARIAN = possibly Marian Evelyn Cox (Pathé and related labels)

CRESCENT TRIO = Charles Hart, Lewis James (tenors), Elliott Shaw (baritone) (Pathé, various minor brands)

CRITERION QUARTET (I) = Robert R. Rainey, William A. Washburn (tenors), Reinald Werrenrath (baritone/manager), Walter A. Downie (bass) (early 1900's issues on Columbia and related labels, Edison, Leeds and related labels, Zon-O-Phone).

CRITERION QUARTET (II) = John Young, Horatio Rench (tenors), George Reardon (baritone), and Donald Chalmers (bass). Frank Moeller replaced Reardon in 1921. (numerous 1920's labels)

CROSS, HENRIETTA — Suggested by several researchers as a pseudonym for Dolly Kay, based on aural evidence. Not supported by Plaza Music Company files, but Plaza sometimes logged sessions pseudonymously. (Domino)

CROXTON QUARTET = Agnes Kimball (soprano), Nevada Van Der Veer (contralto), Reed Miller (tenor), Frank Croxton (bass). Walsh cites an early Gennett release on which personnel was Inez Barbour (soprano), Van Der Veer, Henry Burr (tenor), and Croxton (bass). (Emerson, Gennett, Okeh and other minor labels)

CROXTON TRIO = Agnes Kimball (soprano), Reed Miller (tenor), Frank Croxton (bass). Personnel is per Edison file; Walsh lists personnel on Okeh as Inez Barbour (soprano), Henry Burr (tenor), and Croxton (bass).

CUMMINGS, JAMES = Vernon Dalhart

CURTIS, HARRY = Charles Hart (Regal and related labels, except as noted); Charles Harrison (Regal 954)

DALE, CHARLES = Franklyn Baur; Arthur Fields; Lewis James (all on Grey Gull, Radiex and related labels); Arthur Fields (Globe and probably other Grey Gull products; Paramount, Puretone, Puritan, Triangle and related labels, from New York Recording Laboratories masters); Irving Kaufman (Madison and probably other Grey Gull products). Not to be confused with vaudevillian Charles Dale, of Avon Comedy Four and Smith and Dale fame, who did not record under his own name during this period.

DALE, EDWIN = Charles Hackett (Columbia)

DALE, FLORA = Rosa Henderson (Domino)

DALE, TEDDY = Smith Ballew (Broadway)

DALE, WALTER H. = Arthur Fields

DALHART & WELLS = Vernon Dalhart and Carson Robison (Columbia)

DALHART TRIO = Vernon Dalhart (vocal/harmonica), Carson Robison (vocal/whistling/guitar), Adelyn Hood (vocal/violin) (Cameo)

DALTON, CHARLES = Vernon Dalhart; Charles Hart (Oriole, Regal)

DALTON, JACK = Jack Kaufman (Edison; various minor brands)

DALTON, WALTER (& HIS GUITAR) = Frankie Marvin (Pathé, Perfect and related brands)

DANIELS, HELENE = Helen Rowland (performing under her married name) (Associated transcriptions, Liberty Music Shop, late 1930's)

DANIELS, WALLACE = Ernest Hare (Perfect)

DANIELS, WALTER = Frank Luther (Champion)

DARE, DOT = Annette Hanshaw (Harmony, Puritone and related labels)

DAVE & HOWARD = Dave McCarn and Howard Long (Victor)

DAVIS, ERNEST — Aural evidence suggests Walter Van Brunt on certain New York Recording Laboratories (Paramount) masters; however, the name was used on numerous minor labels by other unidentifiable performers as well.

DAVIS, LILLIAN = Marguerite Dunlap (Victor 17000 series). Not to be confused with British performer Lillian *Davies,* who recorded several sides for His Master's Voice (British) at the Victor studios in 1926.

DAVIS, RED HOT SHAKIN' = Madlyn Davis (Paramount)

DAY, BILLY = Irving Kaufman (Columbia)

DAY, J.W. = Jilson Setters (Victor)

DEEP RIVER PLANTATION SINGERS = Nazarene Congregational Church Choir of Brooklyn, New York (Champion)

DE KAISER, MARIE = Marie Kaiser

DE KYZER, MARIE = Marie Kaiser

DEL CAMPO, SIGNOR A. = Alberto De Bassini (Berliner)

DELL, VERNON = Vernon Dalhart

DE MARCO, ANGELINO = Vaughn De Leath

DENTON, TOM = Sid Garry (Champion)

DE REX, BILLY = Billy Jones (Gennett and related labels)

DE WEES, GEORGE = Irving Kaufman (Challenge, Champion, Silvertone)

DEXTER, CHARLES = Arthur Fields (Van Dyke)

DIAMOND COMEDY FOUR = Len Spencer, Steve Porter, Billy Golden (vocals/speech), Vess L. Ossman (banjo) (early disc and cylinder brands, *c.* 1898-1900)

DIAMOND FOUR = Albert Campbell, James Kent Reynard (tenors), Steve Porter (baritone), Will C. Jones (bass) (Berliner, late 1890's)

DIANNO, JOSEFHA = Regina Vicarino (Broadway, National Music Lovers; from Olympic masters)

DICKSON, BOB = Dick Robertson (Victor)

DICKSON, CHARLES = Irving Kaufman (usually); unknown others (occasionally) (Challenge, Jewel, Oriole and related labels)

DI GIOVANNI, EDOARDO = Edward Johnson (Columbia)

DITTMAN, EVANS — A Crescent issue under this name derives from a Pathé release credited to George Stewart (probably a pseudonym itself).

DIX, BOBBY = Dick Robertson (Clarion, Harmony and related labels; Okeh)

DIXIE JUBILEE SINGERS = Pace Jubilee Singers (Champion, Gennett)

DIXIE SONGSTERS = Charioteers (Associated transcriptions, 1938)

DIXIE STARS = Al Bernard and J. Russell Robinson (Cameo, Columbia, Pathé, Perfect, Starck and many others)

DIXON & ANDREWS = Vernon Dalhart and Carson Robison (Van Dyke)

DIXON, BOB = Dick Robertson (Victor)

DIXON, CHARLES = Irving Kaufman (minor labels)

DIXON, MARTIN = Vernon Dalhart (Van Dyke); Frank Luther (Van Dyke 74118; probably others)

DIXON, RAYMOND = Lambert Murphy (Victor)

DONIVETTI, HUGO = Charles Harrison; possibly others (National Music Lovers)

DONNELLI, JOSEPHA = Regina Vicarino (National Music Lovers, from Olympic masters)

DONOVAN, HUGH = Charles Harrison (in nearly all cases, on a variety of labels). Isolated Donovan releases by Arthur Fields, Ernest Hare, and possibly others, have been reported on Grey Gull and related labels.

DOOLEY & SHEA = Irving and Jack Kaufman (Vocalion)

DOUGLAS & KIRK = Kirk McGee and Blythe Poteet (Champion)

DOUGLAS, DAISY = Virginia Childs (Columbia)

DOUGLAS, WALTER = Howard Hafford (Champion)

DOWE, JOHN = Irving Kaufman (Broadway, Paramount, Puritan, Supertone; probably other New York Recording Laboratories products)

DUFFY, TOM = Irving Kaufman (Pathé, Perfect)

DUKE & HIS UKE = Johnny Marvin (Gennett)

DUKE, BERNICE = Elzadie Robinson (Broadway)

DUKE, HENRY & HIS UKE = Johnny Marvin (National Music Lovers)

DUKE, HONEY (& HIS UKE) = Johnny Marvin (numerous labels)

DURANT, EDWARD = Ernest Davis (*q.v.*; possibly a pseudonym itself) (Banner, Domino and related labels)

DWYER, GERTRUDE = Vaughn De Leath (?) (Bell, Emerson; Harmony and related labels)

EARLE, EMILY = Elizabeth Lennox (Brunswick)

EDISON COMIC OPERA COMPANY -- Personnel undoubtedly varied. Members in 1910 included Edith Chapman, Edna Stearns, Cornelia Marvin, John Young, and Steve Porter.

EDISON (MALE) QUARTET — Original 1894 personnel included Roger Harding, J.K. Reynard (tenors), S.H. Dudley (baritone), William F. Hooley (bass). By 1896 personnel had become John Bieling (tenor), Jere Mahoney (lead tenor), Dudley, and Hooley. Edison literature credits Harry Macdonough as tenor as early as 1897; he had definitely replaced Mahoney by 1900. This group also made disc records as the American Quartet (I) and Haydn Quartet (*q.v.*).

EDISON MIXED QUARTET — Original 1906 personnel included Florence Hinkel (soprano), Mary Porter Mitchell (contralto), John Young (tenor), Frederick Wheeler (baritone). Margaret Keyes replaced Mitchell in 1909.

EDISON MIXED SEXTET — This group recorded the *Floradora Sextet* on at least two occasions. An early version (not necessarily the first) included Corinne Morgan, Ada Jones, _Hornby, Bob Roberts, James Harrison, and Frank C. Stanley. A more common remake replaced Hornby with Grace Nelson and Harrison with George Seymour Lenox.

EDISON MIXED TRIO = Metropolitan Trio (Edison cylinders)

EDISON (MODERN) MINSTRELS — Personnel varied from 1903 through 1909; members of the company at various times included Arthur Collins, Will F. Denney, William F. Hooley, Eugene Jaudas (director), Harry Macdonough, Ed Meeker, Billy Murray, Dan W. Quinn, and Len Spencer. "Modern" was dropped from the billing in February 1906.

EDISON QUARTET & COMPANY — This odd description appears in a 1906 internal memo reported by Ray Wile and lists Arthur Collins, Byron G. Harlan, Billy Murray, Len Spencer, Harry Macdonough, George Washington Johnson, and Vess L. Ossman. Presumably this group (similar in personnel to the Rambler Minstrel Company) made minstrel and vaudeville routines under various names.

EDISON VAUDEVILLE COMPANY — Byron G. Harlan, Billy Murray (tenors), Ed Meeker (baritone, on occasion), Steve Porter (baritone), Eugene Jaudas (director)

EDWARDS, BILLY = Arthur Fields (Empire, possibly other minor vertical-cut brands)

EDWARDS, BUDDY = Charlie Teagarden (mx. 149953, on Harmony 1104-H and derivative issues); Jack Teagarden (mx. 149954, on Harmony 1099-H and derivative issues), both as band vocalists.

EDWARDS, IRVING = Irving Kaufman (Gennett)

EDWARDS, THOMAS = Elliott Shaw; Arthur Fields (both on National Music Lovers)

EDWARDS, TOM = Irving Kaufman (Columbia)

ELECTRIC CITY FOUR = George Weaver, Jenkin Jones, Martin Size, John Wetter (per Edison supplement; voices not specified) (Edison)

ELLIOTT & SPENCER = Ed Smalle and Gerald Underhill Macy (National Music Lovers)

ELLIOTT, JOSEPH = Pseudonym on National Music Lovers for Vernon Dalhart (1073); Arthur Fields (1103, 1104); Charles Harrison (1092); Charles Hart (1192); possibly others.

ELLIS, GAY = Annette Hanshaw (Harmony and related labels)

ELLIS, JERRY = Jack Golding (Champion)

ELMER & JUDD = Doc Roberts (Champion only); Hobbs Brothers (Banner, Conqueror, Oriole and related labels, from Plaza Music Company/American Record Corporation masters)

ELY, CARL = Walter Van Brunt (conjecture per Walsh; no examples have been located for verification) (Indestructible cylinders)

EMMETT, JANE = Margaret McKee (Grey Gull, Madison and related labels)

EMPIRE VAUDEVILLE COMPANY – Personnel varied from session to session, although Edward Meeker was usually present. At various times the company included Al Bernard, Albert Campbell, Billy Golden, Ada Jones, Billy Murray, and members of the American (Premier) Quartet. Walsh notes that one Empire release, "Casting Bread Upon the Waters" was actually the work of Mr. and Mrs. Edward M. Favor with Steve Porter. (Edison discs and cylinders)

ENDER, JACK = William Robyn (Pathé, Perfect)

ENGLISH SINGERS = Norman Stone (tenor), Norman Notley (baritone), Nellie Carson, Flora Mann (sopranos), Lillian Berger (contralto), under the direction of Cuthbert Kelly (Roycroft)

EPSTEIN, GEORGE = Irving Kaufman (Banner and related labels)

ETON BOYS = Charles Day, Jack Day, Earl Smith, Art Gentry (Victor, mid-1930's)

EVANS & CLARKE = Vernon Dalhart and Carson Robsion (Oriole)

EVANS, CHARLOTTE = Clementine Smith (*q.v.*; possibly a pseudonym itself) (Domino)

EVANS, FRANK = Vernon Dalhart (usually, through 1928); Carson Robison (occasionally, late 1920's-early 1930's); Arthur Fields (instances reported but not confirmed) (all on Oriole)

EVANS, FRANKLIN = Carson Robison

EVANS, HAL = Vernon Dalhart (Van Dyke)

EVANS, HAPPY DICK = Les Backer (Champion)

EVANS, HARRY = Evan Williams (Victor only). Julian Morton Moses notes that Victor went so far as to publish a photograph of someone other than Evan Williams and caption it "Harry Evans" to protect Williams' identity! Greek Evans (whose full name was Greek Harry Evans) also used this name on Emerson and related labels.

EVANS, WILLIAM T.* = Evan Williams (Victor)

EVEREADY MIXED QUARTET = Beaulah Gaylord Young (soprano), Rose Bryant (contralto), Charles Harrison (tenor), Wilfred Glenn (bass)

EVERETT, FRANK = Charles Harrison (Van Dyke)

EVERS, FRANK = Eddie Gray (Claxtonola, Paramount)

EVERSON, LOTTIE = Lottie Kimbrough (Champion)

FABER, ED = Carson Robison (Grey Gull, Van Dyke and related labels)

FAIRBANKS & MEYER = Henry Moeller and John H. Meyer (several minor spelling variations of the pseudonym are known) (Grey Gull, Radiex and related labels)

FAIRBANKS, HENRY = Henry Moeller (Grey Gull and related labels)

FARBER GIRLS = Farber Sisters (Pathé)

FARBER SISTERS = Constance and Irene Farber (Pathé)

FENWYCK, JERRY = Smith Ballew; Scrappy Lambert; Dick Robertson (Harmony and related labels). See also Instrumental listing.

FERGUS, JOHN = George Ake (*Sand Cave*); David Miller (*Little Old Log Cabin*) (coupled on Silvertone 4019)

FERGUSON & MILLER = Bob and Charlotte Miller (Columbia)

FERGUSON, BOB = Bob Miller (Columbia, Victor)

FERNAND, M. = Emilio de Gogorza (Improved Record [Eldridge R. Johnson], Victor [including Monarch and other label variations])

FERNANDEZ, MILDRED = Lillyn Brown (Regal)

FERRELL, LOUISE = Elizabeth Lennox (1920's minor labels)

FIELDS, EVELYN = Ella Fitzgerald (World transcriptions, late 1930's)

FIFTH AVENUE PRESBYTERIAN CHURCH CHOIR = Mary Hissem de Moss, Cornelia Marvin, Edward Strong, Frederic Martin (per 1910 Edison supplement; voices not specified) (Edison cylinders)

FINNEGAN, JOHN = Walter Van Brunt (Regal)

FISK UNIVERSITY JUBILEE QUARTET — Personnel varied considerably. On its first recordings in 1910, the Quartet included J. M. Work, N. W. Ryder, Rev. J. A. Myers, and A.G. King. L. P. O'Hara replaced King in 1911. By 1912, the Quartet included Work, Roland Hayes, O'Hara, and Charles Wesley. Later personnel is not well-documented; Hayes pursued a solo career in Europe after World War I, so can be eliminated from later personnel. (Columbia, Edison, Victor)

FLANNERY SISTERS = Allie Flannery (vocal/guitar) and Billie Flannery (vocal) (Decca)

FLOYD, CAROLINE & MAY = Alta Browne and Bertha Powell (Champion)

FLYNN, JIMMY — According to John McAndrew (*Record Research* 11/1965), Jimmy Flynn was an actual Irish tenor who recorded for Pathé and Harmony before his death in 1926. No material has yet been found to verify the existence of Flynn; later issues under this name, however, are unmistakably the work of Irving Kaufman. (Harmony, Velvet Tone and related labels; Pathé, Perfect and related labels)

FORD, EDDY = Irving Kaufman

FOSTER, AL = Sid Garry (usually) (Oriole, Romeo and related labels); William Robyn (occasionally) (Cameo only); possibly others

FOSTER, CHARLES = Fred Hillebrand (Regal)

FOSTER, EVELYN = Clara Herring (Champion)

FOSTER, JIM = Sam Collins (Champion, Silvertone, Superior)

FOUR ARISTOCRATS = Fred Weber, Bert Bennett, Ed Lewis, Tom Miller (Edison, Victor)

FOUR SERENADERS = Gennett Songsters (Champion)

FOUR SOUTHERN SINGERS = Owen, Robert, James and Annie Laurie Ward (various labels, early 1930's)

FROLICKERS = Arthur Hall, John Ryan (tenors), Ed Smalle (tenor; piano accompaniment, when used) (Edison)

FRANCISCO, CARLOS = Emilio de Gogorza (Climax Record, Improved Gram-O-Phone, Lambert cylinders, Victor [including Monarch and other label variations], Zon-O-Phone)

FRANCISCO, E. = Emilio de Gogorza (Berliner, probably other early disc brands)

FRANCISCO, SEÑOR = Emilio de Gogorza (Victor)

FRANCISCO, SGR. / SIG. = Emilio de Gogorza (Berliner, Victor)

FRANKIE & JONES = Maude Mills and Jack Jones (Banner and related labels)

FRANKLIN, EDWARD = Emilio de Gogorza (Climax Record, Zon-O-Phone, possibly other early brands)

FRANKLIN, FRED = William Robyn (Romeo)

FRAWLEY, TOM – Used indiscriminately for several band vocalists *c.* 1929-1932. In general, Frawley was Irving Kaufman (Okeh), Tom Stacks (Harmony, Velvet Tone and other Columbia budget labels, *c.* 1929-1930), Scrappy Lambert (Harmony, early 1930's), or Bill Coty (with Jack Albin's Orchestra only, early 1930's) (Harmony and related labels). There are undoubtedly exceptions.

FREDERICKS, WILLIAM = Percy Hemus (Columbia). Identification per Peter Burgis; Walsh identified Fredericks as Frank C. Stanley, but no examples have been found to support this.

FREER, MARGARET A. = Marcia Freer (Victor)

FRENCH, GEORGE = Arthur Fields (per Walsh; no label cited)

FRENCH, MAE = Peggy English (Regal)

FULLER, JEFF = Vernon Dalhart (Grey Gull and related labels)

FULLER, JEP = Vernon Dalhart (Grey Gull and related labels)

GAIETY MUSICAL COMEDY CHORUS = The Revelers (Brunswick)

GALE & FISHER = Billy Jones and Ernest Hare (Cameo)

GALE, EDDIE – Considerable confusion surrounds this name. Various accounts list Gale as a pseudonym for Ben Pollack; others credit him as a performer in his own right. No documentation has been found to support either view, and aural evidence is inconclusive.

GARGOLO, UGESO = Billy Jones (per Walsh; no label cited)

GARLAND, DOROTHY = Delores Valesco (Champion)

GAUNT, JOE & ZEB = Arthur Fields and Fred Hall (Clarion, Harmony and related labels)

GAYLE, NORMAN = G.B. Grayson and/or Henry Whitter (Champion)

GEAR, GLORIA* = Vaughn De Leath (Emerson and related labels)

GEER, GLORIA = Vaughn De Leath (Banner, Cameo, Triangle and many other minor brands) (see also previous entry)

GEER, GEORGIA = Vaughn De Leath (Puritan, Triangle and related labels)

GENE & GLENN = Gene Carroll and Glenn Rowell (of WLS-Chicago) (Gennett, Silvertone and related labels)

GENT & WHEELER = Arthur Fields with an unknown female partner (Romeo)

GEORGIA BILL = Blind Willie McTell (Okeh)

GEORGIA TOM = Thomas A. Dorsey (numerous brands). This is the blues (and, later, gospel) performer and songwriter, not to be confused with bandleader Tommy Dorsey.

GEORGIA WILDCATS = Tom Darby and Jesse Pitts (Victor)

GIBBONS, IRENE = Eva Taylor (Columbia)

GIBSON, CLEO — Although there has been speculation for many years that this was a pseudonym (including totally unsupported statements that Gibson was actually Ma Rainey or Bessie Smith), Gibson appears to have been an actual performer. A performance by Cleo Sephus Gibson is mentioned in a *Billboard* review for October 27, 1923.

GIBSON, CLIFFORD = Curley Weaver (and Eddie Mapp, -A side) (label error on Q-R-S 7082 only)

GILBERT & NELSON = Arthur Hall and John Ryan (Oriole)

GILBERT, LAWRENCE E. = Thomas Chalmers (Edison Blue Amberol)

GILBERTS, THE = Russ and Lovina Gilbert (Roycroft)

GILLETTE, IRVING = Henry Burr (Crescent, Edison Blue Amberol; other disc and cylinder brands)

GITFIDDLE JIM = Kokomo Arnold (Victor)

GODDARD, CHARLES = Henry Moeller (Champion)

GODDARD, HERBERT = Emilio De Gogorza (Improved Record [Eldridge R. Johnson], Victor [including Monarch and other label variations])

GOLD DUST TWINS = Earl Tuckerman and Harvey Hindermeyer (Edison)

GOODMAN SACRED SINGERS = McDonald Quartet (Champion)

GOODWIN, GOODY = Irving Mills (as a band vocalist) (Pathé, Perfect)

GOODWIN, HARRY = Irving Kaufman

GOOLD, EDITH C. = Edith Chapman

GORDON & GLOVER = Frank Bessinger and Frank Wright; possibly others (Champion)

GORDON, CHARLES = Percy Hemus (minor labels)

GORDON, WESTELL = Charles Harrison; possibly others (Grey Gull, Radiex and related labels)

GOSPEL MINNIE = Memphis Minnie (Decca)

GOULD = Charles Harrison (aural identification per Bill Bryant) (Operaphone 8" vertical-cut)

GRAHAM, LEONARD = Noble Sissle (Regal)

GRAHAM, LUCKY = Frank Luther (Champion)

GRAHAM, LUCKY & LUCILLE = Frank Luther and an unknown female partner (Champion)

GRANT, ARTHUR = Arthur Hall; Ernest Hare (per Walsh; no labels given)

GRANT, RACHEL = Gladys Rice (Edison discs and cylinders)

GRANT TRIO = Graham Brothers (Victor)

GRAVELLE, BUDDY = William Robyn (Lincoln, Romeo)

GRAY, DIXIE = Billy (Jazz Caspar) Higgins (Domino)

GRAY, HENRY = Arthur Fields

GRAYSEN & LOTTY = G.B. Grayson and Henry Whitter (Champion)

GREAT GAP ENTERTAINERS = Lookout Mountain Boys (Broadway)

GREAT WHITE WAY QUARTET = Harmonizers

GREATER NEW YORK QUARTETTE = Roger Harding, Will C. Jones (tenors), Steve Porter (baritone), (?) Hargrave (bass) (Columbia cylinders, 1900-1901)

GREEN, ALICE = Olive Kline (Victor)

GREEN, BERT = Jack Kaufman

GREEN, FRANK = Clarence Todd (Oriole 650, 674 only)

GREEN, JACK = Victor Fletcher (Black Swan, from an Olympic master). Fletcher may have been a pseudonym itself; the Olympic Disc Record Corporation was owned by *John* Fletcher.

GREEN, JIMMY = Smith Ballew (Broadway); Scrappy Lambert (Broadway 1357); there may be other isolated exceptions as well.

GREEN, MARION = Wilfred Glenn (Lyric)

GREEN, MAZIE = Josie Miles (Silvertone); probably others

GREEN, SADIE* = Bessie Brown (Oriole); another, unknown (Pathé, Perfect)

GREEN, VIOLET = Clara Smith (Okeh)

GREY, HAROLD = Porter Grainger (Victor)

GRIMES, BETTY = Vaughn De Leath (Champion)

GRINSTED, WILLIAM S. = Frank C. Stanley (performing under his given name, both as vocalist and banjo soloist) (early cylinders)

GUITAR EVANGELIST = Edward W. Clayborn (Vocalion 1082, later re-pressed with labels crediting Clayborn)

GUNBOAT BILLY & THE SPARROW = Arthur Fields and Fred Hall (Victor); probably the same (Crown, Paramount)

HADLEY, ELDER J.J. = Charley Patton (Paramount)

HAHL, ADOLPH J. = Arthur Hall (performing under his birth name) (Edison)

HAINES, RALPH = Scrappy Lambert, possibly others (Jewel, Oriole); William Robyn, possibly others (Domino, Regal)

HALE, CHESTER* = Scrappy Lambert (Banner, Pathé, Perfect and related labels)

HALEY, HARRY = Henry Burr (Banner and related labels; Cameo; possibly others)

HALL, EDGAR = Andrea Sarto (Columbia)

HALL, FREDDY = Billy Jones (Champion). Vocals only; not to be confused with bandleader Fred Hall.

HALL, JAMES = Andrea Sarto

HAM, HAMFOOT = Joe McCoy (virtually all Decca issues except 7484; Vocalion, except as noted); Herb Morand (Decca 7484, Vocalion 05136, 05287); Alberta Smith (Vocalion 04828, 04925); Morand and Smith (Vocalion 05136, 05287); Lil Allen (Vocalion 05233)

HAMILTON, EDWARD = Reinald Werrenrath (Victor only); William Robyn (Emerson, Medallion and related labels); others, probably including Robyn (Paramount and related labels)

HAMILTON, RAY = William Robyn (Lincoln)

HAMLIN QUARTETTE = Woodlawn Quartette of Woodlawn, Alabama (Champion)

HAPPINESS BOYS = Billy Jones and Ernest Hare (often with piano accompaniment by Larry Briers [through mid-1925] and Dave Kaplan [from late 1925]) (numerous labels)

HAPPY JACK = J. Donald Parker

HARDY, JOHN = Gene Autry (Van Dyke)

HARE, MR. = Ernest Hare (various children's labels)

HARGENS, TRILBY = Thelma La Vizzo (Herwin)

HARLAN & ROBERTS = John H. Meyer and Charles Hart or Henry Moeller (Late 1920's releases. Not to be confused with veteran comedians Byron G. Harlan and Bob Roberts, both of whom had retired from recording by the time that these issues appeared.) (Champion)

HARLEM HANNAH = Peggy English (Bluebird, Electradisk, Sunrise)

HARMONIZERS (QUARTET) = Charles Hart (tenor), Billy Jones (lead tenor), Steve Porter (baritone), Harry Donaghy (bass) (Edison)

HARMONY BROADCASTERS = Billy Jones and Ernest Hare; possibly others (Champion)

HARMONY FOUR = Gladys Rice (soprano), John Young, George Wilton Ballard (tenors), Donald Chalmers (bass) (Edison)

HARMONY (MALE) QUARTETTE = Columbia Male Quartet (through mid-1906); Peerless Quartet (from late 1906) (Harmony)

HAROLD, EUGENE = Billy Jones

HARPER, BILLY = Irving Kaufman (Brunswick)

HARRIS & HARRIS = Alfoncy and Bethenea Harris (Victor)

HARRIS & SMITH = Charles Hart and Elliott Shaw (Champion)

HARRIS, DAVID = Irving Kaufman (Columbia); pseudonym on National Music Lovers for Irving Kaufman (1233, 1234); Vernon Dalhart (1074, 1075); Arthur Fields (1102, 1104, 1119, 1204); Ernest Hare (1096); Dan Hennessey (mx. 2692, on NML 1225), Billy Jones (1075); Walter Van Brunt (mx. 2624, on NML 1225). National Music Lovers releases by Charles Harrison and Elliott Shaw has also been reported under this name, but have not yet been verified.

HARRIS, FRANK = Irving Kaufman (Banner and related labels; Columbia)

HARRIS, HARRY = Vernon Dalhart (National Music Lovers)

HARRIS, HELEN = Lillian Miller; Hattie Snow (Champion)

HARRIS, HENRY = Vernon Dalhart

HARRIS, MAE = Hazel Meyers (Domino)

HARRIS, MAGNOLIA (& HOWLING SMITH) = Victoria Spivey and Big Bill Broonzy (identification per Victoria Spivey, in a 1965 *Record Research* interview) (Melotone, Vocalion)

HARRIS, MAMIE = Rosa Henderson (Pathé, Perfect; Domino except as noted): Hazel Meyers (Domino 361, 362)

HARRIS, MAXINE = Mae Matthews (Champion)

HARRIS, PEARL = Josie Miles (Olympic, except as noted); Mary Straine (Olympic/Majestic 1522, from Black Swan masters)

HARRIS, SIM = Ernest Stoneman (Oriole)

HARRISON, JAMES = Frederick J. Wheeler (numerous brands)

HARROW & EDWARDS = Billy Jones and Ernest Hare (National Music Lovers)

HART, RUTH = Ruth Carhart (Champion)

HARTLEY, LESTER = Franklyn Baur (?) (Grey Gull and related labels)

HARVEY, HAROLD = Lewis James

HATFIELD, JAMES = John Ryan (Grey Gull and related labels 4117, 4171; probably others)

HAUSER, ROBERT = William O'Connor (of WLS-Chicago) (Champion)

HAWKINS, UNCLE BEN = Ernest Stoneman (Champion)

HAWKINS, UNCLE BEN & HIS BOYS = Ernest Stoneman & the Grayson County Boys (Champion)

HAWLEY = possibly Arthur Collins (Indestructible cylinders). Alleged by Walsh, but no examples have been found to verify this.

HAYDN QUARTET — Several personnels are known for this group, a descendant of the Edison Male Quartet (*q.v.*) . The *Phonoscope* for June 1899 lists personnel as Fred Rycrofe, Charles Belling (tenor), S.H.Dudley (baritone), William F. Hooley (bass). A 1900 Berliner document lists Fred Rycrof*t* (tenor), Harry Macdonough (lead tenor), Dudley (baritone), Hooley (bass). Dudley recalled the 1901 Victor personnel as Albert Campbell (tenor), W.T. Leahy (lead tenor), Dudley (baritone), Hooley (bass). By 1902-1903 personnel had become John Bieling (tenor), Macdonough (lead tenor), Dudley, and Hooley. Reinald Werrenrath replaced Dudley after 1913. (Berliner, Improved Gram-O-Phone, Victor [including DeLuxe, Monarch, and other early label variations])

HAYDEN QUARTET = modified spelling for the Haydn Quartet, adopted in 1913 (Victor)

HAYES, DADDY MOON & HIS BOYS = Harvey Hull & His Down Home Boys (Champion)

HAYES, ETHEL = Monette Moore (Harmograph)

HAYES, LOU = Vernon Dalhart

HAYWIRE MAC = Harry McClintock (Decca)

HAZELTON, JOE = Frank Kamplain (Van Dyke)

HEIDELBERG QUINTET = Will Oakland (counter-tenor), John Bieling (tenor), Billy Murray (lead tenor), Steve Porter (baritone), William F. Hooley (bass) (Victor)

HENDERSON, CATHERINE = Eva Taylor (Diva, Velvet Tone)

HENDERSON, FRANK = Harry Frankel (Champion)

HENDERSON, ROSE = Rosa Henderson (label errors on Paramount, Pathé and Perfect)

HERMAN BROTHERS = Hobbs Brothers (Broadway)

HEROLD, FRANCIS = Arthur Fields (Grey Gull and related labels)

HIGGINS, SI = Arthur Fields (Harmony and related labels)

HILL, BOB = Bob Miller (Victor)

HILL, SAM = Gene Autry (Grey Gull and related labels). Not to be confused with Sam Hill and His Orchestra on Oriole, which is usually a pseudonym for Fletcher Henderson's Orchestra.

HILLER, JOSEPHINE = possibly Dolly Kay, based on aural evidence (Cameo)

HILLY, DAN = Arthur Fields (Clarion, Columbia and related labels)

HILTON, CHARLES = Charles Harrison

HOBBS, HERB = Arthur Fields (Pathé, Perfect)

HOLLAND, BYRON = Byron G. Harlan (Supertone)

HOLMES, DICK = Jack Kaufman (Jewel, Oriole)

HOLMES, JOHN = Irving Kaufman

HOLT & SINGER = Scrappy Lambert and Bill Hillpot (Jewel, Oriole)

HOLTON & CROSS = Scrappy Lambert and Bill Hillpot (Oriole)

HOLTON, LARRY = Scrappy Lambert (Jewel, Oriole and related brands)

HOMESTEAD TRIO = Gladys Rice, Betsy Lane Shepherd (sopranos); Amy Ellerman (contralto). Elizabeth Spencer replaced Rice in 1921 (Edison).

HOMETOWNERS = Arthur Fields and Fred Hall (vocals). This name was also used frequently by Fred Hall's Orchestra. (Bell, probably other minor labels)

HONEY DUKE (& HIS UKE) = Johnny Marvin (numerous labels)

HONEY GAL & SMOKE = Gene ("Honey Gal") Cobb and Jack ("Smoke") Gray (Champion)

HORTON, ROBERT = Ed Allington (an actual performer and composer) (Crescent)

HOWARD & DORAN = Gerald Underhill Macy and Ed Smalle (Oriole)

HOWARD & MITCHELL = Frederic Baer and Henry Moeller (Champion)

HOWARD, ALBERT = Eddie Nelson (Regal)

HOWARD, ANNA = Lucy Isabelle Marsh (Victor)

HOWARD, FATSO = Bob Howard (Clarion, Velvet Tone)

HOWARD, FRANK = Albert Campbell (Zon-O-Phone, Oxford and other early brands); Arthur Hall and possibly others (Silvertone and other 1920's brands); Clarence Todd (Silvertone 2770 only)

HOWARD, TOM = Tom Stacks (Edison)

HOWARD, WILLIAM = Frederic Baer (Champion)

HOWE, PAUL = Willard Robison (Harmony)

HUBBARD, GEORGE = George P. Watson (National Music Lovers)

HUDSON MALE QUARTET = Shannon Four; Revelers (Pathé, Perfect and related labels)

HUGHES, DAN = Billy Murray (Oriole)

HUGHES, PHIL = Scrappy Lambert (Harmony and related labels; Okeh); Dick Robertson (Okeh)

HUGHEY, DAN = Bradley Kincaid (Champion)

HUGUET, JOSEFINA = Giuseppina Huguet (Victor)

HUNT, DAVE = Willie Stoneman (Champion)

HUNTER & JENKINS = Leola B. Wilson and Kid Wesley Wilson (Vocalion)

HUNTER, JAMES = Arthur Fields (Clover, Emerson, and probably other Consolidated Record Corporation brands; National Music Lovers 1444)

HUTCHENS & ALSTON = John McGhee and _Cogar (Champion)

HUTCHENS BROTHERS = John McGhee and Frank Welling (Champion)

HUTCHENS FAMILY TRIO = John and Alma McGhee, Frank Welling (Champion)

HUTCHENS, JOHN = John McGhee (Champion)

"IKE" = Cliff Edwards (Harmograph)

IMPERIAL MINSTRELS — Personnel varies, but usually includes Roger Harding, Harry Macdonough (tenors), Len Spencer, Steve Porter (baritones) (Columbia cylinders, 1900-1901)

IMPERIAL QUARTET — Personnel unknown. This group is unrelated to the later Imperial Quartet of Chicago (see next entry). (early discs and cylinders, *c.* 1898-1900)

IMPERIAL QUARTET (OF CHICAGO) = Wallace Moody, C.R. Wood, Ben Q. Tufts, Oliver Johnson (Victor). This group should not be confused with the much earlier Imperial Quartet (see previous entry).

INK SPOTS = Charles Fuqua (tenor voice/guitar/ukulele), Bill Kenny (tenor voice/cymbal), Ivory Watson (baritone voice/guitar), Orville Jones (bass voice/ string bass) (Bluebird, Decca and related labels, Victor)

INTERNATIONAL ASSOCIATION QUARTET = Paul J. Gilbert, P.H. Metcalf, C.M. Keeler, Edward W. Peck (Edison cylinders)

INVINCIBLE FOUR (I) = Invincible Male Quartet (Edison cylinders, early 1900's)

INVINCIBLE FOUR (II) = Peerless Quartet (Pathé and related labels, c. 1918-1919; probably others). Not to be confused with the earlier Invincible Male Quartet, which made discs and cylinders *c.* 1904-1906.

INVINCIBLE MALE QUARTET = Byron G. Harlan, George Seymour Lenox (tenors), Arthur Collins (baritone), Frank C. Stanley (bass). Albert Campbell replaced Lenox on Columbia and possibly other labels. (American Odeon Record, American Record Company and related labels, Columbia and related labels, Edison cylinders, probably others *c.* 1904-1906)

IRVING, HENRY = Irving Kaufman

IRVING, JOHN = Irving Kaufman (Parlophone PNY- series [American])

IRVING, MILTON = Irving Mills (as a band vocalist) (Brunswick, Vocalion, probably others)

IRVING, REX = Irving Kaufman

IRVINGS & JACKSON = Irving and Jack Kaufman (Cameo)

IRVINGS BROTHERS = Irving and Jack Kaufman

JACKSON, CHARLES = Louis Winsch (Operaphone). Not to be confused with blues performer Papa Charlie Jackson on Paramount.

JACKSON, HAPPY = Frank Luther (Herschel Gold Seal)

JACKSON, SADIE — This has been suggested as a pseudonym for Zaidee Jackson (*q.v.*), but aural evidence is inconclusive. (Columbia)

JACKSON, SMILIN' TUBBY = Chubby Parker (Champion)

JACKSON, VIOLET = Hattie Garland (Gennett 6090); Eloise Bennett (Gennett 6147)

JACKSON, ZAIDEE — Contrary to some conjecture, this was not a pseudonym. Jackson was an actual performer, appearing and recording in London in 1929-1933. (Pathé, Perfect)

JACOBS, WALTER = Walter Vinscon (Bluebird, Montgomery Ward, Okeh)

JAMES, LEWIS & MARRON, JOHN = Billy Jones and Ernest Hare (label error on Silvertone 2556 only)

JAMES, PAULINE = Hattie Garland (Gennett 6147)

JAMIESON & TURNER = Charles Hart and Elliott Shaw (Phantasie Concert Record)

JARVIS, HOTSY = Evelyn Preer (Banner, Domino and related labels)

JASPER & BENNETT = Sammy Fain and Artie Dunn (Jewel)

JAZZ CASPAR = Billy Higgins (Banner, probably others)

JEANETTE = Jeanette James (Paramount)

JEFFERSON, GEORGE = Sam Collins (*Hesitation Blues* on Champion 15472; reverse side is by another unknown performer)

JENNINGS BROTHERS = Tweedy Brothers (Champion)

JENNINGS, HERB = Welby Toomey (Champion)

JEWEL TRIO = Vernon Dalhart (vocal/harmonica), Carson Robison (vocal/ guitar), Adelyn Hood (vocal/violin) (Jewel)

JIMSON BROTHERS = Frank Luther and Carson Robison (Edison)

JOHNSON, ARTHUR = Noble Sissle (Crescent)

JOHNSON, BABE = Edmonia Henderson (Silvertone)

JOHNSON, BESSIE = Margaret McKee (Black Swan only, from Olympic masters). Whistling solos, not to be confused with later gospel releases on Okeh by the actual Bessie Johnson.

JOHNSON, CHARLES = Royal Dadmun; Lane Rogers (both on Regal)

JOHNSON, EDWARD = George Ake (Champion)

JOHNSON, EMMA = Helen Clark (Edison)

JOHNSON, ERNEST = Ernest Thompson (Harmony, Velvet Tone and related labels)

JOHNSON, FANNIE = Viola McCoy (Cameo, Romeo)

JOHNSON, GENE = Gene Autry (Timely Tunes)

JOHNSON, GLADYS = Viola McCoy (Variety)

JOHNSON, MARTHA = Lottie Kimbrough (Superior)

JOHNSON, PORKCHOP = Leothus ("Porkchop") Green (Champion)

JOHNSON, WILLIAM = Billy Jones

JONES & CRAWFORD = Billy Golden and Billy Heins (Diva, Harmony and related labels, reissued from earlier Columbia masters)

JONES & HARROLD = Henry Creamer and J. Turner Layton (Claxtonola, Paramount)

JONES & MOORE = Flournoy Miller and Aubrey Lyles (Jewel, Oriole)

JONES & WHITE = Ernest Hare and Al Bernard (Black Swan)

JONES, BESSIE = Mae Glover (Supertone)

JONES, DUNCAN = Cal Stewart (with Ada Jones on *Uncle Josh & Aunt Mandy* [sic] *Put Up the Kitchen Stove*; with Gilbert Girard on *Uncle Josh at the Dentist*) (Grey Gull, Radiex and related labels, reissued from earlier Emerson masters)

JONES, HENRY = Ernest Hare

JONES, LOUELLA —Confirmed as a pseudonym for Alberta Perkins (Mrs. Bob Fuller) by Louis Hooper in a 1966 *Record Research* interview (Hooper was the pianist in Bob Fuller's trio and was present at the "Jones" sessions) (Domino). Rust also lists Jones as a pseudonym for Monette Moore on Regal.

JONES, MAMIE = Aileen Stanley (Black Swan only, from Olympic masters); Ethel Waters (Silvertone only)

JONES, MARTHA = Lottie Kimbrough (Superior)

JONES, MAUDE = Lillyn Brown (Medallion)
JONES, MR. = Billy Jones (various children's brands)
JONES, REESE = Billy Jones (Edison)
JONES, REV. JORDAN = Rev. Emmet Dickinson (Oriole)
JONES, REV. SAM HALL = Rev. J. M. Gates (Oriole)
JONES, SADDIE = Eliza Christmas Lee (Rich-Tone)
JONES, W. REESE = Billy Jones (performing under his given name)
JONES, WALLACE = Thomas Warner (Champion)
JONES, WILLIE = Willie Baker (Supertone only). Not to be confused with
  the actual Willie Jones, who recorded during the same period for Gennett,
  Vocalion, and other labels as pianist, vocalist, and director.
JONES, WILLY = Billy Jones (minor labels)
JORDAN BROTHERS = Charles Hart and Elliott Shaw
JORDAN, HENRY = Charles Hart (Puretone, Puritan and related labels)
JORDAN, JAMES = Charles Hart (various minor brands); Elliott Shaw
  (Okeh only)
JORDAN, JENNIE = Hattie Garland (Champion)
JORDAN, TOMMY = Lonnie Johnson (Columbia)
JORDAY, BILLY = Dock Roberts (Champion)
JOY BOYS = Sammy Fain and Artie Dunn (Banner, Regal and related labels)
JOYCE, RANDOLPH = Jan Peerce (Associated transcriptions, mid-1930's)
JORDAN, JESSIE = Hattie Garland (Champion)
JUDSON, ROBERT = Ernest Hare (Pathé, Perfect and related labels)
JUDSON SISTERS = WSAI Maids Of Melody (Champion)

KAUFMAN BROTHERS = Phil and Jack Kaufman (Edison, possibly others,
  1916); Irving and Jack Kaufman (minor labels, from 1917)
KEAP, OSCAR = Louis Winsch (Crescent)
KEENE, CHARLES = Charles Kaley (Banner and related labels). British
  Imperial issues of the same masters were credited correctly to Kaley. Walsh's
  identification of Keene as Gene Austin is incorrect.
KELLY, WILLIE = Roosevelt Sykes (Victor)
KENDALL & KELLY = Redferne Hollinshead and Charles Harrison
  (Champion)
KENDALL, EDWARD = Willie Weston (Crescent). Walsh listed Weston as a
  pseudonym in his 1944 list, but later discovered that Weston was an actual
  performer.
KENT, FRANKLIN = Joseph A. Phillips (Okeh)
KENTUCKY MOUNTAIN BOYS = Lester McFarland & John Gardner
  (Supertone)
KENYON, JANE = Elizabeth Wheeler
KERN, JIMMY = Arthur Fields (Harmony, Velvet Tone and related labels;

Gennett, Silvertone [from Gennett masters] and related labels; Apollo, Pathé, Perfect)

KERNELL, FRANK = S.H. Dudley (Victor)

KILLEEN, PETE = Irving Kaufman (Pathé, Perfect)

KIMBROUGH, LENA = Lottie Kimbrough (Meritt)

KINCAID, JOE = Vernon Dalhart

KING, AL = Henry Burr (Oriole)

KING, DAISY = probably Vaughn De Leath (Oriole)

KING, FRED = Vernon Dalhart

KING, HENRY = Arthur Fields

KING, MARTIN = Scrappy Lambert; possibly others (Domino)

KINGSTON, KATHLEEN = Mary Carson (Edison)

KLINE, DAVID = Monroe Silver (Regal)

KNAPP, FRANK = Henry Burr (Harmony and related labels)

KNICKERBOCKER QUARTET (I) — Original 1909 personnel included John Young, George M. Stricklett (tenors), Frederick Wheeler (baritone), and Gus Reed (bass). After 1912 there was no consistent personnel; Edison files list Robert D. Armour, John Finnegan, Royal Fish, Harvey Hindermeyer, William F. Hooley, Reinald Werrenrath, Frederick Wheeler, and John Young as participating in various sessions.

KNICKERBOCKER QUARTET (II) = George Eldred, Lewis James, William Morgan, Glenn Howard (Columbia)

KNICKERBOCKER QUINTET = Parvin Witte, Charles H. Bates, Geoffrey O'Hara, Walter C. White, Leon Parmett (per 1905 Edison supplement; voices not specified) (Edison cylinders)

KYZER, MARIE = Marie Kaiser (Gennett)

LAKESHORE CLUB QUARTET = Peerless Quartet (Champion)

LANCE, ROLAND = Scrappy Lambert (Banner, Broadway and related labels)

LANDON, LEE = Hoke Rice (Champion)

LANE & HARRIS = Louis John Johnson and Ben Alley (Champion)

LANE, JACK & HIS UKE = Johnny Marvin (Champion)

LANG, HAROLD = Scrappy Lambert (Perfect)

LAWRENCE, HARRY = Joseph A. Phillips (Rex; probably related vertical-cut brands)

LAZY LARRY = Frank Marvin (Romeo and related labels)

LEAVITT, ROBERT = Carson Robison (Van Dyke)

LE FEVRE, EDWARD = Edward M. Favor (early cylinders)

LEE, BESSIE = Trixie Smith (Broadway, Silvertone)

LEE, BUDDY — Contrary to conjecture, this was not a pseudonym. Lee replaced Cliff Edwards in the 1926 London production of *Lady Be Good*. Not to be confused with a 1950's rock-and-roll performer of the same name. (Gennett)

LEE, CAROLINE = Bessie Brown (Oriole 698, 716, 746, 771); Josie Miles (Oriole, except as noted for Bessie Brown)

LEE, MANDY* – At least three separate performers, none of whom resemble the others vocally, recorded under this name in the 1920's. 1923 Gennett releases are possibly by Vaughn de Leath, based on aural identification. Two other unknown performers recorded as Mandy Lee, one for Pathé and one for the Plaza Music Company (Banner), in 1926.

LEE, VIRGINIA = possibly Vaughn De Leath (Gennett; Harmony and related labels)

LEIGHTON, CHESTER = Dick Robertson; probably others (Harmony and related labels, Okeh)

LEJEUNE, GABRIELLE = Mme. Charles Gilibert (performing under her maiden name) (Victor 70025)

LeMAIRE, PETE = Pete La Mar (Victor)

LENOX & JOHNSON = Reed Miller and Lane Rogers (Banner, Regal and related labels)

LENOX & ROBERT = Reed Miller and Nevada Van Der Veer (Grey Gull, Oriole and related labels)

LENOX, GEORGE = Reed Miller (Oriole, Regal and probably others, from Emerson and possibly other sources)

LENOX, RUTH = probably Helen Clark; possibly others (Okeh, Pathé and related labels, other minor brands)

LEON, ALBERT = Ernest Hare (National Music Lovers)

LEROY'S BUDDY = Bill Gaither (Decca)

LESLIE, WALTER = Ernest Hare (Cameo)

LEWIS & SCOTT = Billy Jones and Ernest Hare

LEWIS, HOWARD = Arthur Hall

LEWIS, IDA = Viola Bartlette (Silvertone)

LEWIS, JUSTICE = Louis Winsch (Pathé and related labels); possibly Joseph A. Phillips (per Walsh) (Okeh, Rex and related labels)

LEWIS, KATE = Ida Cox (Broadway)

LEWIS, ROBERT = Lewis James (Columbia, Oriole)

LEWIS, RODMAN = Scrappy Lambert (Banner, Conqueror, Jewel and other Plaza Music Company /American Record Corporation brands; possibly other non-Plaza/ARC brands)

LEWIS, UNCLE = Lewis James (various children's brands)

LEWIS, WILLIAM = Arthur Fields

LIBERTY (MALE) QUARTET = Shannon Four (Emerson and related labels)

LINCOLN, CHESTER = Byron G. Harlan (Champion)

LINCOLN, MAC = Arthur Fields (Van Dyke)

LINN, BEN – Walsh's 1962 listing incorrectly claimed this as a pseudonym on Emerson for Eddie Nelson. In fact, Linn was a performer in his own right whose voice and style bore only slight resemblance to Nelson's.

LITCHFIELD, BEN = possibly Franklyn Baur (aural identification per Walsh) (acoustically recorded Grey Gull, Nadsco, Radiex and related labels); Arthur Fields (Grey Gull mx. 2516; Van Dyke 75215); Jerry White (*q.v.*) (Van Dyke 74261, 74262, 74267, 74268); probably others (Grey Gull, Radiex and related labels)

LITTLE SISTER = Irene Scruggs (Varsity 6063, dubbed from Gennett)

LITTLE, TOBE = Vernon Dalhart (Okeh)

LIVINGSTON = John Bieling (early cylinders). Conjecture per Walsh; no examples have been located for verification.

LLOYD, ED = Ed Kirkeby (director of the California Ramblers, occasionally featured as vocalist) (Pathé, Regal, Silvertone, many others)

LOEW, JACK = Irving or Jack Kaufman (Romeo)

LONESOME PINE TWINS = Frank & James McCravy (Banner, Regal, Supertone and other minor labels)

LONE STAR RANGER = Whitey Johns (per American Record Corporation files). Identification as Vernon Dalhart or Arthur Fields (per Walsh and others) is probably incorrect, at least for the ARC-derived Broadway issues under this name.

LONG BROTHERS = Gene Autry and Jimmie Long (Victor)

LONG, TOM = Gene Autry (Sunrise)

LORD, JACK = Scrappy Lambert (Velvet Tone and related labels)

LORIN, BURT = Scrappy Lambert (Victor)

LOTTY, WILL = Henry Whitter (Champion)

LOTUS QUARTET = George Seymour Lenox, George M. Stricklett (tenors), Charles Lewis (baritone), Frank C. Stanley (bass) (Edison cylinders)

LOYD, EDDIE = Eddie Kirkeby (director of the California Ramblers, occasionally featured as vocalist) (Bluebird)

LUMBERJACKS = Arthur Fields and Fred Hall, sometimes with an additional unknown singer. This name was also used as a pseudonym for several dance orchestras on Cameo, Romeo, and other minor labels.

LUTHER & FABER = Frank Luther and Carson Robison (Van Dyke)

LUTHER BROTHERS = Frank Luther and Carson Robison (Broadway, Paramount)

LUTHER, FRANCIS = Frank Luther (Champion and other labels)

LYBOULT, WALTER = Al Shayne (Champion)

LYONS & HEILMAN = Billy Jones and Ernest Hare

LYONS, BILLY = Billy Jones

LYRIC MALE QUARTET = Shannon Four (1920's issues on Edison, Harmony, and various minor brands). Not to be confused with the earlier Lyric Quartet on Victor.

LYRIC CHOIR = Lyric Trio (I) (Victor)

LYRIC QUARTET – Original 1906 personnel included Elise Stevenson (soprano), Corinne Morgan (contralto), Harry Macdonough (tenor), Frank C. Stanley (baritone-bass). In late 1910 or early 1911, the quartet was reorganized as Olive Kline (later replaced by Elsie Baker) (soprano), Marguerite Dunlap (contralto), Macdonough, and Reinald Werrenrath (baritone). (Victor)

LYRIC TRIO (I) – Original 1898 personnel included Estella Louise Mann (soprano), John Havens (tenor), William F. Hooley (bass). Harry Macdonough replaced Havens in August 1899 (Edison and Lyric cylinders, the latter manufactured by Ms. Mann's short-lived Lyric Record Company). By 1900, personnel was Grace Spencer (soprano), Harry Macdonough (tenor), William F. Hooley (bass). (Berliner, Improved Gram-O-Phone and Victor [including Monarch and other label variations]).

LYRIC TRIO (II) = Will Oakland (counter-tenor), Albert Campbell (tenor), Henry Burr (lead tenor) (Victor, 1914-1915)

"MAC" = Harry McClintock (early 1930's RCA products)

MacDONALD & BROONES = Johnny Marvin (as a soloist, despite the duet designation) (Champion)

MacDONALD, HARRY = Harry Macdonough (Reed and Dawson cylinders, probably other early disc and cylinder brands)

MacFARLAND, BOB = Irving Kaufman (Broadway)

MACK & MITCHELL = Billie Wilson and Eddie Green (Silvertone)

MACK, ARTHUR = Arthur Fields

MACK, BOBBY = William Robyn (Muse)

MACY, JERRY = Gerald Underhill Macy (Gennett)

MAGEE, ERWIN = Irving Mills (as a band vocalist) (Pathé)

MANDEL SISTERS = Joe and Dan Mooney (Supertone S- series)

MANDER, AMBROSE = Arthur Fields (Crescent, Pathé and related labels); another, unknown but definitely not Fields (Crescent)

MANHANSETT QUARTET – First listed by Edison in 1890, although no personnel was given. By 1892 the group was recording for New Jersey cylinders and was identified in their catalog as George J. Gaskin, Gilbert Girard (tenors), Joe Riley (baritone), and (?) Evans (bass). By the mid-1890's, personnel included John Bieling, Gaskin (tenors), Riley (baritone), and Jim Cherry (bass). Cherry was later replaced by Walter Snow. (Edison and various early regional cylinder brands)

MANHATTAN LADIES' QUARTET = Irene Cummings, Mabel Meade Davis, Annie Laurie McCorkle, Anne Winkoop (personnel per 1912 Edison supplement; voices not given) (Edison cylinders)

MANHATTAN QUARTET —— Personnel unknown, although Walsh listed Arthur Hall (tenor) as one member. (Edison, Victor)

MANHATTAN TRIO = Metropolitan Mixed Trio (Edison cylinders)
MANN, ESTELLE = Bertha Henderson (Broadway)
MANN, FRANK = Ernest Hare (Pathé and related labels)
MARCO, ANGELINA = Vaughn De Leath (Harmony and related labels)
MARK, FREDDIE = Irving Kaufman (Harmony and related labels)
MARLOW & YOUNG = Rutherford & Foster (Champion)
MARLOW, ANDY = Howard Keesee (Champion)
MARRON, JOHN = Ernest Hare (Silvertone)
MARSDEN, VICTORIA = Gladys Rice
MARSHALL, FRANK = Tom Morton (Original Indiana Five drummer, as vocalist with his band; identification per Rust) (Jewel, Oriole)
MARTIN, HAPPY = Jack Kaufman
MARTIN, JACK = Arthur Fields
MARTINI, ENRICO = John Charles Thomas (Lyric vertical-cut)
MARTINI, PIETRO = Max Bloch (National Music Lovers, from Emerson masters); unknown (National Music Lovers, from Lyric masters)
MASKED MARVEL = Charley Patton (Paramount)
MASSEY, BOB = Vernon Dalhart (minor labels)
MASSEY, GUY = Vernon Dalhart (minor labels). Dalhart borrowed this name from his cousin, disputed composer (or co-composer, or appropriator, depending upon the account) of *The Prisoner's Song.*
MATER, FRANK = Rudy Vallee (Harmony and related labels)
MATTHEW, J. = Henry Burr (Medallion)
MAUER, RUSSELL = J. Lynn Griffin (Champion, Supertone)
MAY, JIMMY = Johnny Marvin (Bell, Emerson and possibly other Consolidated Record Corporation labels)
MAYNARD, JAMES = Arthur Hall (Champion)
McCLASKEY & MEYERS = Henry Burr and John H. Meyer (Gennett)
McCLASKEY, HARRY = Henry Burr (performing under his given name) (Crescent, Okeh, Paramount, Pathé and related labels, many others)
McCLASKEY, SHAMUS = Henry Burr (Emerson and related labels)
McCOY, VIOLET = Viola McCoy (Cameo, possibly others)
McHUGH, MARTIN = Walter Van Brunt (National Music Lovers)
McLAUGHLIN, GEORGE = Vernon Dalhart
MEADOWS, ARTHUR = Arthur Fields
MELODY THREE = J. Donald Parker, Will Donaldson and Phil Dewey (various labels)
MELODY TWINS = probably Ed Smalle and Gerald Underhill Macy (Oriole)
MEN ABOUT TOWN = J. Donald Parker, Will Donaldson and Phil Dewey (Edison)
MENDELSSOHN MIXED QUARTET = Edith Chapman (soprano), Corinne Morgan (contralto), George Morgan Stricklett (tenor), Frank C. Stanley (baritone-bass) (Edison cylinders)

MEREDITH, MAY = Helen Clark (Columbia)

MERRYMAKERS = Revelers (Brunswick)

MERWIN, BART = Robert Merwin

MERWIN, ROBERT — This was an actual performer, although Rust once contended that Merwin "is almost certainly a pseudonym." Merwin's existence was verified in a 1976 letter to *Record Research* by his son.

MESSON, SARA = Clementine Smith (*q.v.*; possibly a pseudonym itself) (Oriole 325)

METROPOLITAN ENTERTAINERS = Elizabeth Spencer (soprano), Charles Harrison (tenor), Ernest Hare (baritone) (Edison)

METROPOLITAN MIXED TRIO — Original 1904 personnel on Edison cylinders was Corinne Morgan (contralto), George Seymour Lenox (tenor), Frank C. Stanley (baritone-bass) (Edison cylinders). Later disc and cylinder issues on various brands featured Elise Stevenson (soprano), Henry Burr (tenor), Stanley (baritone-bass).

METROPOLITAN QUARTET = Florence Hinkle (soprano), Margaret Keyes (contralto), John Young (tenor), Frederick Wheeler (bass) (Edison cylinders, 1908-1913). Edison disc and cylinder issues after 1913 drew on available studio performers and personnel was not consistent, although Walsh notes that Young, Wheeler, and Elizabeth Spencer (soprano) were present at many sessions.

MEYER, SAUL = Monroe Silver (Champion)

MEYERS & GILLETTE = John H. Meyer and Henry Burr (Okeh)

MEYERS & HART = John H. Meyer and Henry Moeller (Champion)

MEYERS, JOHN = John H. Meyer (Lyric, Okeh, probably others)

MIAMI VALLEY TRIO = Sterling Trio (in its later form, without Henry Burr) (Champion)

MILLER & MILLER = Bob and Charlotte Miller (Okeh 45000 series)

MILLER, DAISY = Catherine Boswell ("The Sunshine Girl," per Gennett ledger) (Champion)

MILLER, DAVID = Holland Puckett (label error on Champion 15298 only)

MILLER, KENNETH = Charles Harrison (Champion)

MILLER'S BULLFROG ENTERTAINERS = Bob Miller and unknown group (Okeh 45000 series)

MILLS BROTHERS = John Mills, Jr. (vocal/guitar) with Herbert, Harry and Donald Mills (vocals). John Jr. died in 1936 and was replaced briefly by Bernard Addison (guitar) in London. John Mills, Sr. took his son's place when the group returned to the United States in late 1936. (Brunswick, Decca and related labels)

MILLS, JOSIE = Josie Miles (Emerson)

MILLS, LILLIAN = Lillian Miller (Gennett)

MILLS, VIOLET = Julia Moody (Domino)

MINSTRELS — Generic description used on Columbia and derivative labels as well as Columbia, Indestructible, Lakeside, Oxford, U.S. Everlasting, and other cylinder brands. Personnel varies considerably, but a large number of pre-1909 releases are by the Rambler Minstrel Company (*q.v.*). From 1909 onward, the Peerless Quartet (*q.v.*) was responsible for many anonymous Minstrel releases.

MISS ANNETTE = Annette Hanshaw (Pathé, Perfect and related labels)

MISS FRANCIS = Adeline Francis (Indestructible cylinders and derivative brands)

MISS FRANKIE = Jane Howard (Banner, Domino and Regal); unknown other (possibly Howard) (Pathé, Perfect; Grey Gull, Radiex and related labels)

MISS LEE = Eliza Christmas Lee (Connorized)

MISSISSIPPI MATILDA = Matilda Powell (Bluebird)

MITCHELL & WHITE = Vernon Dalhart and Ed Smalle (Pathé, Perfect)

MITCHELL, SIDNEY = Franklyn Baur (Oriole); Irving Kaufman (Clover, Silvertone and other minor brands); unknown (definitely not Kaufman) (Triangle)

MITCHELL, WARREN = Vernon Dalhart (Pathé, Perfect)

MITTELSTADT, EDOUARD = Arthur Middleton

MITZI – Rust notes that Mizzi Hajos performed in the mid-1920's as "Mitzi." However, the Gennett recordings issued under that name (entered in the Starr Piano Company files simply as "Mitzi") are not definitely verified as Hajos' work.

MODERNAIRES – Original mid-1930's personnel included Hal Dickinson, Ralph Brewster, Chuck Goldstein, Bill Conway. Later frequent personnel changes are beyond the scope of this book. (Bluebird, Decca)

MOONLIGHT TRIO = Gladys Rice (soprano), George Wilton Ballard (tenor), Donald Chalmers (bass) (Edison)

MOONSHINE DAVE = B.L. ("Sunshine") Pritchard (Champion)

MOORE, BUDDY = Al Bernard (Van Dyke)

MOORE, HARRY A. = Vernon Dalhart (Black Swan 2090-A, 18047-A); Charles Harrison (Black Swan 2090-B, 18047-B) (all from Olympic masters)

MOORE, WEBSTER = Bill Coty (with Jack Albin's Orchestra only, Harmony and related labels); Scrappy Lambert (Harmony and related labels)

MORELEY, HERBERT = Morton Harvey

MORGAN, ICKY = Dick Morgan (banjo/guitarist with Ben Pollack's Orchestra, occasionally featured as vocalist) (Regal and related labels)

MORRIS & ELLIOTT = Charles Hart and Elliott Shaw (?) (National Music Lovers 1102)

MORRIS, JAMES = Vernon Dalhart (Black Swan, from Olympic masters)

MORRIS, WILLIAM = Billy Jones (National Music Lovers)

MORROW, GEORGE = Irving Kaufman (Harmony and related labels)

MORSE, DICK = Vernon Dalhart (Oriole)

MORTON, GEORGE = Chick Bullock (Banner, Perfect, Romeo and other American Record Corporation brands; Victor)

MORTON, JAMES = Morton Downey (Edison)

MR. X = Arthur Fields (usually); Vernon Dalhart (rarely); probably others on occasion (Grey Gull and related labels)

MURPHY & SHEA* = Albert Campbell and Jack Kaufman (Gennett)

MURRAY, DICK = Harry Reber (band vocalist with Devine's Wisconsin Roof Orchestra) (Oriole 1313)

MURRAY, GLADYS = Clementine Smith (*q.v.*; possibly a pseudonym itself) (Banner, Regal)

MURRAY QUARTET = American Quartet (Aeolian-Vocalion)

MURRAY'S TRIO = Billy Murray, Carl Matthieu, Monroe Silver (Victor)

MUSIC LOVERS (MALE) QUARTET – Several labeling variations exist, including Music Lovers Male Quartet and Music Lovers Stellar Quartet. The Criterion Quartet (on NML 1108, 1194) and Shannon Four were responsible for many issues, but NML drew on masters from numerous sources, and other groups probably also appear under this name (*see also* NML Male Quartet).

MYERS & FAIRBANKS = John H. Meyer and Henry Moeller (Grey Gull and related labels)

MYERS, JOHN = John H. Meyer (Grey Gull and related labels)

MYRICK, RUSSELL = Henry Moeller (Champion)

NANCE, MABEL = Thelma La Vizzo (Silvertone)

NASH, GRACE = Louise McMahon (Columbia)

NATIONAL (MALE) QUARTET = Clarence Da Silva, Lloyd Wiley (tenors), Harry Jockin (baritone), Harry Donaghey (bass). By 1926, Da Silva and Wiley had been replaced by Arthur Hall and John Ryan, respectively. (Edison; Pathé, Perfect and related labels; probably other minor brands)

NAZARENE CHOIR = Nazarene Congregational Church Choir of Brooklyn, New York (Champion)

NELSON & GWYNNE = George Wilton Ballard and William Wheeler (Oriole)

NELSON, CHARLES = Irving Kaufman (Oriole)

NELSON, GERALD = Scrappy Lambert (Oriole)

NELSON, SONNY BOY = Eugene Powell (Bluebird)

NEW YORKERS = (?) Shope, (?) Preston, Ed Smalle, Colin O'More (tenors) (Edison)

NICHOLS, FRANK = Arthur Hall (Pathé, Perfect)

NIELSON, JANE = Esther Nelson (Okeh)

NIELSON, VARNA = Aileen Stanley (Symphony Concert Record)

NML MALE QUARTET = Four Harmony Kings (mx. 41950, on National Music Lovers 1000); Stellar Quartet (mx. 41276, on NML 1000); (*see also* Music Lovers [Male] Quartet)

NOBLE, HAROLD = Scrappy Lambert (Broadway)
NORTH, HATTIE = Edith North Johnson (Vocalion)
NORTON, JAMES = Jack Norworth (Cleartone 803 only)
NORTON, WALTER = William Robyn (Muse, Tremont); Arthur Fields (Grey Gull, Radiex and related labels)

OAKLAND, CHARLES = Louis Winsch (Crescent)
OAKLAND QUARTET = Will Oakland (counter-tenor), possibly with John Bieling (tenor), Steve Porter (baritone), and William F. Hooley (bass) (Edison cylinders; U.S. Everlasting, Lakeside and related cylinder brands)
O'BRIAN, PADRIC = Arthur Fields
O'BRIEN, JOHN = Walter Van Brunt (Oriole)
O'BRIEN, PAT = Matthew (Mattie) Haskins (Oriole)
O'BRIEN, PAT & MARY = Matthew (Mattie) & Mary Haskins (Oriole)
OLD KING COLE = Bob Pierce (Edison)
OLD MAN SUNSHINE = Bob Pierce (Edison)
OLD SOUTH QUARTET = James L. Stamper and three unknown others. Polk Miller is featured with this group on Edison cylinders, credited under his name. A similarly named group, performing the same type of material and possibly including some or all of the original members (but without Miller, who died in 1913), recorded for Q-R-S in 1928.
OLYMPIA QUARTET – Reputed to include William Robyn (tenor); other members unknown (Victor)
OLIVER, PAUL = Frank Munn
O'MALLEY, DENNIS = Billy Jones
ORIOLE MALE QUARTET = National Male Quartet (Oriole 400)
ORIOLE TRIO = Vernon Dalhart (vocal/harmonica), Carson Robison (vocal/guitar) and Adelyn Hood (vocal/violin) (Oriole)
ORPHEUS QUARTET = Lambert Murphy (tenor), Harry Macdonough (lead tenor), Reinald Werrenrath (baritone), William F. Hooley (bass) (Victor)
ORPHEUS TRIO = Crescent Trio (Pathé and related labels)

PALMER & OLIVER = Virginia Rea and Frank Munn (Edison)
PALMER, BILL = Bob Miller (Bluebird, Electradisk, Victor)
PALMER, (BILL) TRIO = Bob Miller Trio (Bluebird, Electradisk, Victor)
PALMER, BOB = Bob Miller (Electradisk)
PALMER, OLIVE = Virginia Rea (Edison)
PARKER, JACK = J. Donald Parker (Edison)
PARSONS, (HAPPY) JIM = Irving Kaufman
PATRICOLA, (MISS) = Isabella Patricola (Pathé, Victor)

PATTEN, KENNETH = Norman Wallace (Champion)

PATTERSON, FLORENCE = Helen Ohlheim (World Program Service transcriptions, 1930's)

PATTERSON, LILA = Ma Rainey (Broadway)

PATTI, ORVILLE = Irving Kaufman (Champion)

PEARL, JACK = Jan Peerce (Crown, Gem and related labels; Perfect and related labels)

PEARL, PINKIE / PINKY = Jan Peerce (Crown; Oriole, Perfect and related labels)

PECELLI, MARIA = Florence Cole-Talbert (National Music Lovers, from a Black Swan master)

PEERLESS FOUR = Shannon Four (Okeh, Gennett, and various minor labels). Not to be confused with the Peerless Quartet, an unrelated group.

PEERLESS MINSTRELS = Peerless Quartet (early disc and cylinder brands)

PEERLESS QUARTET – A reorganized version of the Columbia Quartet (*q.v.*). Original 1906 personnel included Albert Campbell (tenor), Henry Burr (lead tenor), Steve Porter (baritone), Frank C. Stanley (bass/manager). Arthur Collins replaced Porter almost immediately, and John H. Meyer replaced Stanley after the latter's death in December 1910. Frank Croxton (bass) replaced Collins in 1918. In mid-1925, Burr reorganized the quartet to include Carl Mathieu (tenor), Burr (lead tenor), Stanley Baughman (baritone), James Stanley (bass). (numerous brands 1906-1920; exclusive to Victor, 1920-1928)

PEERLESS TRIO = Billy Murray, Byron G. Harlan (tenors), Steve Porter (baritone) (Indestructible and derivative cylinder brands)

PERRY, GEORGE = Arthur Hall (Pathé, Perfect and related labels)

PHIL & HIS BOYFRIEND SAM = Phil Cook (Edison)

PHIL & JERRY = Phil Cook (Edison)

PHILLIPS, CURT = Ernest Hare; possibly others (Silvertone)

PHILLIPS, JOE = Joseph A. Phillips (Okeh)

PICKENS SISTERS = Helen, Georgia and Patti Pickens (vocals) (Victor)

PIEDMONT MELODY BOYS = Frank Stamps All Star Quartet (Victor)

PINCKNEY, HENRY = Reed Miller (Emerson, Medallion and related labels)

PINE MOUNTAIN BOYS = Dock Walsh and Garley Foster (Victor)

PINETOP & LINDBERG = Sparks Brothers (Victor)

PINEWOOD TOM = Josh White (Oriole, Perfect and other American Record Corporation brands)

PIPPINS, CYRUS = Byron G. Harlan (Edison cylinders)

PITKIN, CY = Billy Murray (Edison)

PLATT, JAMES = Teddy Moss (Champion)

PLEASANT FAMILY = Pickard Family (Broadway)

PORTER, FLOSSIE = Caroline Johnson (Champion)

POST, IRVING = usually Franklyn Baur (Blu-Disc, Clover, Oriole, Triangle and other minor brands). Isolated issues by Irving Kaufman have also been reported by several collectors, but no detailed listing supplied.

POTTER, NETTIE = Monette Moore (Pathé, Perfect)

POWELL, ROY = William Robyn (Challenge, Oriole)

POWERS, JULIA = Ida Cox (Harmograph)

POWERS, JULIUS = Ida Cox (label error on Harmograph 872)

PREMIER QUARTET = American Quartet (Aeolian-Vocalion, Edison and others, through mid-1920); The Harmonizers (Edison only, from late 1921)

PREMIER-AMERICAN QUARTET = American Quartet (Emerson and other minor brands, pre-1921)

PRESCOTT, CARRIE = Marian Evelyn Cox (Crescent and possibly other Pathé-derived brands); Cora Tracey (of the De Koven Light Opera Company) (Crescent 10053 only)

PRESCOTT, GEORGE = Louis Winsch (Pathé)

PRICE, JIMMY = Frankie Marvin (Romeo)

PRIME, ALBERTA — Contrary to Rust and others, this was not a pseudonym for Alberta Hunter on Blu-Disc. Prime was an actual performer whose voice bore only a slight resemblance to Hunter's; she was interviewed by Len Kunstadt in 1967, shortly before her death.

Q**UARTET/QUARTETTE** = Generic description on Columbia and derivative brands for the Columbia Male Quartet (through mid-1906); Peerless Quartet (from late 1906) (most issues on Columbia and Columbia derivatives, including Diamond, Harmony, Lakeside, Oxford, Standard, United and many others; Little Wonder; Columbia, Indestructible, Lakeside, Oxford and U.S. Everlasting cylinders)

R**ADIO ACES** = Gerald Underhill Macy and Ed Smalle (minor brands, late 1920's)

RADIO BOYS = Arthur Hall and John Ryan (?)

RADIO CHEF (& HIS BOYFRIEND SAM) = Phil Cook (Edison)

RADIO EDDIE = Scrappy Lambert (Banner, Regal)

RADIO FRANKS = Frank Bessinger and Frank Wright. Jerry White replaced Wright in the later 1920's. (Edison, Gennett, and numerous minor brands)

RADIO GIRL = Vaughn De Leath (Edison)

RADIO IMPS = Gerald Underhill Macy and Ed Smalle (Banner, Regal and related labels)

RADIO JOE = Ernest Hare

RADIO KINGS = Billy Jones and Ernest Hare; Frank Bessinger and Frank Wright; possibly others (all on Gennett). This name was also used on Brunswick and probably other labels for instrumental duets featuring Harry Reser.

RADIO MAC = Harry McClintock (Victor and other early 1930's RCA products)

RADIO RED* = Wendell Hall (Banner and related labels)

RAMBLER MINSTREL COMPANY = Byron G. Harlan, Billy Murray (tenors), Arthur Collins, Steve Porter (baritones) (Columbia and derivative brands, Zon-O-Phone, other early disc and cylinder brands)

RANDALL, CLARK = Frank Tennille (Banner, Perfect and other American Record Corporation labels)

RANDALL, ROY = Arthur Fields (Pathé)

RANKIN, RUBY = Ivy Smith (Champion)

RANSOM, DOLLY = Clementine Smith (*q.v.*; possibly a pseudonym itself) (Domino)

RAY, JOEY = Barney Burnett (Grey Gull & related labels)

RAY, WALTER = William Robyn (Tremont)

RAYMOND, HARRY = Vernon Dalhart (Silvertone)

RAYMOND, RALPH = Harry Macdonough (Harms, Kaiser & Hagen cylinders). No examples have been located for verification, but this information was related to Jim Walsh by Macdonough himself.

RAYMOND, RAY = Dick Robertson (Melotone)

RECORD BOYS = Al Bernard and Frank Kamplain with piano accompaniment by Sam Stept (Harmony, Diva and related labels; probably other minor brands). Walsh cites a later group including Kamplain, Tom Ford, and Lew Cobey. This name was also used by an unknown country music group (Vocalion 5000 series only).

RED HEADED BRIER HOPPER = Leroy Anderson (Champion)

RED ONION JOE & HIS UKE = Joe Linthecome (Champion)

RED PEPPER SAM* = Billy Costello (Perfect, probably other American Record Corporation masters). Costello was the original voice of Popeye.

REED, JAMES = Reed Miller (various minor brands)

REED, SADIE = Elizabeth Washington (Champion)

REES, WILLIAM = Billy Jones

REESE, CLAUDE = possibly Sunny Clapp (conjecture per Connor & Hicks) (Harmony, Velvet Tone and related labels).

REESE, WILLIAM = Billy Jones (Brunswick)

REEVE, FLOYD = Steve Porter (Van Dyke)

REGAL RASCALS = Vernon Dalhart (vocal/harmonica), Carson Robison (vocal/guitar), Adelyn Hood (vocal/violin) (Regal)

REMINGTON, JOE = Louis Winsch (Pathé)

REVELERS —Originally Lewis James, Franklyn Baur (tenors), Ed Smalle (tenor and piano/arranger), Elliott Shaw (baritone), Wilfred Glenn (bass) (an outgrowth of the Shannon Four, *q.v.*). Smalle left the group when it sailed for England in October 1926 and was replaced upon its return in November by Frank Black (piano). Charles Harrison, Frank Luther, and Ed Smalle occasionally replaced James and/or Baur throughout 1927. By November 1927 personnel had stabilized as Lewis James and James Melton (tenors), Shaw (baritone), Glenn (bass), and Black (piano, when used). Others who occasionally performed with the Revelers included Phil Dewey (as a temporary replacement for Shaw in the late 1920's), Robert Simmons, and J. Donald Parker (who replaced Melton on several unissued Victor sides in 1929 and 1934).

REYNOLDS, DICK = Will Osborne (World Program Service transcriptions, mid-1930's)

RHAN, JACK = John Ryan

RHYTHM BOYS = Bing Crosby, Al Rinker (vocals), Harry Barris (vocal/piano) (Columbia, Victor)

RICE, ROBERT = Henry Burr (Emerson and related labels)

RICHARDS, CHARLES = Arthur Fields (National Music Lovers 1119)

RICHARDS, DAISY = Vaughn De Leath (Banner)

RICHARDS, HELEN = possibly Vaughn De Leath, based on aural evidence (Banner and related labels). Plaza/ARC sessions are logged under this name, raising the possibility that this was an actual performer.

RICHARDS, UNCLE CHARLIE = Blind Richard Yates (Pathé, Perfect)

RIFFERS = Eva Taylor and Lil Hardin Armstrong (Columbia)

RITZ, SALLY = Rosa Henderson (using her sister's name) (Banner, Harmograph, Regal)

ROBBINS & UKE = Johnny Marvin (Challenge, Champion)

ROBERTS, BEN = Dick Robertson (Broadway, Crown)

ROBERTS, CHARLES = Smith Ballew (Victor)

ROBERTS, ED = Irving Kaufman (Oriole)

ROBERTS, HAPPY JACK = Bernie Grauer (Champion)

ROBERTS, HELEN = Alberta Hunter (Silvertone)

ROBERTS, JOHN = Scrappy Lambert (National Music Lovers, New Phonic)

ROBERTS, ROBERT = Bob Roberts (Rex and related labels)

ROBERTS, ROY = Ernest Hare

ROBERTS, SALLY = Sara Martin (Okch)

ROBERTS, STICKNEY & GRISELLE = Henry Moeller and unknown partner with piano accompaniment by Thomas Griselle (Gennett)

ROBERTS, VICTOR = Billy Jones (Victor)

ROBINOW, WILLIAM = William Robyn (Victor)

ROBINSON, PAUL = Jan Peerce (World Program Service transcriptions, mid-1930's)

ROBINSON QUARTETTE = Criterion Quartet (Champion)

ROBINSON, WILLIAM = William Robyn (Emerson, Medallion)

ROBISON, (CARSON) TRIO = Carson Robison, Frank Luther, and Phil Crow. Some duets by Luther and Robison were also issued under the Trio name. (Banner and related labels, Okeh, numerous others)

ROBISON, C.J. = Carson Robison (Grey Gull, Van Dyke and associated labels)

ROBYN, ("WEE") WILLIE* = William Robyn (Banner, Cameo, Crown, Oriole and numerous other minor labels)

RODOLFI, MARIO = Mario Chamlee (Lyric vertical-cut)

ROE, TURNER = Percy Hemus (Pathé)

ROGERS, DUKE – Several researchers have suggested this as a pseudonym for Bert Williams, a conjecture not at all supported by the performance itself (a single Edison release).

ROGERS, GENE = Morton Harvey

ROGERS, MAY = Marie Ginter (Champion)

ROLAND & YOUNG = Andy Patterson and Warren Caplinger (Champion)

ROMEO BOYS = Billy Jones and Ernest Hare (Romeo)

ROSE, LUCY = Louise Anderson (Champion)

ROSS, LUCY = Alura Mack (Champion)

ROSS, MARIAN = Vaughn De Leath (Cameo)

ROSS, TED = Horace Smith (Champion)

ROTTER, ALMA = Alma Henderson (Okeh)

ROUNDERS = Dudley B. Chambers, Ben McLaughlin, Otto Plotz (tenors); Richard C. Hartt (baritone); Armand L'Ecuyer (bass) (Victor). This name was also used for various dance orchestras on minor labels.

ROXY QUARTET = Criterion Quartet (late 1920's minor labels)

RUBAN, GEORGE = William Robyn (Operaphone 41000 series)

RUBIN, CANTOR WILLIAM = William Robyn (performing as a cantor under his given name) (Pilotone, 1940's)

RUBINOFF, WILLIAM = William Robyn (Pathé, Perfect)

RUNDALL, WILLIAM = Charles Harrison (Perfect)

RUNDLE, WILLIAM = Charles Harrison (Actuelle, Pathé and related labels)

RUNNELS & SMYSER = Roy Harvey and Bob Hoke (Champion)

RUNNELS, GEORGE = Roy Harvey (Champion)

RUSH, LILLIAN = Alice Clinton (Champion)

RUSSELL, AL = Irving Kaufman (Broadway)

RUSSELL, ROY = Scrappy Lambert (Broadway)

RUTHERS, GEORGE "HAMBONE" = F.T. Thomas (Champion)

RYAN, JIMMY = Arthur Fields

RYAN, JOHN = Joe Rines (1930's-1940's party records only, including material on the John Ryan label). The actual John Ryan was a prolific studio free-lance tenor in the 1920's and apparently was not connected with these releases.

SALLY SAD = Hattie Snow (Varsity 6033); Mae Glover (Varsity 6066); Ivy Smith (Varsity 6040, 6066) (all dubbed from Gennett originals)

SALT & PEPPER = Frank Kurtz and Jack Cully (Cameo). Various sources, including earlier editions of *Jazz Records*, state incorrectly that Salt and Pepper was Vernon Dalhart and Ed Smalle or Dalhart with an unidentified partner. Contemporary sheet music and promotional photographs prove otherwise.

SALTY DOG SAM = Sam Collins (Oriole, Perfect and other American Record Corporation brands)

SAM & OSCAR = Sam Theard & John Oscar (Brunswick)

SAMUELS, CLAUDE = Carson Robsion (Broadway)

SANDERS, BESSIE = Alberta Jones (Champion)

SANDS, ROBERT = Robert Merwin

SAUNDERS & WHITE = Billy Murray and Walter Van Brunt (Banner, Regal and related labels)

SAWYER, CHARLES = Henry Moeller (Champion)

SCANLAN, WALTER = Walter Van Brunt (Edison, Emerson and numerous other major and minor brands)

SCARPIOFF, WILLIAM = William Robyn (Columbia)

SCHUBERT TRIO = Elise Stevenson (soprano), Harry Macdonough (tenor), Frank C. Stanley (baritone-bass) (Victor)

SCOTT, GENEVIA = Hannah Sylvester (recording under her mother's name) (Pathé, Perfect)

SCOTT, HENRY = William Robyn (Cameo). Not to be confused with concert artist *Henri* Scott on Columbia and Edison.

SEANEY, UNCLE JIM = Ernest Stoneman (Champion)

SEELIG, ARTHUR = Irving Kaufman (Harmony and related labels)

SHANNON FOUR – Original 1917 personnel included Charles Hart, Harvey Hindermeyer (tenors), Elliott Shaw (baritone), Wilfred Glenn (bass). Lewis James replaced Hindermeyer in 1918. Franklyn Baur replaced Hart in 1923, at which time the group changed its name to Shannon Four. In 1925 the group was reorganized as the Revelers (*q.v.*), but occasionally reverted to the Shannon Quartet name on minor labels.

SHANNON QUARTET = Shannon Four (minor labels)

SHANNON, THOMAS = Charles Harrison (Plaza Music Co. mx. 5394); Walter Van Brunt (Emerson mx. 41235) (coupled National Music Lovers 1082)

SHAW, EDDIE = William Robyn (Muse)

SHAW, JANET = Annette Hanshaw (Parlophone PNY- series [American])

SHEA, JACK = Irving Kaufman (Vocalion)

SHAW, JESSIE = Peggy English (Romeo)

SHELTON BROTHERS = Bob and Joe Shelton (Decca)

SHUFFLIN' SAM = Clarence Todd (Columbia); possibly another, unknown (Columbia)

SILVER, RAY = Brad Mitchell (Oriole)

SILVER-MASKED TENOR = Joseph M. White (Victor and others)

SILVERTONE QUARTET (I) = Columbia Male Quartet (through mid-1906); Peerless Quartet (from late 1906) (Columbia-produced Oxford and Silvertone issues)

SILVERTONE QUARTET (II) = Criterion Quartet (Black Swan, from Olympic masters). The Criterion Quartet was probably also responsible for many other issues under this name on the Silvertone label (*see also* Silvertone Quartet [I]).

SIMS, HOWARD = Ollie Powers (as a vocalist) (Harmograph)

SIMS, REV. GEORGE H. & CONGREGATION = Evangelist R.H. Harris and Pentecostal Sisters (Champion)

SIMS, SKEETER = Al Bernard (Regal and related labels)

SINGER & HOLTON = Scrappy Lambert and Bill Hillpot

SINGIN' SAM = Harry Frankel (Melotone, Oriole, Perfect, other 1930's American Record Corporation brands; Beacon, Gennett, Joe Davis, other minor 1940's brands)

SINGING SOPHOMORES = Revelers (Columbia)

SKOOT, SKEETER = Bob Howard (Okeh)

SLIM & SLAM = Slim Gaillard (vocal/guitar/vibraphone) and Slam Stewart (vocal/string bass) (Vocalion)

SLOANE, JOHN = Arthur Fields

SLOPPY HENRY = Waymon Henry (Okeh)

SMITH, ANNE = Ma Rainey (Harmograph)

SMITH, BARNEY = Bert Lewis (of the Club Kentucky, per Gennett ledger) (Champion)

SMITH, BERTRAM = Billy Jones

SMITH BROTHERS = William and Roosevelt Smith (Victor V-40000 series). Not to be confused with the pop vocal duet of the same name (see next entry).

SMITH BROTHERS (TRADE & MARK): Scrappy Lambert and Bill Hillpot (Domino and related labels; Victor; probably others). Not to be confused with the country-music duo of the same name (see previous entry).

SMITH, CLARA — Black Patti issued several sides under this name in 1927, from masters recorded for them in St. Paul. It is not known if this was a pseudonym or an actual performer, but it is definitely not Columbia's star of the same name.

SMITH, CLEMENTINE — Confusion surrounds this name. It is confirmed as a pseudonym for Helen Gross on Pathé and Perfect issues pressed from Ajax masters. Plaza Music Company issues (Banner, Regal and related labels) credited to Clementine Smith are by a different performer; it is not known whether that Clementine Smith was a pseudonym or an actual performer.

SMITH, DAN = Andy Razaf (Jewel, Oriole)

SMITH, GUY = John Erby, per Erby's 1973 *Record Research* interview. Erby recalled using this pseudonym on Okeh, although the only known issues are on Paramount.

SMITH, HARRY = Irving Kaufman (confirmed on Romeo and related labels). Brooks also lists this as a possible pseudonym for William Robyn on Romeo.

SMITH, HONEY BOY & SOUTHERN JACK = Tampa Red and Georgia Tom (Supertone)

SMITH, JANE = Ida Cox (Silvertone)

SMITH, JIMMIE* = Gene Autry. Not to be confused with *Jimmy* Smith, who recorded country-style harmonica solos for Victor in 1926. (Victor, Timely Tunes, possibly other early 1930's RCA brands)

SMITH, JOSEPHUS = Vernon Dalhart

SMITH, JULIA = Mandy Lee (*q.v.*; possibly a pseudonym itself) (Oriole)

SMITH, LOUELLA = Hazel Meyers (Oriole)

SMITH, MANDY = Lizzie Miles (Jewel, Oriole)

SMITH, OLIVER = Frank Munn (Brunswick)

SMITH, SUSIE = Monette Moore (Ajax)

SMITH, WINI = Frances Sper (Romeo)

SMOKEHOUSE CHARLEY = Georgia Tom (Champion)

SMOOTHIES, THE = Babs Ryan, Charlie Little, Melvin Little (Bluebird, Decca)

SNOW, MARGIE = Anna Lee Chisholm (Silvertone)

SNYDER, BOBBY = Chick Bullock (Vocalion, late 1930's)

SOUTHERNERS = Frank Luther and Carson Robison (Victor)

SOUTHERN SINGERS = Mills Brothers (World transcriptions, mid-1930's)

SPEAR, JOHN = William Robyn (Banner, Cameo, Lincoln, Oriole and related labels)

SPEARS, BLOSSOM = Katie Winters (Champion)

SPENCER & HARRIS = Billy Jones and Ernest Hare (National Music Lovers)

SPENCER, ERNIE = Ernest Hare

SPENCER, (LEN) TRIO — Personnel varied considerably. Walsh cites Len Spencer, Billy Golden, and Steve Porter as usual members beginning in 1897 and notes that George P. Watson and George Washington Johnson may have participated in some sessions. An 1899 Berliner catalog lists personnel as Roger Harding (tenor), Steve Porter, Len Spencer (baritones). Later Columbia disc issues included Spencer and Billy Murray.

SPENCER, MAMIE = Helen Baxter (Oriole 795)

SPENCER, SAMUEL = Arthur Fields (usually, except as noted): Cliff Edwards (NML 1091 only); possibly others (National Music Lovers)

STAIGER, ARTHUR = Seger Ellis (Supertone S- series, from Brunswick masters)

STANDARD (MALE) QUARTETTE = Columbia Quartet (through mid-1906); Peerless Quartet (from late 1906) (Standard, United and probably other Columbia-derived brands)

STANLEY, WILLIAM = William Robyn (Jewel)

STEAMBOAT BILL & HIS GUITAR = Willie Baker (Champion)

STEBBINS, CY = Byron G. Harlan

STELLAR (MALE) QUARTET = Columbia Stellar Quartet (Columbia); Criterion Quartet, Shannon Four and probably others (1920's minor labels)

STERLING, FRANK = Elliott Shaw (Pathé, Perfect and related labels)

STERLING TRIO — Original 1916 personnel included Albert Campbell (tenor), Henry Burr (lead tenor), and John H. Meyer (bass) (Columbia, Victor and numerous other major and minor labels; exclusive to Victor after 1920). When the Trio recorded for Gennett beginning in 1926, Burr (who was under exclusive Victor contract) was replaced by Henry Moeller.

STEVENSON, ALICE C. = Elise Stevenson (Zon-O-Phone)

STEWART, AMY = Elizabeth Spencer (Grey Gull and related labels)

STEWART, CLIFF = Vernon Dalhart; Arthur Fields; Arthur Hall (Domino and related labels)

STEWART, J.M. = James Stewart (of motion picture fame, performing as vocalist with the Princeton Triangle Band) (Columbia Personal Record)

STEWART, MAY = Priscilla Stewart (Silvertone)

STODDARD, EDGAR = Andrea Sarto (Columbia)

STONE, EDWARD = Vernon Dalhart (National Music Lovers 1075), Charles Hart (NML 1074); probably others (NML)

STONE, FRED = Arthur Fields (minor 1920's labels). Not to be confused with vaudevillian Fred Stone, who recorded several sides with partner David Montgomery for Victor in 1911.

STONE, JIMMY = John Ryan (Van Dyke)

STRAND QUARTET = Criterion Quartet (Brunswick, Regal, probably others)

STRONG, ARTHUR = Joseph A. Phillips (Crescent)

STUART, BILLY = Vernon Dalhart

STUART, HERBERT = Albert Weiderhold (Columbia)

SULLIVAN, WALTER = Charles Harrison (?) (Symphonola)

SUNDAY, BLACK BILLY = Rev. Calvin P. Dixon (minor labels)

SUNNY JIM & WHISTLIN' JOE = Daddy Stovepipe and Whistling Pete (Champion)

SUNSHINE BOYS* = Joe and Dan Mooney (Columbia, Melotone)

SUTTON, BUDDY = Slim ("Red") Johnson (Champion)

SWEET PEAS = Addie ("Sweet Pease") Spivey (Victor, Bluebird)

SWEET WILLIAM & BAD BILL = William LeMaire and John Swor (Brunswick)

TATE, ROSE = Katherine Baker (Champion)

TAYLOR, LOUELLA = Clementine Smith (*q.v.*; possibly a pseudonym itself) (Domino)

TAYLOR, NOEL = Irving Kaufman (Okeh)

TED & NED = Ed Smalle and Gerald Underhill Macy (Champion)

TERRALL, LOUISE = Elizabeth Lennox. Pseudonym derives from Lennox's family name (Tyrrell) according to Tom De Long.

TERRELL, LOUISE = Elizabeth Lennox (Gennett, Grey Gull and related labels, Silvertone, probably other minor brands) (see previous entry)

TERRILL, NORMAN = Charles Harrison (Champion)

TERRY, BERT = Byron G. Harlan (Actuelle, Pathé and related labels)

TERRY, WILL = Vernon Dalhart

TEAXS DRIFTER = Goebel Reeves (Decca, Melotone, Vocalion)

TEXAS RANGER = Frankie Marvin (Varsity)

"THAT GIRL" QUARTET = Harriett Keys, Allie Thomas, Precis Thompson, Helen Summers (Edison cylinders; U.S. Everlasting cylinders and derivative brands; Victor)

THOMAS & WEST = Billy Jones and Ernest Hare (minor labels)

THOMAS, BESSIE = Lillian Miller (Supertone)

THOMAS, BOB — Although this name is associated almost exclusively with Ernest Hare on numerous minor labels, there are occasional exceptions. Arthur Fields is confirmed on Grey Gull mx. 3819, and there are unconfirmed reports of Fields on Triangle under this name. A third performer, so far unidentified, recorded as Thomas on Grey Gull mx. 2731, and there are probably other isolated exceptions.

THOMAS, BUD = F.T. Thomas (Supertone)

THOMAS, COTTON — Rust notes that material by Frankie "Half-Pint" Jaxon is thought to have been issued on Supertone under this name, but this has not been confirmed.

THOMAS, FRED* = Art Gillham (Ajax , from Pathé masters)

THOMAS, GRAYSEN = G.B. Grayson (Champion)

THOMAS, HARRY = Tom Stacks (Velvet Tone and related labels). Vocals only, not to be confused with pianist Harry Thomas.

THOMAS, JOHN = Ernest Hare

THOMAS, JOSEPHINE = Rosa Henderson (Pathé, Perfect)

THOMAS, MARIE = Dorothy Dodd (Royal)

THOMAS, SIPPIE = Sippie Wallace (Victor)

THOMAS, WASHINGTON = W.E. (Buddy) Burton (Champion)

THOMPSON, BUD = Frank Luther

THOMPSON, CONRAD = Herbert Waterous (Pathé and related labels)

THOMPSON, MADGE = Vaughn De Leath

THREE 'BACCER TAGS = Stapleton Brothers (Victor)

THREE KAUFIELDS = Arthur Fields, Irving and Jack Kaufman (Emerson and related labels)

THREE KEYS = George (Bon Bon) Tunnell (vocal), Bob Pease (piano), Slim Furness (guitar) (Brunswick)

THREE TWEEDY BOYS = Tweedy Brothers (Champion)

TILLOTSON, MERLE = Merle Alcock

TOBIN, RALPH = Skinnay Ennis (World Program Service transcriptions, mid-1930's)

TOMPKINS, JED = Ernest Thompson (Columbia)

TOOMEY, WELBY – Suggested by several researchers as a Vernon Dalhart pseudonym. However, Toomey appears to have been an actual performer. Sessions are listed under his name in the Gennett ledgers, and the voice is definitely not Dalhart's. (Gennett, Silvertone, Supertone)

TOPNOTCHERS = Billy Jones and Ernest Hare (Bell)

TREADWAY, DEACON = Byron G. Harlan (Pathé)

TREE, JAMES = Sam Ash (Lyric vertical-cut)

TREMAINE BROTHERS* = Frank Bessinger and Frank Wright (Gennett and related labels)

TREVOR, BERT = Arthur Fields (Banner, Regal and related labels)

TRIX SISTERS = Helen and Josephine Trix (Victor, Edison)

TURNER, ALLEN – This pseudonym was used indiscriminately on various minor brands in the early 1920's. Material by Vernon Dalhart, Charles Hart, and Elliott Shaw has been reported, but precise data is lacking. Not to be confused with concert tenor *Alan* Turner.

TURNER, HOBO JACK = Ernest Hare (Diva, Harmony and related labels).

TURNER, SID = Vernon Dalhart

TURNEY BROTHERS = Frank Luther and Carson Robison (Victor)

TUTTLE, FRANK = Vernon Dalhart; Carson Robison

TWITCHELL, ATWOOD – Once identified as George Alexander by Walsh, who later found references in the *Phonoscope* suggesting (but not definitely confirming) that Twitchell was an actual performer. (Harms, Kaiser and Hagen cylinders; Zon-O-Phone; probably other early disc and cylinder brands)

TWO BLACK DIAMONDS = Doe Doe Green and Paul Floyd (National Music Lovers)

TWO DARK KNIGHTS = Phil Cook and Victor Fleming (Edison)

TWO FRANKS = Frank Bessinger and Frank Wright (Cameo)

TWO KAUFIELDS = Arthur Fields with Irving or Jack Kaufman (Emerson and related labels)

UKULELE BAILEY = Webb Hahne (Cameo)

UKULELE IKE = Cliff Edwards (occasionally used on minor labels as a pseudonym, but usually appended to Edwards' name on his Columbia, Pathé and Perfect releases)

UNCLE BILLY = Billy Jones (children's records)

UNCLE ERNEST = Ernest Hare (children's records)

UNCLE ERNIE = Ernest Hare (children's records)

UNCLE JOE = Al Bernard (Romeo)

UNCLE JOSH = Cal Stewart (virtually all issues except for a few very early and rare cylinders by Matt Keefe). Byron G. Harlan recorded *several Uncle Josh* routines for Brunswick after Stewart's death but was credited on the labels.

UNCLE LEWIS = Lewis James (children's records)

UNDERHILL, JERRY = Gerald Underhill Macy (Oriole)

UNIVERSAL QUARTET = possibly Geoffrey O'Hara (tenor), unknown (lead tenor), Reinald Werrenrath (baritone), Walter McPherson (bass) (Zon-O-Phone)

U. S. MINSTRELS = Peerless Quartet (U. S. Everlasting cylinders)

VALLEY INN QUARTET = Four Hooligans (Champion)

VASSAR GIRLS QUARTET = Katherine Armstrong, Lovira Taft, Florence Fiske, E. Eleanor Patterson (Edison cylinders)

VAUGHAN HAPPY TWO = A.B. Sebren and C.G. Wilson (Bluebird, Victor, Vaughan, possibly others)

VAUGHAN QUARTET = Hillman Barnard, Otis L. McCoy (tenors), W.B. Walbert or G. Kieffer Vaughan (baritone), A.M. Pace (bass) (Bluebird, Electradisk, Victor V-40000 series, probably other early 1930's RCA products). A group using the same name, of unknown personnel, recorded Ku Klux Klan material for the Vaughan label in 1924.

VAUGHN, CAROLINE = Beaulah Gaylord Young

VAUGHN, EDITH = Julia Moody (Oriole)

VERNON, BILL = Vernon Dalhart

VERNON, HERBERT = Vernon Dalhart

VERNON, WALTER = Billy Jones (Champion)

VERNON, WILL = Vernon Dalhart

VETERAN, VEL = Vernon Dalhart (usually, on Grey Gull, Radiex and related labels); Arthur Fields (Grey Gull mx. 2511-B; probably many other Grey Gull masters; Broadway and related labels); Irving Kaufman (Grey Gull and related labels 4174, 4183; probably other Grey Gull issues)

VICTOR LADIES' QUARTET = Elizabeth Wheeler, Olive Kline (sopranos), Elsie Baker, Marguerite Dunlap (contraltos)

VICTOR (LIGHT) OPERA COMPANY — Personnel varied from session to session; performers known to have participated *c.* 1909-1912 include Elsie Baker, Inez Barbour, John Bieling, George Carre, S.H. Dudley, Marguerite Dunlap, Frederick Gunster, William F. Hooley, Ada Jones, Hariett Keys, Harry Macdonough, Lucy Isabelle Marsh, Billy Murray, Steve Porter, Walter B. Rogers (director), Elise Stevenson, John Barnes Wells, Reinald Werrenrath, Elizabeth Wheeler, and William Wheeler. Prominently featured performers *c.* 1913-1918 were Baker, Dunlap, Hooley, Olive Kline, Macdonough, Lambert Murphy, and Werrenrath. 1920's issues often featured Baker, Franklyn Baur, Wilfred Glenn, Charles Harrison, Lewis James, Kline, and Elliott Shaw. (Victor)

VICTOR MALE QUARTET = Orpheus Quartet (Victor)

VICTOR MINSTRELS / MINSTREL COMPANY = Haydn Quartet, often with the addition of Len Spencer (pre-1906); Rambler Minstrel Company (1906-1909); Peerless Quartet (sometimes augmented) (from 1909, on the "state" series [*i.e.*, Virginia Minstrels]).

VICTOR MINSTRELS OF 1929 = Billy Murray, Henry Burr, Frank Crumit, James Stanley, and the Cavaliers

VICTOR OPERA SEXTET = Lucy Isablle Marsh (soprano), Marguerite Dunlap (contralto), William Wheeler, Harry Macdonough (tenors), Reinald Werrenrath (baritone), William F. Hooley (bass) (1911). The group recorded again in 1915 with Olive Kline (soprano), Dunlap (contralto), Lambert Murphy, Macdonough (tenors), Werrenrath (baritone), Wilfred Glenn (bass).

VICTOR SALON GROUP = The Revelers (sometimes augmented and accompanied by various studio ensembles under the direction of Nathaniel Shilkret)

VICTOR VAUDEVILLE COMPANY — Personnel varied from session to session. Early issues. *c.* 1908, featured Billy Murray, Byron G. Harlan, and Steve Porter. Later releases featured members of the Peerless Quartet (*q.v.*), sometimes augmented.

VIRGINIA POSSUM TAMERS = Paul Miles & his Red Fox Chasers (Champion)

VOGT, HELEN = Ruth Roye (Crescent)

VERNON, MARY = Henrietta Wakefield (Symphony Concert Record)

VOLEVI, MARIE = Henrietta Wakefield (National Music Lovers, from Olympic masters)

WAINWRIGHT SISTERS — Walsh's identification as Brox Sisters is incorrect. The Wainwright Sisters were actual performers.

WALLACE, BRUCE = Royal Dadmun (Victor); Lewis James (Okeh)

WALLACE, FRANCIS (& HIS GUITAR) = Frankie Marvin (minor labels)

WALLACE, FRANKIE (& HIS GUITAR/ & HIS UKE) = Frankie Marvin (Edison, Gennett, Paramount and many other major and minor labels)

WALLACE, TED = Ed Kirkeby (director of the California Ramblers, sometimes featured as band vocalist) (Columbia, Okeh and others)

WALLACE, TRIXIE = Kitty Irwin (Claxtonola)

WALSH, CHARLOTTE = Anna Lee Chisholm (Silvertone)

WALTERS, KENNETH = Robert Howe

WALTERS, NAT = Ernest Hare

WALTON, MISS — Apparently not a pseudonym. Victor files list the performer precisely this way, with no first name given. (Victor)

WANNER, ENOS = W.C. Childers (Champion)

WANNER, ENOS & MRS. = Mr. and Mrs. W.C. Childers (Champion)

WARD, AMY = Sodarisa Miller (Silvertone)

WARD, SLEEPY = Irving Kaufman (Harmony)

WARFIELD, LEWIS = Frankie Marvin (Broadway)

WARNER, FLORENCE = Aileen Stanley (Banner)

WARNER, YODELIN' JIMMY = Frankie Marvin (Champion)

WARREN, CHARLES = Charles Hart (Pathé, Perfect and related labels)

WASHBURN & HALL = Mae Glover and John Byrd (Superior)

WASHBURN, ALBERTA = Mae Glover (Superior)

WATERS, FRANKIE = William Robyn (Cameo)

WATSON, HARVEY = Holland Puckett (Champion)

WATSON SISTERS = Kitty and Fanny Watson (Columbia, Okeh)

WATSON, NORA = Elsie Baker

WATSON, TOM = Vernon Dalhart (Silvertone)

WEARY WILLIE = Frankie Marvin (usually); Jack Kaufman (occasionally) (Pathé, Perfect and related labels); Frank Luther and Carson Robison (Cameo and related labels) (all 1920's issues).

WEARY WILLIE TRIO = Billy Murray (tenor), Ed Meeker (baritone) and Donald Chalmers (bass) (Edison, 1916)

WEBSTER, FRANK = Albert Campbell (Pathé)

WEE WILLIE = William Robyn (minor labels)

"WE GIRLS" QUARTET = Gladys Rice, Betsy Lane Shepherd (sopranos), Marion Evelyn Cox, Amy Ellerman (contraltos) (Edison)

WELCH, BARREL HOUSE = Nolan Welsh (Paramount)

WELLS, LORENZO = Charles Hart (Black Swan 2031); Percy Hemus (Black Swan 2091) (from Olympic masters)

WELSH, CORINNE MORGAN = Corinne Morgan (performing under her legal name) (Edison)

WEST & THOMAS = Billy Jones and Ernest Hare (numerous minor labels)

WEST, BILLY = Billy Jones (numerous labels)

WEST, JACK = Frankie Marvin (Broadway)

WEST, MABEL = Elsie Baker (Victor)

WEST, WILLIAM = Billy Jones (numerous labels)

WESTON, WILLIE — Contrary to Walsh's original listing, this was not a pseudonym. Weston, who recorded for Victor and several minor brands before 1920, was a performer in his own right.

WEST VIRGINIA RAIL SPLITTER, THE = The Arkansas Woodchopper (Champion)

WHEELER & MORSE = Albert Campbell and Jack Kaufman (Madison)

WHISPERING PIANIST = Art Gillham

WHITE & GRAY = Viola McCoy and Billy (Jazz Caspar) Higgins (Domino)

WHITE, BILLY = Arthur Fields (Jewel)

WHITE, BOB = Vernon Dalhart (Regal)

WHITE, CLARA = Viola McCoy (Oriole)

WHITE, E. = Lulu Whidby (Famous 3049)

WHITE, ELLEN = Katie Crippen (Famous 3048)

WHITE, GEORGE = Vernon Dalhart (Pathé, Perfect and related labels); Frankie Marvin (Okeh 45000 series); Georgia White (label error on Decca 7216 only)

WHITE, GRACE = Monette Moore (Silvertone)

WHITE, JANE = Josie Miles (mx. 5910); Kitty Brown (mx. unknown) (same pseudonym used for different performers on either side of Emerson 10874)

WHITE, JERRY – Some confusion surrounds this name. Plaza Music Company/American Record Corporation masters by both Jack Kaufman and William Robyn were issued on Banner and related labels under Jerry White's name. Jerome (Jerry) White was an actual performer, however, and was employed as an arranger by Irving Berlin in the 1920's. He performed on radio both as soloist and as one of the Radio Franks (*q.v.*); Edison, Gennett, and at least some Plaza/ARC issues under his name are credited correctly.

WHITE, JOE = Billy Jones (minor label, early 1920's); Joseph M. White (late 1920's-early 1930's)

WHITE, LEE = Noble Sissle (Okeh only). Not to be confused with the British female vocalist of the same period.

WHITE, ROBERT = Vernon Dalhart (Columbia)

WHITE, SLIM = Al Bernard (Black Swan)

WHITEMAN, PAUL'S RHYTHM BOYS = Bing Crosby (lead vocal) with Al Rinker (vocal) and Harry Barris (vocal/piano) (Columbia, Victor)

WHITLOCK, WALTER = Vernon Dalhart

WHITNEY BROTHERS QUARTET = Alvin, Edwin M., William, and Yale Whitney (Edison cylinders, Victor)

WIGGINS, PETE = Frank Luther (?) (Okeh)

WILBUR, JOHN = John H. Meyer (using his uncle's name) (Victor)

WILKINS, TIM = Robert Wilkins (Vocalion)

WILLIAMS & DALE = Viola McCoy and Billy (Jazz Caspar) Higgins (Domino)

WILLIAMS BROTHERS = Frank Luther and Carson Robison (Harmony)

WILLIAMS SISTERS = Dorothea and Hannah Williams (the latter was Mrs. Jack Dempsey) (Victor)

WILLIAMS, BESSIE = Viola McCoy (Domino)

WILLIAMS, CARL = Howard Shelly (possibly a pseudonym itself) (Grey Gull, Oriole, Master Tone and others)

WILLIAMS, CARLTON = Billy Jones

WILLIAMS, FRANK = Dan W. Quinn (Columbia and derivative brands, including Diamond, Standard and United, early 1900's); Vernon Dalhart (Cameo and other minor brands, 1920's); possibly others (1920's minor brands)

WILLIAMS, GEORGE S. = Frank C. Stanley (as a banjo soloist on Edison cylinders; as a vocalist, sometimes self-accompanied on banjo on Reed Dawson & Co. and Harms, Kaiser & Hagen cylinders)

WILLIAMS, HARRY = Louis Winsch (Lyric)

WILLIAMS, IRENE = Eva Taylor (Okeh only). Not to be confused with concert soprano Irene Williams, who recorded for Brunswick in the early 1920's.

WILLIAMS, RABBIT'S FOOT = Jay Bird Coleman (Black Patti, Champion, Silvertone)

WILLIAMS, SUSAN = Viola McCoy (Lincoln)

WILSON, ARTHUR = Charles Hart (Pathé, Perfect)

WILSON, FRED = Riley Puckett (Harmony and related label)

WILSON, GEORGE = James Harrod (Columbia)

WILSON, LUCKY & HIS UKE = Buddy Lee (*q.v.*) (Champion)

WILTON, GEORGE = George Wilton Ballard (Federal, Resona, Silvertone, and related labels; Gennett and related labels; probably others)

WINDY CITY DUO = Vernon Dalhart and Ed Smalle (Gennett)

WINTERS, HORACE = Walter Woolf (Champion 15218 & 15219 only); Irving Kaufman (all other Champion issues)

WISEMAN QUARTET – Probably similar to the Bethel Jubilee Quartet (*q.v.*); Rev. T.H. Wiseman, director. (Gennett, Rainbow)

WISEMAN SEXTET – Probably similar to the Bethel Jubilee Quartet (*q.v.*), with the addition of two unknown members, one of them female; Rev. T.H. Wiseman, director. (Gennett, Rainbow)

WOOD, ELSIE = Elise Stevenson

WOOD, ROBERT – Used indiscriminately *c.* 1928-1932 for several band vocalists. In general, Wood was Bill Coty (with Jack Albin's Orchestra only, on Harmony, Velvet Tone and related labels); Arthur Fields (Columbia Special Records [Publix, Metro-Goldwyn-Mayer, etc.], Harmony and related labels, late 1920's); and Dick Robertson or Scrappy Lambert (Harmony and related labels, early 1930's). There are undoubtedly exceptions.

WOODS, EVA = Ozie McPherson (Silvertone)

WOODS, GEORGE = Vernon Dalhart

WOODS, GLADYS = possibly Vaughn De Leath (Oriole). Plaza Music Company files list these sessions under the name of Helen Richards, a possible De Leath pseudonym.

WOODS, GRACE = Helen Clark (Edison)

WOODS, HARRY = Scrappy Lambert and Bill Hillpot (Broadway 1055 only)

WYNKEN, BLYNKEN & NOD = Gertrude and Lucille Matthews, Greta Woodson) (Victor)

WYOMING COWBOY = Charles Baker (Champion)

YACHT CLUB BOYS = Adler, Kelly, Kern and Mann (first names not known) (Brunswick, Columbia)

YAS YAS GIRL = Merline Johnson (Banner, Conqueror, Oriole, and other American Record Corporation labels; Okeh)

YODELING TWINS = Garner Eckler and Roland Gaines (Champion)

YOUNG, CLARENCE = Ollie Powers (Harmograph only); Frank Welling (Champion only)

YOUNG, JACK = Bill Marshall (Champion only); John Young (Gennett)

YOUNG, JACKSON = Ben Jarrell (Champion)

YOUNG, MARVIN = Irving Kaufman (Harmony and related labels)

YOUNG, PATSY = Annette Hanshaw (Harmony and related labels)

YOUNGER, EDDIE & HIS MOUNTAINEERS = Arthur Fields and Fred Hall (Clarion, Diva and related labels)

ZA ZU GIRL = Elton Spivey Harris (Banner, Perfect and other American Record Corporation brands)

ZONOPHONE QUARTET = Rambler Minstrel Company (Zon-O-Phone)

ZORA = Zora Layman (Decca)

Vocalists and Vocal Groups: Foreign Issues

*Pseudonyms appear in **bold type**, followed by artist identification.*

This listing includes foreign-label issues by American performers, derived from American-made masters. Country of issue is shown in brackets, followed by the American master source when known.

It is interesting to note that in some cases, material issued under fictitious names in the United States appeared properly credited in Great Britain. This is particularly true in the case of Plaza Music Company/American Record Corporation masters; material by Fletcher Henderson, Charles Kaley, Irving Kaufman and many others, issued pseudonymously in the States, appeared correctly credited on Imperial and related British labels.

Pseudonyms followed by an asterisk (*) also appear in the domestic listing, but are not necessarily assigned to the same performers.

ALLISON, JAMES = William Robyn (Worth [Australian])

BART, JOHN = Henry Burr (Aurora [Canadian], from Victor masters)

BELLWOOD & BURR = Albert Campbell & Henry Burr (Scala [British], from American masters of unknown origin)

BERT, FLO* – not a pseudonym, despite conjecture by Rust that this was a pseudonym for Florence Cole-Talbert (see explanation in domestic vocal listing) (Starr Gennett [Canadian], from Gennett masters)

BILLINGS, BUD & JOE* = Frank Luther & Carson Robison (Zonophone [British], from Victor masters)

BINGHAM, ETHEL = Annette Hanshaw (Key [British], from American Record Corporation [Banner] masters)

BLACK BROTHERS* = Frank Luther & Carson Robison (Parlophone [British], from Okeh masters)

BLUE, BUDDY* = Smith Ballew (Imperial [British], from Plaza Music Company/American Record Corporation masters)

BLUE, JACK = Smith Ballew (Imperial [British], from Plaza Music Company /American Record Corporation [Banner] masters)

BOLTON, JAMIE = William Robyn (Angelus [Australian], from American Record Corporation masters)

BROOKES, ARTHUR T. = Robert Howe (Coliseum [British], probably from Gennett masters)

BRUCE, A.L. = Scrappy Lambert (Edison Bell Winner [British], probably from the Brunswick /American Record Corporation master pool)

BUCK & BUBBLES* = Buck Washington & John ''Bubbles'' Sublett (Columbia [British], from Columbia masters)

BURKE, TERRANCE = Joseph M. White (Aurora [Canadian], from Victor masters)

BURTON, MAURICE = Maurice Burkhardt (Columbia [British], from Columbia masters)

BURTON, SAMMY* = Irving Kaufman; unknown others, thought to be American. (Guardsman [British], from Vocalion masters)

CAMPBELL, GEORGE = Scrappy Lambert (Edison Bell Winner [British], probably from the Brunswick/American Record Corporation master pool)

CARROLL, JACK = Jack Kaufman (Apex, Domino, Microphone, Sterling, and other Canadian brands, pressed by the Compo Company from Plaza Music Company [Banner] masters)

CHESTER & ROLLINS = Frank Luther & Carson Robison (Aurora [Canadian], from Victor masters)

CLARKE, ETHEL = Corinne Morgan (Zonophone [British], from Victor masters)

CLARKE, WALTER = William Robyn (Melotone [Australian], from Brunswick masters)

CLIFF, DAISY = Viola McCoy (Guardsman [British], from Vocalion masters)

COLMAN, NELLY = Lena Wilson (Guardsman [British], from Vocalion masters)

DALTRY, LILLIE = Peggy English (Guardsman [British], from Vocalion masters)

DAVIS, JOHNNY = Paul Small (His Master's Voice [British], La Voce del Padrone [Italian], from Victor masters)

DAY, J.W.* = Jilson Setters (Aurora [Canadian], from Victor masters)

DESMOND DUO = Joe & Dan Mooney (Embassy [British], from Brunswick masters)

DI GIOVANNI, EDOARDO* = Edward Johnson (Columbia [British & South American issues], from Columbia masters)

DONOVAN, HUGH* = Charles Harrison (Imperial [British], from Plaza Music Company masters; probably others)

EVANS, WILLIAM T.* = Evan Williams (Gramophone & Typewriter, His Master's Voice [British]; His Master's Voice-Victor [Canadian]; probably others, all from Victor masters)

FORSYTHE, REG = William Robyn (Embassy [Australian])

FOSTER, AL* = William Robyn (Angelus [Australian], from American Record Corporation masters)

FOSTER, NANCY* = Vaughn De Leath (Ariel [British], from Okeh masters)

FRANCISCO, E.* = Emilio de Gogorza (International Concert Zon-O-Phone Record [British], from Zon-O-Phone masters; probably other Zon-O-Phone and Victor affiliates)

FRANKLIN, EDWARD* = Emilio de Gogorza (International Concert Zon-O-Phone Record [British], from Zon-O-Phone masters; probably other Zon-O-Phone and Victor affiliates)

FRANKS, SINCLAIR = Evelyn Preer (Bon Marche [Australian], from Plaza Music Company [Banner] masters)

GARNETT, JIM = Noble Sissle (Ariel [British], from Okeh masters)

GEAR, GLORIA* = Vaughn De Leath (Grafton [British], from Emerson masters)

GILLETTE, HENRY = Henry Burr (Aurora [Canadian], from Victor masters)

GREEN, SADIE* = Beth Challis (Parlophone R-3421); Vaughn De Leath (Parlophone R-3386) (British, both from Okeh masters)

HADDON, CHARLES = Seger Ellis (Kismet [Australian], from Okeh masters)

HALE, CHESTER* = Scrappy Lambert (Imperial [British], from American Record Corporation [Banner] masters)

HARMONY TWINS = Sunshine Boys (Joe & Dan Mooney) (Mayfair [British], from Brunswick masters)

HART, CHARLES = William Robyn (label error on an Angelus [Australian] release, reported by Brooks)

HART, EARL = Russell Douglas (Parlophone [British], from Okeh masters)

HENDERSON, LARRY = William Robyn (Starr [Canadian])

HENRY, LAWRENCE = William Robyn (Electron [Australian])

HILLMAN, BOB = William Robyn (Regent [Australian])

HOLT, ARTHUR = Irving Kaufman (Homochord [British], from Vocalion masters)

HOPWOOD, FRANCIS = Annette Hanshaw (Peacock [British], from Brunswick masters)

JOHNSON, GENE* = Gene Autry (Aurora [Canadian], from RCA masters)

JOHNSON, MARGARET = Sara Martin (label error on Parlophone R-3506 [British], from Okeh masters).

JOHNSTON, AL = William Robyn (Golden Tongue [Australian])

JONES BROTHERS = Vernon Dalhart & Carson Robison (Panachord [Australian], from American Record Corporation masters)

JONES, HARRY = Carson Robison (Regal [British], from American Columbia masters)

KAUFMAN, IRVING = Evelyn Preer (label error on Imperial 1645 [British] only, from a Plaza Music Company [Banner] master; other Kaufman issues are correct as credited)

LAMBERT, HAROLD = William Robyn (label error on Australian Paramount, reported by Brooks)

LEE, ALBERT = William Robyn (Grand Pree [Australian], probably from Plaza Music Company masters)

LEE, MAMIE* = Vaughn De Leath (Parlophone [British], from Okeh masters)

LEE, MARION = Annette Hanshaw (Mayfair [British], from American Record Corporation masters)

LISLE, ERNEST = Seger Ellis (Ariel [British], from Okeh masters)

MELOTONE BOYS* = Sunshine Boys (Joe & Dan Mooney) (Panachord [British], from Brunswick masters)

MILLER BROTHERS = Lester McFarland & Bob Gardner (Aurora [Canadian], from Brunswick masters)

NEVILL, TOM = Irving Kaufman (Coliseum [British], from Vocalion masters)
NEW, JIM = Newton Gaines (Aurora [Canadian], from Victor masters)

O'SHEA, ALLEN = William Robyn (Sterling [Australian])
O'SHEA, JOHN = William Robyn (Angelus [Australian])

PARKER, H.C. = Frank C. Stanley (Columbia [British], from Columbia masters)
PETERS & JONES = Vernon Dalhart & Carson Robison (Regal [British], from Columbia masters)
PETERS, SADIE = Isabella Patricola (Aco [British], from Vocalion masters)
PETERS, SAM = Vernon Dalhart (Regal [British], from Columbia masters)
PLAYMAN, EDMUND = William Robyn (Gracelon [Australian])

RADIO MAC* = Harry McClintock (Aurora [Canadian], from Victor masters)
RADIO RED* = Evelyn Preer (Imperial 1777, 1788 [British], from Plaza Music Company masters); unknown others (Imperial [British], from Plaza Music Company [Banner] masters)
RED PEPPER SAM* = Billy Costello (Imperial [British], from American Record Corporation [Banner] masters). Costello was the original voice of Popeye.
REMICK, WALTER = William Robyn (Electron [Australian])
RICHARDS, EDGAR = William Robyn (Grand Pree [Australian])
RICHARDS, WALTER = William Robyn (Grand Pree [Australian])
RICKMAN, EDDIE = William Robyn (Sterling [Australian])
ROBERTS, BILLY = William Robyn (Crown, Domino, Sterling and probably other Compo Company labels [Canadian], from Plaza Music Company /American Record Corporation masters)

ROBERTS, LEWIS = William Robyn (Crown, Domino, Sterling and probably other Compo Company labels [Canadian], from Plaza Music Company / American Record Corporation masters)

ROBIN, WYLLIE = William Robyn (Perfect [British], from Pathé or Plaza Music Company masters)

ROBYN, ("WEE") WILLIE* = William Robyn (various Canadian and Australian brands)

ROBYN, WYLLIE = William Robyn (Perfect [British], from Pathé or Plaza Music Company masters)

ROTTER, ALMA = Alma Henderson (Okeh; Parlophone [British], from Okeh masters)

SAM & BILL = Emmett Miller & Charlie Chiles (Parlophone R-1155 [British], from Okeh masters); unknown others are also reported (Parlophone)

SANDFORD, LEILA = Annette Hanshaw (Ariel [British], from Okeh masters)

SANGSTER, RALPH = Bob McGimsey (Aurora [Canadian], from Victor masters)

SMITH, JIMMIE* = Gene Autry (not to be confused with *Jimmy* Smith, who recorded country harmonica solos for Victor in 1926) (Aurora [Canadian, from RCA masters)

SPEAR, JOHN* = William Robyn (Angelus [Australian], from Cameo or Plaza Music Company/American Record Corporation masters)

SUNSHINE BOYS* = Joe & Dan Mooney (Panachord [British], from Brunswick masters)

TERRY, ARTHUR = Smith Ballew (Parlophone E-6329, E-6392 [British]); Seger Ellis (Parlophone E-6356, E-6362 [British]) (all from Okeh masters; there are probably other similar issues)

THOMAS, BRIAN = William Robyn (Worth [Australian])

THORNE, NORMAN(D) = Seger Ellis (Ariel [British], from Okeh masters)

TURNER, RAY = William Robyn (Melotone [Australian], from Brunswick masters)

VIVIAN, LILA = Edna Hicks (Guardsman [British], from Vocalion masters)

WATT, BRIAN = Irving Kaufman (Ariel [British], from Okeh masters)
WESTON, LES = William Robyn (Worth [Australian])
WRIGHT, JIM & HIS GUITAR = Frankie Marvin (Aurora [Canadian], from Victor masters)
WRIGHT, JOE & HIS GUITAR = Frankie Marvin (Aurora [Canadian], from Brunswick masters)

YOUNG, LOUIS = William Robyn (Grand Pree [Australian])

Instrumental Soloists and Groups

*Pseudonyms appear in **bold type**, followed by artist identification.*

Pseudonym use on instrumental recordings is generally more complicated than on vocal issues. Both major and minor companies assigned fictitious names indiscriminately, often releasing material by several different bands under a single pseudonym (or, in some cases, under the names of competing bands). Many listings, therefore, are on an issue-by-issue basis. A group's use of a pseudonym on one issue does not necessarily mean that similarly credited issues are also by that group. Pseudonyms listed here are primarily for established bands and orchestras; informal "pickup" groups and house organizations have not been included, in general, to avoid repeating previously published personnel details (see References).

ADAMS, CHARLES (director) = Charles A. Prince (Columbia)

AKANA & KEI (Hawaiian instrumental) = Cecil & Esther Ward, of WLS-Chicago (Champion)

ALABAMA CREOLE BAND = Bailey's Dixie Dudes (a California Ramblers unit) (Claxtonola 40397)

ALABAMA FUZZY WUZZIES = Frank Bunch & his Fuzzy Wuzzies (Champion)

ALABAMA JAZZ BAND = Joseph Samuels' Jazz Band (Operaphone 31161)

ALABAMA JIM & GEORGE = William E. (Buddy) Burton (piano/cello/vocal), Marcus Normand (drums) (Champion, Gennett, Silvertone)

ALABAMA JOE (banjo) = Roy Smeck (Columbia 14000-D series)

ALABAMA RASCALS = Memphis Night Hawks (Oriole, Perfect, Romeo and related labels)

ALABAMA RED JACKETS = Harry Pollock's Blue Diamonds (Champion)

ALABAMA SERENADERS = Harry Pollock's Blue Diamonds (Champion)

ALAMAC HOTEL ORCHESTRA = California Ramblers (Domino 3471, 3474)

ALAMO GARDEN JAZZERS = Joe Candullo's Everglades Orchestra (Champion)

ALL STAR TRIO = Wheeler Wadsworth (saxophone); Victor Arden (piano); George Hamilton Green (xylophone/percussion) (Okeh, Victor, others)

ALLEN'S CREEK PLAYERS = Jim Booker (violin), Marion Underwood (banjo), Willie Young (guitar) (Champion)

AMES, MELVILLE (guitar) = Charlie Dixon (Domino)

ANDERSON, ERNIE (banjo) = Fred J. Bacon (Edison)

ANDREWS INSTRUMENTAL TRIO = Henry Lange Trio (Perfect)

ANDREWS, JIMMY (piano) = Frank Banta (Banner)

ARMSTRONG, BEN'S ORCHESTRA = Victor Arden & his Orchestra (World Program Service transcriptions, early 1930's)

ARMSTRONG, FRED & HIS SYNCOPATORS = Blanche Calloway & her Joy Boys (Aurora [Canadian], from Victor masters)

ARTISTIC TRIO = usually a Grey Gull house band (*q.v.*)

ARTO BLUE FLAME SYNCOPATORS = Jimmie (James P.) Johnson's Jazz Boys (Arto 9096). Not to be confused with Lucille Hegamin's Blue Flame Syncopators (an unrelated group) on the same label.

ASH, PAUL & HIS MERRY MAD MUSICAL GANG = Fred Rich & his Orchestra (Columbia mxs. 150817, 150908, on Harmony and related labels)

ASTORITES = a unit of Fred Rich's Orchestra (Harmony & related labels)

AUBURN, FRANK & HIS MUSIC/ORCHESTRA = Smith Ballew & his Orchestra (Clarion 5187-C); Sam Lanin & his Orchestra (Okeh mx. 404467, on Harmony and related labels); Fred Rich & his Orchestra (Clarion 5179-C, 5180-C; Harmony 1240-H, 1249-H; Columbia mxs. 100483, 100488, 100501-100503, 151328, 151330, on Harmony and related labels); Ben Selvin & his Orchestra (Columbia mxs. 151426, 351059, 351063, on Harmony and related labels)

AURORA ARISTOCRATS = King Oliver & his Dixie Syncopators (Aurora [Canadian] 22001, 22002, from Brunswick masters)

AVALONIANS = Clarence Williams' Bottomland Orchestra (Vocalion 15577)

AYRES, JOHN'S ORCHESTRA = Jack Purvis & his Orchestra (Parlophone [American] PNY-34084, 34085)

BADGERS = Pseudonym on Broadway for Fletcher Henderson & his Orchestra (1130); Jack Pettis & his Band (1055); Ben Pollack & his Orchestra (1409)

BALTIMORE BELLHOPS = Fletcher Henderson & his Orchestra (Columbia 2449-D only)

BALTIMORE BLUES ORCHESTRA = Pseudonym on Black Swan for Bennie Krueger's Orchestra (2069, 10065); Sam Lanin's Roseland Orchestra (2064 [*Saturday On*]); Club Maurice Orchestra (2064 [*Dapper Dan*])

BALTIMORE SOCIETY ORCHESTRA = Pseudonym on Oriole for the California Ramblers (304, 417, 445); Al Goering's Collegians (569); Lou Gold & his Orchestra (431); Sam Lanin & his Orchestra (581, 666 [*Where'd You Get Those Eyes?*], 667, 675, 849); Ben Selvin & his Orchestra (491 [*Remember*])

BAND -- Generic term on Columbia products, nearly always indicating Columbia or Prince's Band (*q.v.*) (Columbia, including Aretino, Harmony,

Standard, United, and many other derivative labels; Columbia cylinders; Little Wonder and other Columbia special products)

BANDA ESPAÑOLA = Columbia/Prince's Band (Columbia; Manhattan and other Columbia derivatives)

BANDLEADER STARS = Metronome All-Stars (V-Disc, reissued from 1940 commercial masters)

BARBECUE JOE & HIS HOT DOGS = Wingy Mannone & his Orchestra (Champion, Decca)

BARBECUE PETE (piano) = Herve Duerson (Champion)

BARKER, TOM & HIS ORCHESTRA = Frankie Trumbauer & his Orchestra (Parlophone [American] PNY-34084, 34085, 34119, 34120)

BARNES, BILLIE (piano) = Charles Avery (Broadway)

BARRELHOUSE PETE (piano) = Art Gillham (Columbia 14000-D series)

BARTLETT, SLIM & HIS ORCHESTRA = Syd Valentine & his Patent Leather Kids (Superior)

BARTON, JOHN (violin) = John Baltzell (Broadway)

BAT "THE HUMMING BIRD" (piano) = Charles (Cow Cow) Davenport (Varsity, dubbed from Gennett originals)

BAY STATE BROADCASTERS = usually a Grey Gull house band (*q.v.*)

BEALE STREET SERENADERS = Original Memphis Five (Lincoln)

BELL, KYRLE & HIS ORCHESTRA = Smith Ballew & his Orchestra (Parlophone [American] PNY- series)

BENJAMIN, ROBERT & HIS ORCHESTRA = Ben Selvin & his Orchestra (Associated transcriptions, 1930's)

BENNETT BROTHERS = Wheeler Wadsworth (saxophone) and Victor Arden (piano) (Lyric, possibly other related labels)

BENNETT, PHIL & HIS ORCHESTRA = Ben Pollack & his Orchestra (Broadway 1391)

BERNIE & BAKER = Ben Bernie (violin) and Phil Baker (accordion) (Victor)

BIG CITY SIX ORCHESTRA = California Ramblers (Grey Gull 1234, 1285, and derivative issues)

BINNY, JACK & HIS ORCHESTRA = Jack Pettis & his Orchestra (Parlophone [American] PNY-34076)

BIRMINGHAM BLUETETTE = Jimmy Blythe & his Ragamuffins (Herwin 92019 [*Old Man Blues*]); Jones' Paramount Charleston Four (Herwin 92019 [*Homeward Bound Blues*])

BIRMINGHAM FIVE = Original Indiana Five (Champion)

BLACK DIAMOND TWINS (pianos) = W.E. (Buddy) Burton and Bob Hudson (Banner, Oriole, Perfect and related labels)

BLACK, HERMAN & HIS ORCHESTRA = King Oliver & his Dixie Syncopators (Aurora [Canadian] 22008, from Brunswick master)

BLACK, ROBERT (piano) = Eubie Blake (Regal)

BLAINE, REX & HIS ORCHESTRA = Gene Kardos & his Orchestra

(Electradisk 1802)

BLAKE, RUBY (piano) = Eubie Blake (Medallion)

BLAKE'S JAZZONE ORCHESTRA -- According to Charters & Kunstadt, this was a Richmond, Virginia band and not connected with Eubie Blake (Pathé).

BLUE BOYS (mandolin/guitar) = Nap Hayes & Matthew Prater (Okeh)

BLUE DIAMOND ORCHESTRA = Red Nichols & his Orchestra (Supertone S-2167)

BLUE FIVE ORCHESTRA = Clarence Williams' Blue Five (Vocalion 1094)

BLUE JAY BOYS = State Street Ramblers (Decca, reissued from Gennett masters)

BLUE MOON MELODY BOYS = Van & his Half-Moon Hotel Orchestra (Champion)

BLUEBIRDS = probably a Harry Reser unit (Vocalion)

BLYTHE'S BLUE BOYS = State Street Ramblers (Champion)

BOBBY'S REVELERS = Lovie Austin's Blues Serenaders (Silvertone 3537, 3551)

BOHEMIAN TRIO = Venetian Trio (Aurora [Canadian], from Victor masters)

BOSTONIAN SYNCOPATORS = Original Memphis Five (Grey Gull 1137, 1138)

BOUDINI (accordion) = Dan Boudini (Emerson, Medallion, probably other minor labels)

BOUDINI BROTHERS (accordions) = Dan & Phil Boudini (Emerson, Pathé, probably others)

BOURUCHOFF, HANS (violin) = Leopold Lichtenberg (Oriole)

BOYNTON, EDWARD (banjo) = Fred Van Eps (Pathé and related labels)

BRADFORD, LARRY'S ORCHESTRA = Richard Himber & his Orchestra (World Program Service transcriptions, mid-1930's)

BRIGGS, JOE (banjo) = Fred Van Eps (Black Swan, from Olympic masters)

BROADWAY MELODY MAKERS = California Ramblers (Puretone 11349; Puritan/Triangle and related labels 11310, 11320); Fletcher Henderson & his Orchestra (Puritan 11250, 11251, 11270); Indiana Syncopators (Triangle 11200); Original Memphis Five (Broadway/Puritan 11213); Al Siegel & his Orchestra (Puretone 11373)

BROADWAY PICKERS = Paramount Pickers (Broadway 5069)

BROADWAY RASTUS (piano) = Frank Melrose (Paramount)

BROADWAY SEVEN = Original Memphis Five (Grey Gull 1190, 1192)

BROWN & EDWARDS (accordions) = Dan & Phil Boudini (Lyric)

BROWN BROTHERS SAXOPHONE QUINTET = Five Brown Brothers (Columbia)

BROWN, FRANK & HIS TOOTERS = Duke Ellington & his Orchestra (Parlophone [American] PNY- series)

BROWN, GEORGE (piano) = Lindsay McPhail (Black Swan, from Olympic masters)

BROWN, JOE'S ALABAMA BAND = Yerkes' Master Players (Black Swan 2041, from Olympic master)

BROWN, WILLIE & HIS SIZZLING SYNCOPATORS = Noble Sissle & his Sizzling Syncopators (Medallion)

BROWNE, SAM & HIS ORCHESTRA = Red Perkins' Dixie Ramblers (Superior)

BURKHARDT, ABNER (harmonica/guitar) = Walter C. Peterson (Champion)

BURTON, DAVID (Hawaiian guitar) = Sam Ku West, accompanied by James Kohono (Oriole 1004) and Ernest Manase (Oriole 972)

BURTON, DICK & HIS ORCHESTRA = Carl Fenton & his Orchestra (Champion)

BUSTER & JACK = Jack Cawley's Oklahoma Ridge Runners (Victor)

CALIFORNIA MELODIE SYNCOPATORS = Fletcher Henderson & his Orchestra (Emerson 10852)

CALIFORNIA RAMBLERS = Charlie Barnet & his Orchestra (Variety, 1937 issues only)

CALIFORNIA VAGABONDS = a unit of the California Ramblers (Gennett)

CALIFORNIAN RAMBLERS = California Ramblers (Vocalion, various minor labels)

CALLOWAY, JEAN & HIS ORCHESTRA = Gene Kardos & his Orchestra (Victor 22959)

CALLOWAY'S HOT SHOTS = Roane's Pennsylvanians (Bluebird B-4921, B-5108, Sunrise S-3191, Victor 24037)

CAMPBELL, BUDDY & HIS ORCHESTRA = Ben Selvin & his Orchestra (Okeh)

CANDY & COCO = Candy Candido (string bass) and Otto (Coco) Heimal (guitar), sometimes with Gene Austin (vocal/piano) (Banner, Brunswick, Perfect and related American Record Corporation brands; Decca)

CAPTIVATORS = Red Nichols & his Orchestra (Brunswick 4591; Melotone)

CARDINAL DANCE ORCHESTRA = Bailey's Lucky Seven (Cardinal 523, 571)

CAROLINA COLLEGIANS = Carolina Club Orchestra (Banner, Conqueror, Domino, Regal)

CAROLINA PEANUT BOYS = Memphis Jug Band (Victor, except as noted): Noah Lewis' Jug Band (*Sellin' the Jelly*), Charles Nickerson (*Goin' Back*) (coupled on Victor 23319)

CAROLINIANS = Fletcher Henderson & his Orchestra (Silvertone 2399); Original Memphis Five (Federal 5428, Resona 75428)

CARR, STEVE'S RHYTHM ACES = Fletcher Henderson & his Orchestra (Broadway 5020)

CARROLL, ROY & HIS (SANDS POINT) ORCHESTRA = Pseudonym on Clarion, Harmony, and related labels for Fred Rich & his Orchestra (Columbia mxs. 151325-151327, 351016, 351024-351027, 351034, 351035, 351042, 351054, 351107); Jack Teagarden & his Orchestra (Columbia mxs. 151839-151842)

CARSON, LENNY & HIS ORCHESTRA = Larry Clinton & his Orchestra (Associated transcriptions, 1930's)

CAUSER, BOB & HIS CORNELLIANS/ORCHESTRA = pseudonym on Melotone, Perfect, Romeo and other American Record Corporation labels for Bunny Berigan & his Orchestra (mxs. 13236, 13288-13291); Chick Bullock & his Levee Loungers (mxs. 15695, 15697); Jimmy Hunter & his Orchestra (mxs. 19924, 19926); Gene Kardos & his Orchestra (mxs. 22290, 22293, 22377, 22378); Don Redman & his Orchestra (mx. 14315)

CAVALIERS = Ben Selvin & his Orchestra (Columbia)

CHAMPION DANCE KINGS = Elmer Grosso & his Orchestra (Champion)

CHAMPION MELODY BOYS = Willie Creager's Rhythm Aces (Champion)

CHARLES, HENRY (piano) = Henry Brown (Broadway)

CHENSKI, IVAN (violin) = Richard Czerwonky (Globe, Grey Gull, Nadsco and other Grey Gull brands; Oriole; probably others)

CHERNIAVSKY TRIO = Michael Cherniavsky (violin), Leo Cherniavsky (cello), Jan Cherniavsky (piano) (Edison)

CHICAGO BLUES DANCE ORCHESTRA = Midway Gardens Orchestra (Columbia)

CHICAGO FOOTWARMERS = Duke Ellington & his Orchestra (Okeh 8675)

CHICAGO HOT FIVE = Washboard Rhythm Kings (Victor)

CHICAGO RHYTHM KINGS = Tempo King & his Kings of Tempo (Bluebird B-6690)

CHICAGO STOMPERS = State Street Ramblers (Champion 16297, 16350; 40009, 40013 (the latter two items reissued by Decca from Gennett masters)

CHICLET ORCHESTRA = California Ramblers (Domino 414, 417, 418)

CHOCOLATE DANDIES = McKinney's Cotton Pickers (Okeh 8627, 8668); Mills' Blue Rhythm Band (Vocalion 1646); King Oliver & his Orchestra (Vocalion 1610, 1617)

CHOO CHOO JAZZERS = Original Memphis Five (Ajax 17038)

CLARK, DICK & HIS ORCHESTRA = Joe Haymes & his Orchestra (Electradisk 2509)

CLEARTONE JAZZ BAND = Joseph Samuels' Jazz Band (Cleartone 802)

CLEVELANDERS = a Harry Reser unit (Brunswick, except as noted): Carolina Club Orchestra (Supertone S-2192)

CLICQUOT CLUB ESKIMOES = Harry Reser's Orchestra (Columbia, various minor labels)

CLOVERDALE COUNTRY CLUB ORCHESTRA = Ben Selvin & his Orchestra (Okeh 41520, 41539); Jack Teagarden & his Orchestra (Okeh 41551 [*Chances Are*])

CLUB ALABAM ORCHESTRA = Fletcher Henderson & his Orchestra (Domino)

CLYDE, BILLY & HIS ORCHESTRA = Clyde McCoy & his Orchestra (Champion, from Decca masters)

COLE, KING & HIS MUSIC WEAVERS = Bert Lown & his Orchestra (no connection to Nat King Cole) (Timely Tunes C-1589)

COLLINS, BRAD & HIS ORCHESTRA = Bob Crosby & his Orchestra (Associated transcriptions, late 1930's)

COLLINS, ROY & HIS ORCHESTRA = California Ramblers (Domino 3446); Willie Creager & his Orchestra (Oriole 844); Sam Lanin & his Orchestra (Oriole 457, 825); used most often as a pseudonym for Plaza Music Company studio groups under the direction of Adrian Schubert (Jewel, Oriole).

COLUMBIA BAND/ORCHESTRA — Studio band or orchestra under the direction of Charles A. Prince. In 1910 the name was changed to Prince's Band or Orchestra, although Columbia continued to occasionally issue material under the older names.

COLUMBIA PHOTO PLAYERS = Ben Selvin & his Orchestra (Columbia)

CONNIE'S INN ORCHESTRA = Fletcher Henderson & his (Connie's Inn) Orchestra (numerous labels, 1931-1932)

CONNOR, LOU'S COLLEGIANS = Sam Lanin & his Orchestra (Jewel 5012); pseudonym on Oriole for the Buffalodians (670, 684); Sam Lanin & his Orchestra (1097, 1105, 1124, 1126, 1133); Rounders (1205); Whoopee Makers (1483)

CONNORIZED JAZZERS = Original Memphis Five (Connorized)

CONTINENTAL DANCE ORCHESTRA = Eddie Peabody & his Orchestra (Oriole 516)

COREYPHONIC ORCHESTRA = California Ramblers (Bell P-196)

COTA, EL (xylophone) = Lawrence Albert Coates (Columbia [American]; British Columbia and Regal issues were credited to Lawrence Coates)

COTTON BLOSSOMS ORCHESTRA = California Ramblers (Grey Gull/Radiex 1245)

COTTON PICKERS = Original Memphis Five (often augmented) (Brunswick, through 2532 only; personnel varied on later issues); Andy Mansfield & his Band (Gennett). See also next entry.

COTTON PICKERS ORCHESTRA = usually a Grey Gull house band (*q.v.*)

COUNTY CORK TRIO = Flanagan Brothers (Oriole)

CRANE, MARK'S ORCHESTRA = Fred Hall & his Orchestra (Parlophone [American] PNY-34034, PNY-34042)

CRAWFORD, JACK & HIS BOYS = Emil Seidl & his Orchestra (Champion)
CRESCENT CITY RED JACKETS = Fred Rich & his Orchestra (Champion)
CROSS TOWN RAMBLERS = Hitch's Happy Harmonists (Champion 15039)
CUBAN DANCE PLAYERS = Brad Gowan's Rhapsody Makers (Challenge 210)
CURRAN, JOE & HIS ORCHESTRA = Smith Ballew & his Orchestra (Parlophone [American] PNY-41282); Fred Hall & his Orchestra (Parlophone PNY-41310)

D & R (MILITARY) BAND = Columbia/Prince's Band (D&R blue label)
DALE'S DANCE ORCHESTRA = Bob Haring's Orchestra; probably others (Lincoln)
DALY BROTHERS' ORCHESTRA = Dorsey Brothers Orchestra (World Program Service transcriptions, 1930's)
DALY, FRANK'S BELL RECORD ORCHESTRA = Fletcher Henderson & his Orchestra (Bell 323)
DANCING CHAMPIONS = Fred Rich & his Orchestra (Champion)
DANCING STEVEDORES = Red McKenzie's Candy Kids (Silvertone 3054, 3056)
DANN TRIO = M. Felice Dann (cornet), Blanche L. Dann (violin), Rosalynd J. Davis (piano) (Edison)
DAVE'S HARLEM HIGHLIGHTS = Dave Nelson & his Orchestra (Aurora [Canadian], from Victor masters)
DAVIDSON, JACK & HIS ORCHESTRA = Ernie Golden & his Orchestra (Champion)
THE DEAN & HIS KIDS = Ben Pollack & his Orchestra (Brunswick, Vocalion)
DEAUVILLE SYNCOPATORS = Pseudonym on Parlophone (American PNY- series) for Fred Rich & his Orchestra, except as noted: Smith Ballew & his Orchestra (PNY-34149); Sam Lanin & his Orchestra (PNY-34140, 34144, 34145, 34199)
DICKSON'S HARLEM ORCHESTRA = Gene Kardos & his Orchestra (Victor 23377)
DIGGS, DUKE & HIS ORCHESTRA = Alphonse Trent & his Orchestra (Supertone)
DIXIE BOYS = California Ramblers (Champion, Claxtonola), except as noted: Andy Preer & the Cotton Club Orchestra (Champion 15227)
DIXIE DAISIES = Sam Lanin & his Orchestra (Pathé 36602, 36628; Perfect 14809, 14783). This name was more often used on Cameo for its house band.
DIXIE JAZZ BAND = Charles Booker's Jazz Band (Oriole 315, 347); California Ramblers (Oriole 475 [*Foot Loose*], 1022); Joe Candullo's

Everglades Orchestra (Jewel 5048; Oriole 674, 682 [*Jackass Blues*], 685, 688, 691, 705 [*I Wonder What's Become of Joe*], 723, 748, 952 [*St. Louis Blues*], 1287, 1313, 1339, 1343, 1346); Willie Creager & his Orchestra (Jewel 5488, 5490; Oriole 1447,1450, 1454, 1457); Dubin's Demons (house band) (Oriole 1515 [*St. Louis Blues*]); Duke Ellington & his Orchestra (Oriole 1730); Arthur Fields & the Noodlers (Oriole 1504, 1507); Five Birmingham Babies (*q.v.*) (984); Fred Hall's Jazz Band (Jewel 5412; Oriole 1371 [*West End Blues*], 1416); Fletcher Henderson's Collegians (Jewel 5145, 5171; Oriole 1071, 1100); Fletcher Henderson & his Orchestra (Oriole 528); Joe Jordan's Ten Sharps & Flats (Oriole 717); Sam Lanin's Orchestra (424 [*Flag That Train*]); Al Lentz & his Orchestra (Oriole 778); Al Lynch & his Orchestra (Oriole 1046); Toots Mendello's Five Gee-Gees (Oriole 1360, 1363, 1371 [*Cool Papa*], 1387, 1396); Ken (Goof) Moyer's Novelty Trio (Oriole 762); New Orleans Jazz Band (Oriole 269, 271, 291, 413 [*Some of These Days*], 445, 464); Original Indiana Five (Challenge 628; Jewel 5067, 5263; Oriole 819, 828, 829, 926, 927, 956, 960, 963, 977, 1171, 1172, 1275 [*Somebody's Making a Fuss*]); Original Memphis Five (Oriole 241); Jack Pettis & his Band (Jewel 5192, 5196; Oriole 799, 804, 846, 1123, 1127, 1131); Harry Reser's Orchestra (Oriole 1256); Luis Russell & his Orchestra (Oriole 1726, 1728); Seven Missing Links (Harry Reser group) (Oriole 443, 475 [*Angry*]); Six Black Diamonds (house band) (Oriole 413, 424); Six Hottentots (Red & Miff's Stompers) (Oriole 880, 883, 952 [*Memphis Blues*]); Whoopee Makers (Challenge 958, 999; Jewel 5547, 5569, 5685; Oriole 1515 [*Icky Blues*], 1537, 1540, 1624, 1668); Clarence Williams' Dixie Washboard Band (Oriole 565).

DIXIE JAZZ HOUNDS = New Orleans Jazz Band (Domino 306, 308, 328, 329)

DIXIE PLAYERS = California Ramblers (Champion)

DIXIE RAG PICKERS = usually a Grey Gull house band (*q.v.*)

DIXIE STOMPERS = a unit of Fletcher Henderson's Orchestra (Diva, Harmony, Velvet Tone)

DIXIE TRIO = usually a Grey Gull house band (*q.v.*)

DIZZY TRIO = Borrah Minevitch (harmonica), Carson Robison (guitar), Roy Smeck (banjo/ukulele) (Victor)

DODGE, BILL'S ORCHESTRA = Benny Goodman & his Orchestra (World Program Service transcriptions, early 1930's)

DOOLEY, PHIL & HIS ORCHESTRA = Joe Haymes & his Orchestra (Victor 24060)

D'ORSAY DANCE ORCHESTRA = Ben Selvin & his Orchestra (mx. 351111, on Clarion, Harmony, Okeh and related labels)

DOTY, MIKE & HIS ORCHESTRA = Joe Haymes & his Orchestra (Electradisk 2508)

DUNN, BLIND WILLIE (guitar) = Eddie Lang (Okeh)

EDISON VENETIAN TRIO = Eugene Jaudas (violin/director), Eugene Rose (flute), Charles Schuetze (harp) (Edison)

EDWARDS, DAVID & HIS BOYS = Sam Lanin & his Orchestra (Okeh 41492)

EDWARDS, WALLY & HIS ORCHESTRA = California Ramblers (Clarion, Harmony, Velvet Tone and related labels)

ELITE ORCHESTRA = Carolina Club Orchestra (Pathé 036197, Starck 197)

ELLINGTON, DUKE & HIS ORCHESTRA = probably a Ben Selvin unit (per Rust) (Blu-Disc T-1004 only)

ELMAN STRING QUARTET = Mischa Elman (1st violin) with Bak, Rissland, and Nagel of the Boston Symphony (acoustic recordings); or Bachmann, Schubert, and Britt (electric recordings) (Victor)

ELSHUCCO TRIO = William Kroll or Elias Breeskin (violin), Willem Willeke (cello), Amelio Giorni (piano) (Brunswick)

EMERSON DANCE ORCHESTRA = California Ramblers (Emerson 10541 [*Fascination*])

EMPIRE DANCE ORCHESTRA = California Ramblers (Pathé 036199/ Perfect 14380 [*Blue-Eyed Sally*])

EMPIRE JAZZ BAND = Joseph Samuels' Jazz Band (Empire, from Pathé masters)

EQUINOX ORCHESTRA OF PRINCETON, NEW JERSEY = Princeton Triangle Band (Columbia Personal Record)

EVANS, BILLY'S HAPPY FIVE = California Ramblers (Domino, Regal and related labels)

EVERETT, ELIOT & HIS ORCHESTRA = Joe Haymes & his Orchestra (Victor 24085); Gene Kardos & his Orchestra (Victor 22987, 24080)

FALKENBURG, FRANZ (piano) = Ernest L. Stevens (Edison)

FENWYCK, JERRY & HIS ORCHESTRA = Ben Selvin & his Orchestra (mxs. 351043, 351044, 351067, 351069, 351070, 351072, 351134, 351141, 351142, on Clarion, Harmony and related labels)

FERERA, FRANK (Hawaiian guitar/ukulele) — Many spelling variations of this performer's name occur, including Ferara, Ferreira (seen on the earliest issues, and possibly the correct spelling according to Walsh), and Ferrera.

FIRST NATIONAL JAZZ BOYS = Sam Lanin's Famous Players (Cardinal 564)

FIVE BIRMINGHAM BABIES = a unit of the California Ramblers (Pathé, Perfect and related labels)

FIVE BROWN BROTHERS (saxophones) = Alec, William, Vern, Fred, and Tom Brown (U.S. Everlasting cylinders)

FLONZALEY QUARTET = Adolfo Betti (1st violin), Alfred Pochon (2nd violin), Ugo Ara (viola), Iwan d'Archambeau (cello). Louis Bailly replaced Ara in 1917; Nicolas Moldavan replaced Bailly in the late 1920's. (Victor)

FOUR ACES & THE JOKER = Jabbo Smith's Rhythm Aces (Brunswick)

FOUR HAWAIIANS = Eddie Lewis Tropical Serenaders (Oriole)

FOUR TROUBADOURS = Eddie Lewis Tropical Serenaders (Oriole)

FRASER, VIC (piano/director) = Victor Arden (World Program Service transcriptions, mid-1930's)

FRIEDMAN, BEN'S PARAMOUNT HOTEL ORCHESTRA = Snooks & his Memphis Ramblers (Aurora [Canadian], from Victor masters)

FRISCO SYNCOPATORS = Fletcher Henderson & his Orchestra (Triangle 11384 [*I Can't Get the One I Want*]); Original Memphis Five (Puritan 11330 and derivative issues; Resona 11359); Charley Straight & his Orchestra (Paramount mxs. 1445, 1446, 1505-1507, 1511-1513, 1542, 1543, 1616, 1617, on Claxtonola, Puritan, Triangle and related labels)

FRY'S MILLION DOLLAR PIER ORCHESTRA = Fletcher Henderson & his Orchestra (Pathé 036122, Perfect 14303 only). This was an actual Atlantic City-based orchestra and is correct as credited on other issues (Edison, Pathé and related labels, Victor).

FULLER, BOB TRIO = Bob Fuller (clarinet), Louis Hooper (piano), Elmer Snowden (banjo). Although the banjo is traditionally attributed to Buddy Christian, there is very strong evidence (including contemporary group photos and a 1966 *Record Research* interview with Hooper) that Snowden was actually the banjoist.

FUTURIST JAZZ BAND = Joseph Samuels' Jazz Band (Arrow)

GALLOWAY, BOB & HIS ORCHESTRA = Cab Calloway & his Orchestra (Crown)

GENDRON, HENRI'S STRAND ROOF ORCHESTRA = Fletcher Henderson & his Orchestra (Banner 1490 only). This was an actual orchestra and is correct as credited on other issues (Banner, Cameo, Edison, Paramount and related labels).

GENE & HIS GLORIANS = Gene Kardos & his Orchestra (Aurora [Canadian], from Victor masters; Timely Tunes)

GEORGE & ROSCOE = possibly Horace George (clarinet/vocal) and Q. Roscoe Snowden (piano/vocal) (identification per Rust) (Columbia)

GEORGIA COLLEGIANS = Willie Creager's Orchestra (Champion)

GEORGIA GRINDER (piano) = Charles (Cow Cow) Davenport (Vocalion, dubbed from Gennett originals)

GEORGIA SYNCOPATORS = Duke Ellington & his Orchestra (Melotone M-12444, Oriole 2528, Perfect 15649)

GEORGIANS – Used for various unknown orchestras on late 1920's Cameo, Supertone, and other minor brands. The actual Georgians, a unit from the Paul Specht Orchestra under the direction of Frank Guarente, recorded exclusively for Columbia and its budget line (Diva, Harmony, Velvet Tone, etc.).

GLORIA PALACE ORCHESTRA = Gene Kardos & his Orchestra (Electradisk 1803, 1807)

GOLDEN GATE ORCHESTRA = California Ramblers (numerous major and minor labels, except as noted): New Orleans Jazz Band (Triangle 11382); Original Indiana Five (Silvertone 21506); Sammy Stewart's Orchestra (Broadway/Lyratone 11404); Al Turk's Princess Orchestra (Pennington 1436); there are undoubtedly other exceptions.

GOLDEN GATE SYNCOPATORS = California Ramblers (Bell P-278)

GOLDEN MELODY MEN = Preston Jackson & his Uptown Band (Challenge 803)

GOLDEN TERRACE ORCHESTRA = Ben Selvin & his Orchestra (Okeh 41500, 41508, 41510, 41512, 41517)

GOODWIN, EARL & HIS ORCHESTRA = Ernie Golden & his Orchestra (Broadway 1214)

GOOFUS FIVE = a unit of the California Ramblers (Okeh)

GORDON, EDDIE'S BAND = Miff Mole's Little Molers (Odeon [American] ONY-41153, 41273)

GORMAN, ELWOODS'S (MILITARY) BAND = Edwin Franko Goldman's Band (World Program Service transcriptions, mid-1930's)

GORMAN'S SUNDOWNERS = California Ramblers (Challenge 736)

GOTHAM CLUB ORCHESTRA = Original Memphis Five (Silvertone 2400)

GRAUB, CARL & HIS ORCHESTRA = Johnny Hamp & his Orchestra (Aurora [Canadian], from Victor masters)

GRAY, DON & HIS COLLEGIANS = Franchini's South Sea Serenaders (Champion 15478)

GRAY, HAROLD (piano) = Porter Grainger (Victor)

GREAT GAP ENTERTAINERS = Lookout Mountain Boys (Broadway)

GREEN, BOB'S (DANCE) ORCHESTRA = Pseudonym on Oriole for Willie Creager & his Orchestra (1390); Devine's Wisconsin Roof Orchestra (1313); Sam Lanin & his Orchestra (620, 635, 643, 689, 724, 733, 753, 849, 850, 926, 929); Al Lentz & his Orchestra (717)

GREEN, HARRY'S RHYTHM BOYS = Gene Kardos & his Orchestra (Bluebird B-5519)

GREEN, SONNY & HIS ORCHESTRA = Sunny Clapp & his Band o' Sunshine (Aurora [Canadian], from Victor masters)

GREER, SONNY & HIS MEMPHIS MEN = Duke Ellington & his Orchestra (Columbia)

GREY GULL HOUSE BAND — A small group of studio musicians, usually including Mike Mosiello (trumpet), Andy Sannella (reeds/guitar/steel guitar/banjo/ukulele/string bass), Charlie Magnante (piano/accordion), George Hamilton Green (xylophone/marimba/percussion), and Arthur Fields (vocal) was responsible for a tremendous number of instrumental sides issued both anonymously and under a bewildering assortment of pseudonyms on the Grey Gull chain (Bingola, Globe, Grey Gull, Madison, Radiex, Sunrise, Supreme, and Van Dyke, among others; electric recordings, 1926-1930).

GRIMES, GORDON & HIS ORCHESTRA = California Ramblers (Champion)

GRINDERINO, SIGNOR = hurdy-gurdy solos, allegedly cranked by an actual New York organ-grinder (Victor)

GRINSTED, WILLIAM STANLEY (banjo) = Frank C. Stanley, recording under his own name (see also vocal listing) (Edison cylinders)

GUILLERMO, CLARENCIO (piano/director) = Clarence Williams (Okeh [Mexican], from American masters)

HACKEL-BERGE ORCHESTRA — see Taylor Trio

HALE, JIMMY'S ORCHESTRA = Isham Jones' Orchestra (World Program Service transcriptions, mid-1930's)

HALL, GOLDIE (piano) = Lovie Austin (Harmograph)

HALL, GOLDIE & HER BLUES SERENADERS = Lovie Austin & her Blues Serenaders (Harmograph)

HAMILTON, GEORGE (piano) = Charles (Cow Cow) Davenport (Champion)

HAMILTON, GEORGE (xylophone/marimba) = George Hamilton Green (minor brands *c.* 1918-1921)

HAPPY HOUR ORCHESTRA = Fred Rich & his Orchestra (Okeh)

HARLAN, EARL & HIS ORCHESTRA = Don Redman & his Orchestra (Banner, Melotone, Romeo and related labels)

HARLEM FOOTWARMERS = Duke Ellington & his Orchestra (Okeh 8720, 8840, 8869)

HARLEM HOT CHOCOLATES = Duke Ellington & his Orchestra (Hit of the Week)

HARLEM HOT SHOTS = Billy Banks & his Orchestra (Domino 123 [early 1930's series]); Joe Haymes & his Orchestra (Bluebird B-5481); Henny Hendrickson's Louisville Serenaders (Electradisk 1931 [*I Ain't Got Nobody*]); Dave Nelson's Harlem Hot Shots (Electradisk 1931 [*St. Louis Blues*])

HARLEM MUSIC MASTERS = Duke Ellington & his Orchestra (Odeon [American] ONY- series; Okeh 41468)

HARLEM TRIO = George McClennon (clarinet) with unknown piano and banjo accompaniment (Okeh)

HARLEM WILDCATS = Joel Shaw & his Orchestra (Varsity, dubbed from Crown originals)

HARMOGRAPH DANCE ORCHESTRA = Pseudonym on Harmograph for California Ramblers (804); Cameo Dance Orchestra (744); Fletcher Henderson & his Orchestra (803); Charley Straight & his Orchestra (862, 889)

HARMONIANS = a Ben Selvin unit (virtually all Harmony issues, except as noted): California Ramblers (Harmony 1135-H only)

HARMONICA TIM = Blues Birdhead (Clarion, Velvet Tone)

HARRY'S RECKLESS FIVE = Kansas City Frank (Melrose) & his Footwarmers (Broadway)

HAWAIIAN SERENADERS = Pseudonym on Oriole for Frank Ferera's Hawaiians (474, 863, 892, 1088, 1116, 1117, 1145, 1168, 1169, 1192, 1245, 1499, 1500, 1531, 920 [*Honolulu Home*], 1031 [*Lonely Nights*]; Ferera & Paaluhi (508, 744, 770, 785, 813, 1057, 1087, 1031 [*My Hawaiian Melody*]; Lani's Hawaiians (1379, 1381); Roy Smeck (1221); South Sea Islanders (840, 943, 920 [*One-Two*], 1003; Waikiki Hawaiians (1442)

HAWAIIAN TRIO = Helen Louise, Frank Ferera, and Irene Greenus (various labels)

HAWKINS, UNCLE BILLY (violin) = William B. Houchens (Champion)

HAYMES, JOE & HIS ORCHESTRA = Roane's Pennsylvanians (Victor 24353 only).

HAYNES' HARLEM SYNCOPATORS = Pseudonym on Black Swan for Earl Fuller's New York Orchestra (2058 [*Melody in F*]); Palace Trio (2059 [*You Ought to See My Baby*]); Rudy Wiedoeft's Californians (2058 [*Hawaiian Blues*]); other unidentified white groups (all from Olympic masters)

HEINS, JOE & HIS ORCHESTRA = Joe Haymes & his Orchestra (Associated transcriptions, 1930's)

HELMS, BUD & HIS BAND = John Williams & his Memphis Stompers (Champion)

HENDERSON'S DANCE ORCHESTRA = Pseudonym on Black Swan for Bennie Krueger's Orchestra (20280/10076 [*Wang Wang Blues*]); Sam Lanin's Roseland Orchestra (2073/10069 [*Jane*], 2080/10076 [*Lucky Dog*]); Merry Melody Men (2073/10069 [*Last Waltz*]); Original Memphis Five (2034); probably others (all from Olympic masters)

HENDERSON'S NOVELTY ORCHESTRA = Irving Weiss & his Ritz Carlton Orchestra (Black Swan 2025, from Olympic masters)

HENDERSON'S WONDER BOYS = Fletcher Henderson & his Orchestra (Pathé 036157)

HERWIN HOT SHOTS = Paramount Pickers (Herwin 93015)

HICKORY KNOLL PAVILLION KINGS = California Ramblers (Champion)

HIGH SOCIETY SEVEN = usually a Grey Gull house band (*q.v.*); Fletcher Henderson & his Orchestra (Oriole 226)

HILL, SAM (piano) = Fletcher Henderson (Oriole)

HILL, SAM & HIS ORCHESTRA = Fletcher Henderson & his Orchestra (Oriole), except as noted: unidentified, possibly a house band (Oriole 410)

HILL TOP INN ORCHESTRA = Pseudonym on Champion for Jimmy Carr & his Orchestra (15293); Johnny Clesi's Areolinas (15203); Willie Creager's Orchestra (15167); Guy Lombardo's Royal Canadians (15031)

HOFFMAN, HARVEY & HIS ORCHESTRA = Jimmy Wade's Club Alabam Orchestra (Champion)

HOLLYWOOD DANCE ORCHESTRA = Lou Gold & his Orchestra (Oriole 1982); Sam Lanin & his Orchestra (Oriole 1684); Johnny Sylvester & his Orchestra (Pathé 036211, Perfect 14392)

HOLLYWOOD SHUFFLERS = Reuben Reeves & his River Boys (Vocalion 15837, 15841)

HOLLYWOOD SYNCOPATORS = Original Memphis Five (Nordskog 3013, from Arto masters)

HOMETOWNERS = Fred Hall & his Orchestra (Oriole 1885)

HONOLULU TRIO = Ferera and Franchini (Champion); Ferera, Franchini and Greenus (Gennett); probably similar personnel on many other minor labels

HOT DOGS = Lovie Austin's Blues Serenaders (Silvertone 3551, 3562, 3572); unknown band (not Austin) (Silvertone 3574)

HOT HENRY'S LUCKY SEVEN = Joe Candullo's Everglades Orchestra (Variety 5002)

HOTEL COMMODORE DANCE ORCHESTRA = Ben Selvin & his Orchestra (mxs. 371074, 351077, on Clarion, Harmony and related labels)

HOTTENTOTS = Floyd Mills' Marylanders (Supertone 9447)

HUB SYNCOPATORS = usually a Grey Gull house band (*q.v.*)

HUGHES, PHIL & HIS HIGH HATTERS = Sam Lanin & his Orchestra (Clarion 5304-C, Harmony 1313-H, Velvet Tone 2370-V)

IANTES, HARRY (piano) = Harry Jentes (Parlophone [British], from Okeh masters)

IMPERIAL DANCE ORCHESTRA = Sam Lanin & his Orchestra (Oriole 586, 675); Al Lynch & his Orchestra (Oriole 961); Jack Teagarden & his Orchestra (Domino 4646)

INDIANA HOTEL BROADCASTERS = Joe Candullo's Everglades Orchestra (Champion 15110, 15111, 15117, 15119); Harry Pollock's Club Maurice Diamonds (Champion 15186, 15216)

IPANA TROUBADOURS = Sam Lanin & his Orchestra (or a unit thereof) (Columbia, Gennett, Parlophone [American])

JACK'S FAST-STEPPIN' BELL HOPS = Fletcher Henderson & his Orchestra (Champion 15088); Tennessee Ten (Champion 15089); Barney Zeeman's Kentucky Kardinals (Champion 15090, 15093)

JACKSON, (SHOELESS) JOHN = Benny Goodman (with Mel Powell's Orchestra, as credited on the label personnel listing) (Commodore)

JACKSON, EARL & HIS MUSICAL CHAMPIONS = Duke Ellington & his Orchestra (Melotone M-12093; Polk P-9006); Mills' Blue Rhythm Band (Melotone M-12093, M-12164)

JACKSON, FRISKY FOOT & HIS THUMPERS = King Mutt's Tennessee Thumpers (Champion)

JACKSON, LITTLE JOE & HIS BOYS = Frank Bunch & his Fuzzy Wuzzies (Bell)

JACKSON, SLIM TRIO = Bob Fuller Trio (Cameo)

JACKSON, SMOKE & HIS RED ONIONS = Zach Whyte's Chocolate Beau Brummels (Champion)

JAMES, BILLY & HIS ORCHESTRA = Pseudonym on Oriole for Willie Creager & his Orchestra (1503, 1600); Fletcher Henderson & his Orchestra (271); Sam Lanin & his Orchestra (251, 255, 469, 477, 495, 517, 521, 534, 547, 565, 588, 603, 604, 728, 775, 777, 779, 841; Al Lynch & his Orchestra (1098). Billy James was an actual bandleader and songwriter; later Plaza Music Company/American Record Corporation sessions are logged under his name.

JAMES, CORKY & HIS BLACKBIRDS = Blackbirds of Paradise (Bell)

JAZZ-BO'S CAROLINA SERENADERS = Original Memphis Five (Cameo, Muse)

JAZZ HARMONISTS = Wolverines (Claxtonola)

JAZZ HARMONIZERS = Bailey's Lucky Seven (Rich-Tone)

JAZZ MASTERS = Indiana Syncopators (Black Swan 2109, from Olympic masters)

JAZZ PILOTS = Harry Reser's Orchestra (Okeh)

JAZZAZZA JAZZ BAND = Joseph Samuels' Jazz Band (Operaphone, from Pathé masters)

JAZZOPATORS = usually a Grey Gull house band (*q.v.*)

JEFFRIES, SPEED & HIS NIGHT OWLS = State Street Ramblers (Superior)

JEWEL DANCE ORCHESTRA = Fred Rich & his Orchestra (Challenge 999)

JOE'S HOT BABIES = King Brady's Clarinet Band (Paramount 12783)

JOHNSON ALL STAR ORCHESTRA = Irving Weiss & his Ritz Carlton Orchestra (Black Swan 2070/10066 [*Figaro*]); unknown white band, from an Olympic master (Black Swan 2070/10066 [*Song of Love*])

JOHNSON BOYS = Nap Hayes & Matthew Prater (variable instrumentation; both play violin, mandolin and guitar) (Okeh)

JOHNSON, ED (clarinet) = Wilbur Sweatman (Dandy)

JOHNSON, GRAVEYARD & HIS GANG = King Mutt & his Tennessee Thumpers (Supertone)

JOHNSON, JIMMIE (piano/director) = James P. Johnson (Arto, Columbia and others)

JOHNSON, LONNIE'S HARLEM FOOTWARMERS = Duke Ellington & his Orchestra (Okeh 8638)

JOHNSON, PORKCHOP (piano) = Leothus (Porkchop) Green (Champion)

JOHNSON'S JAZZ BAND = Cotton Pickers (*q.v.*) (Silvertone 3101)

JONES, BILLY & HIS ORCHESTRA = Johnny Sylvester & his Orchestra (not connected with recording comedian Billy Jones) (Champion)

JONES, BOBBY & HIS NEW YORKERS = Joe Candullo's Everglades Orchestra (Champion 15177); Johnny Sylvester & his Orchestra (Champion 15202, 15203, 15204, 15294)

JONES, GINGER HANK = Henry Johnson's Boys (Champion)

JONES, HIRAM (violin) = John Baltzell (Oriole)

JONES-SMITH, INCORPORATED = Count Basie Quintet (Vocalion)

JUNGLE BAND = Duke Ellington & his Orchestra (Brunswick), except as noted: Cab Calloway & his Orchestra (Brunswick 4936); pick-up group (see Rust's *Jazz Records*) (Brunswick 4450)

KAHN, ART & HIS ORCHESTRA = Benny Goodman & his Orchestra (label error on Melotone M-12090 only)

KALTENBORN STRING QUARTET = Frank Kaltenborn (1st violin), Herman Kuhn (2nd violin), Max Barr (viola), Max Droge (cello) (Edison cylinders)

KANSAS CITY BLUE BOYS = usually a Grey Gull house band (*q.v.*)

KANSAS CITY FRANK (piano) = Frank Melrose (Brunswick)

KEATING, LLOYD & HIS MUSIC/ORCHESTRA = Pseudonym on Clarion, Harmony and related labels for Smith Ballew & his Orchestra (Columbia mx. 151154); Sam Lanin & his Orchestra (Okeh mx. 404819); Fred Rich & his Orchestra (Columbia mxs. 100367, 100435, 100436, 100440, 100484, 100505, 100506, 151325, 151329); Ben Selvin & his Orchestra (Columbia mxs. 100377, 351028, 351029, 351041, 351047, 351056, 351061, 351062, 351071, 351073, 351075)

KEENE, HALL & HIS ORCHESTRA = Hal Kemp & his Orchestra (World Program Service transcriptions, mid- 1930's)

KELLY, EDWARD (accordian) = John Kimmel (National Music Lovers)

KENDALL, CLYDE (guitar) = Carl Kress (World Program Service transcriptions, mid-1930's)

KENTUCKY BLOWERS = Bailey's Dixie Dudes (a California Ramblers unit) (Gennett 5602)

KENTUCKY GRASSHOPPERS = Whoopee Makers (*q.v.*) (Banner)

KENTUCKY SERENADERS = Original Memphis Five (Regal 9139, 9143)

KEOLE BROTHERS (Hawaiian guitars) = Sam Ku West and Joseph Ikeole (Champion)

KEYES, FRANK & HIS ORCHESTRA = Jack Teagarden & his Orchestra (Perfect 15358)

KILAURA & HANELEI = Lei's Royal Hawaiians (Champion), except as noted: Francis Lei & Chester Smith (of Lei's Royal Hawaiians) (Champion 15469 [*Dreamy Hawaii*] only)

KIMMBLE, JOHN (accordian) = John Kimmel (Edison cylinders)

KIMMEL, JOSEPH (accordian) = John Kimmel

KING COLE & HIS MUSIC WEAVERS = Bert Lown & his Biltmore Orchestra (Aurora [Canadian], from Victor masters)

KING NAWAHI -- see Nawahi's Hawaiians

KING POPS (saxophone) = Sidney Bechet (Bluebird)

KING, REX & HIS SOVEREIGNS = Fred Rich & his Orchestra (Odeon [American] ONY-36204

KING'S HAWAIIANS = King Nawahi's Hawaiians (Aurora [Canadian], from Victor masters)

KING'S MILITARY BAND = Prince's Band (Columbia [British], Regal [British], from American Columbia masters)

KIRILOFF, EFREM (piano) = Mana Zucca (Oriole, Grey Gull and related labels, from Emerson 4100/41000-series masters); unknown (same labels, from Paramount masters)

KNICKERBOCKERS = Ben Selvin & his Orchestra (Columbia 2129-D, probably many other Columbia issues)

KULANI TRIO = Lei's Royal Hawaiians (Champion)

LA PALINA BROADCASTERS = Fred Rich & his Orchestra (Pathé, Perfect)

LADD'S BLACK ACES = Original Memphis Five (Connorized, Gennett, Starr [Canadian] and related labels)

LAKSA, HAL & HIS ORCHESTRA = Casa Loma Orchestra (Parlophone [American] PNY- series)

LANE, AUDREY (cello) = Bernard Altschuler (Black Swan, from Olympic masters)

LANIN, SAM & HIS (ROSELAND) ORCHESTRA — Generally correct as credited, with the following known exceptions: Original Memphis Five (Banner 1182, Emerson 10566); New Orleans Jazz Band (Silvertone 2498); undoubtedly, there are others exceptions.

LANIN'S SOUTHERN SERENADERS = Original Memphis Five (sometimes augmented) (Banner, Emerson, Paramount and other minor labels); aural evidence suggests a different (non-jazz) group on most Arto, Pathé, and derivative brands.

LAUREL DANCE ORCHESTRA = Pseudonym on Black Swan for Green Brothers Novelty Band (2071/10067 [*Learning*]); Bennie Krueger's Orchestra (2071/10067 [*Someone Else*]); Sam Lanin's Roseland Orchestra (2075/10071 [*Cherry Blossoms*]); unknown white band (2075/10071 [*Honeymoon Blues*]) (all from Olympic masters)

LE SIEUR, LEO (organ) = Edmund Cromwell (Regal)

LEI'S ROYAL HAWAIIANS = Francis Lei, Chester Smith; others unknown (Gennett)

LEIGHTON, CHESTER & HIS ORCHESTRA/SOPHOMORES = Pseudonym on Clarion, Harmony and related labels for Sam Lanin & his Orchestra (Okeh mx. 404470); Fred Rich & his Orchestra (Columbia mxs. 150812-150816, 150909-150912, 100435, 100436, 100437, 100439, 100504); Ben Selvin & his Orchestra (Columbia mxs. 351042, 351045, 351074)

LEIHELE TRIO = Kalama Maui Island Trio (Champion)

LEM, HAROLD & HIS ORCHESTRA = Smith Ballew & his Orchestra (Okeh 41465)

LENNOX DANCE ORCHESTRA = Fletcher Henderson & his Orchestra (Perfect 14394)

LEVEE LOUNGERS = Sam Lanin & his Orchestra (Perfect 14979)

LEVEE SYNCOPATORS = usually a Grey Gull house band (*q.v.*)

LEVY'S TRIO = Jules Levy, Jr. (trumpet), Larry Briers (piano), unknown (possibly Harry Reser) (banjo) (Pathé, Perfect)

LEWIS, DANNY (banjo) = Fred Van Eps (Black Swan, from Olympic masters)

LILLARD, PRESTON (piano) = Sammy Brown (Champion)

LITTLE ACES = McKinney's Cotton Pickers (Okeh)

LITTLE RAMBLERS = a unit of the California Ramblers (Columbia, Pathé)

LLOYD, ED (director) = Eddie Kirkeby

LONDON, SID & HIS ORCHESTRA = Ben Selvin & his Orchestra (Associated transcriptions, 1930's)

LORING, STANLEY (organ) = Edmund Cromwell (Oriole)

LOU & HIS GINGER SNAPS = Luis Russell & his Orchestra (Banner, Cameo and related labels)

LOUISIANA JOE & SLIM = William E. (Buddy) Burton (piano/cello/vocal), Marcus Normand (drums) (Champion)

LOUISIANA RHYTHM KINGS = Red Nichols' Five Pennies (Vocalion 15710)

LOUISIANA RHYTHMAKERS = Duke Ellington & his Orchestra (Melotone M-12445, Perfect 15650)

LOUISIANA STOMPERS = Fletcher Henderson & his Orchestra (Paramount)

LOUISVILLE WASHBOARD BAND = Clarence Williams' Dixie Washboard Band (Domino, Oriole)

LOYD, ED (director) = Eddie Kirkeby

LUCKY STRIKE DANCE ORCHESTRA = Lou Gold & his Orchestra (Oriole 434); Sam Lanin & his Orchestra (Oriole 302)

LUDWIG, NORBERT (organ) = Edmund Cromwell (Regal)

LYNN, AL & HIS ORCHESTRA = Al Lynch & his Orchestra (confirmed on Jewel and Oriole); it is not known if Al Lynn's Music Masters on Edison was also Lynch's Orchestra.

MAD HATTERS = Joe Haymes & his Orchestra (Bluebird, Electradisk, Sunrise)

MAJESTIC DANCE ORCHESTRA = Al Lynch & his Orchestra (Oriole 903, 957); Original Memphis Five (Perfect 14391); Fred Rich & his Orchestra (Oriole 1034); Jack Teagarden & his Orchestra (mxs. 10101-10103, on Banner, Cameo, Perfect and related labels)

MANHATTAN BAND = Prince's Band (Manhattan)

MANHATTAN MUSICIANS = Harry Reser's Orchestra (New Phonic 1246); Fred Rich & his Orchestra (New Phonic 1238 [*Old Shoes*]); pseudonym on National Music Lovers for Fred Hall & his Orchestra (1210); Bob Haring & his Orchestra (1218); Fletcher Henderson & his Orchestra (1099); Sam Lanin & his Orchestra (1090, 1215); Fred Rich & his Orchestra (1196)

MANLEY BROTHERS' ORCHESTRA = Dorsey Brothers' Orchestra (Broadway 1352)

MARIMBA PLAYERS = Hurtado's Royal Marimba Band (New Phonic 1239, 1240, 1241, 1242)

MARKS & HIS FIVE OH-MY'S = Toots Mendello & his Five Gee-Gee's (Broadway)

MARLOW, RUDY & HIS ORCHESTRA = Fred Rich & his Orchestra (Columbia mxs. 100340, 100341, on Harmony and related labels); Ben Selvin & his Orchestra (mxs. 100353, 100378, on Harmony and related labels)

MARSH, GILBERT & HIS ORCHESTRA = Miff Mole's Little Molers (Parlophone [American] PNY-34040, 34041, 34038, 34039, 36045)

MARSHALL, TED & HIS BOYS = Travis-Carlton Orchestra (Champion)

MARTIN & ROBERTS = Alfred Martin (guitar) and Robert Cooksey (harmonica/vocal) (Brunswick, Vocalion)

MARTIN, BEN & HIS ORCHESTRA = Eubie Blake & his Orchestra (Broadway 1448)

MARTIN, GUSTAVUS (violin) = Milan Lusk (National Music Lovers)

MARTIN, SARA'S JUG BAND = Clifford's Louisville Jug Band (Okeh)

MARTON, JELLY ROLL = misspelling of Jelly Roll Morton (Paramount and related labels)

MASON, ALBERT & HIS ORCHESTRA = Sam Lanin & his Famous Players (Parlophone [American] PNY- series, except as noted): Smith Ballew & his Orchestra (Parlophone PNY-34069)

MASTER MELODY MAKERS = Fred Rich (New Phonic 1237); pseudonym on National Music Lovers for Bob Haring & his Orchestra (1217); Fletcher Henderson & his Orchestra (1133 [*Then I'll Be Happy*]); Sam Lanin & his Orchestra (1090); Jack Pettis & his Band (1195); Fred Rich & his Orchestra (1210)

MAYNARD, SID & HIS ORCHESTRA = Jack Stillman & his Orchestra (Champion)

McCONNELL, EDWARD (accordian) = John Kimmel

McGINTY'S OKLAHOMA COWBOY BAND = Gray's Oklahoma Cowboy Band (Champion)

MEADE, (OLIVE) QUARTET = Olive Meade (1st violin), Vera Fonaroff (2nd violin), Gladys North (viola), Lillian Littledales (cello) (Edison cylinders)

MEMPHIS DADDY & HIS BOYS = Jelly James & his Fewsicians (Silvertone)

MEMPHIS HOT SHOTS = Pseudonym on Clarion, Velvet Tone and related labels for Duke Ellington & his Orchestra (Okeh mxs. 404802, 404804); Clarence Williams' Jazz Kings (Okeh mxs. 404854-404857)

MEMPHIS JAZZERS = usually a Grey Gull house band (*q.v.*)

MEMPHIS MELODY BOYS = Hitch's Happy Harmonists (Buddy)

MEMPHIS MELODY PLAYERS = Johnny Sylvester & his Orchestra (Challenge 233, 234, 237)

MEMPHIS SHEIKS = Memphis Jug Band (Victor)

MEROFF, BENNY & HIS ORCHESTRA = Frankie Trumbauer & his Orchestra (Okeh 40912)

MEYERS, KEN (clarinet) = Ken (Goof) Moyer's Novelty Trio (Regal)

MIAMI JAZZ BAND = Fletcher Henderson & his Orchestra (Oriole 552); New Orleans Jazz Band (Oriole 253)

MIAMI ROYAL PALM ORCHESTRA = Willard Robison & his Orchestra (Pathé mxs. 108021, 108022, on Cameo and related labels)

MIAMI SOCIETY ORCHESTRA = Devine's Wisconsin Roof Orchestra (Oriole 1479); Sam Lanin & his Orchestra (1125, 1154, 1174, 1180, 1203, 1210, 1235, 1283, 1284, 1573, 1574, 1604, 1609)

MICHALL, ERNEST (& HIS NEW ORLEANS BOYS) = King Brady's Clarinet Band (Black Patti)

MILLS' TEN BLACKBERRIES = Duke Ellington & his Orchestra (Clarion, Diva, Velvet Tone, and related labels)

MISSOURI JAZZ BAND = California Ramblers (Domino 3507); Willie Creager's Orchestra (Banner 6262); Devine's Wisconsin Roof Orchestra (Conqueror 7110, Domino 4184, Regal 8615); Five Birmingham Babies (Domino 4011, Regal 8380); Lou Gold & his Orchestra (Oriole 518, 521); Fletcher Henderson & his Orchestra (Oriole 528 [*Then I'll be Happy*], 536); Sam Lanin & his Orchestra (Banner 1621, Domino 3952, 3610, Oriole 590); Ozzie Nelson & his Orchestra (Supertone S-2172); Samuels' Jazz Band (Regal 9470); Noble Sissle & his Orchestra (Supertone S-2173)

MISSOURI JAZZ HOUNDS = Original Memphis Five (Apex [Canadian] 693, from Pathé master)

MONTAUK TRIO = Stanley Brooks (saxophone), Walter Wooley (piano), Henry L. Taylor (banjo) (Edison)

MOORE, WEBSTER & HIS HIGH HATTERS = Sam Lanin & his Famous Players (Harmony 1197-H)

MORRIS, JOE & HIS (SPECIALTY) ORCHESTRA = Sam Lanin & his Orchestra (Champion)

MOSELY, SID'S BLUE BOYS = Syd Valentine & his Patent Leather Kids (Supertone)

MOSIELLO, MIKE & HIS RADIO STARS = Grey Gull house band (*q.v.*)

MURRAY, BILLY'S MERRY MELODY MEN — Not connected with vocalist Billy Murray, as related to Jim Walsh by Murray himself. Later issues dropped Murray's name. (Olympic, Lyric and other minor labels, *c.* 1919-1920).

MUSE NOVELTY SEXTET = Varsity Eight (*q.v.*) (Muse)

MUSICAL COMRADES = Johnny Johnson & his Orchestra (Muse 416); Varsity Eight (*q.v.*) (Tremont)

NATIONAL MUSIC LOVERS (DANCE) ORCHESTRA = Pseudonym on National Music Lovers for the California Ramblers (1033 [*Who's Sorry Now?*], 1123); Fletcher Henderson & his Orchestra (1097); Hotsey Totsey Boys (a Red Nichols group) (1152 [*Steppin' Along*]); Original Indiana Five (1186); Eddie Peabody & his Band (1137 [*Charleston Mad*]); Adrian Schubert's Dance Orchestra (1084). See also Music Lovers Dance Orchestra and NML Dance Orchestra

NATIONAL MUSIC LOVERS SYNCOPATORS = Bob Fuller Trio (National Music Lovers 1155, 1156)

NATIONAL TRIO = Adler Trio (mx. 42073); Longo Trio (mx. 41835) (coupled on National Music Lovers 1107)

NAWAHI'S HAWAIIANS = Benny Nawahi (steel guitar), James Ferraro (guitar) (Columbia)

NELSON, CHUCK & HIS BOYS = Zach Whyte's Chocolate Beau Brummels (Champion)

NELSON, CLARENCE (piano) = Porter Grainger (Domino)

NEW ORLEANS BLUES BAND = Zach Whyte's Chocolate Beau Brummels (Varsity 6029, dubbed from Gennett original)

NEW ORLEANS FIVE = Original Indiana Five (Cameo 1138, Romeo 370)

NEW ORLEANS LUCKY SEVEN = Bix Beiderbecke & his Gang (Okeh)

NEW ORLEANS PEPSTERS = usually a Grey Gull house band (*q.v.*) (Van Dyke)

NEW ORLEANS RHYTHM KINGS = Jelly Roll Morton's Incomparables (Buddy 8004 only); Gennett issues are correct as credited.

NEW ORLEANS STRUTTERS = Frank Bunch & his Fuzzy Wuzzies (Champion)

NEW SYNCO JAZZ BAND = Joseph Samuels' Jazz Band (Pathé, Perfect and related labels)

NEW YORK SYNCOPATORS = California Ramblers (Okeh 40757, 40965, 41202); Duke Ellington & his Orchestra (Odeon ONY-36189 [*I'm So in Love*], 36190 [*I Can't Realize*]; Sam Lanin & his Orchestra (Odeon ONY-36148 [*It's a Great Life*], 36149 [*When Kentucky Bids*], 36152, 36208 [*Just a Crazy Song*]; Okeh 41003, 41264 [*The One that I Love*]; Fred Rich & his Orchestra (Odeon ONY-36145, 36146, 36148 [*Body and Soul*], 36149 [*Just a Little*], 36157 [*I'll Be Blue*], 36158 [*I Got Rhythm*], 36159 [*Ukulele Moon*], 36163 [*Baby's Birthday*], 36165, 36206 [*Dream a Little Dream*])

NEW YORK TRIO = Louis Edlin (violin), Cornelius Van Vliet (cello), Clarence Adler (piano) (Edison)

NEW YORKERS = Gene Kardos & his Orchestra (Victor 24009)

NICHOLS, BOB (violin) = Clayton McMichen (Columbia)

NICHOLS, LORING & HIS ORCHESTRA = Red Nichols & his Orchestra (Brunswick)

NIGHT CLUB ORCHESTRA = Harry Reser's Orchestra (or a unit thereof) (Harmony and related labels)

NIGHT OWLS = Jimmy Blythe's Sinful Five (Silvertone 3549)

NML DANCE ORCHESTRA = Pseudonym on National Music Lovers for Lou Gold & his Orchestra (1216); Fred Hall & his Orchestra (1195); Six Hottentots (*q.v.*) (1208)

NORTHWEST MELODY BOYS = Walter Anderson & his Golden Pheasant Hoodlums (Champion)

NOVELTY BLUE BLUES = usually a Grey Gull house band (*q.v.*)

NUBIAN FIVE = probably Joseph Samuels' Jazz Band (per aural evidence) (Pathé, Perfect, Harmograph)

O'KEEFE, JIMMY (piano) = Zez Confrey (?) (Puritan, probably others; from Paramount masters)

O'NEIL, JACK'S ORCHESTRA = Jack Stillman's Orchestra (Champion)

OLD SOUTHERN JUG BAND = Clifford's Louisville Jug Band (Vocalion)

OLIVER, EARL'S JAZZ BABIES = a unit of Harry Reser's Orchestra (Edison)

OLVETTI TROUBADOURS = Michael Banner (violin), Roy Butin (guitar) (Edison Amberol cylinders)

ONIVAS, D. (piano/director) = Domenico Savino (Actuelle, Pathé, Perfect and related labels)

ORIGINAL DIXIELAND JAZZ BAND = Original Memphis Five (Arto 9140 and derivative issues only; reported by Rust, but no copies seen for confirmation); other issues are correct as credited.

ORIGINAL MEMPHIS MELODY BOYS = Midway Gardens Orchestra (Cardinal, Champion, Gennett)

ORIGINAL PIANO TRIO = George Dilworth, Edgar Fairchild, Herbert Clair (pianos) (Edison)

ORIGINAL TAMPA FIVE = Original Indiana Five (Dandy 5154, 5248)

ORIOLE DANCE BAND = Bill Haid's Cubs (Oriole 1319)

ORIOLE DANCE ORCHESTRA = Pseudonym on Oriole for the California Ramblers (319 [*Oh Mabel*]); Lou Gold & his Orchestra (434); Sam Lanin & his Orchestra (101, 103, 301, 464, 532, 605, 1256, 1394, 1399, 1513); Fred Rich & his Orchestra (1235, 1575); Joseph Samuels' Orchestra (100, 106, 319 [*Collegiate Walk*], 342 [*Marguerita*]).

ORIOLE VARSITY TEN = Sam Lanin & his Orchestra (Oriole 672, probably others)

OSBORNE, HARRY (piano) = Ernest L. Stevens (Edison)

OSSMAN-DUDLEY TRIO -- Vess L. Ossman (banjo), Audley Dudley (mandolin), Roy Butin or George F. Dudley (harp-guitar) (Columbia and derivative brands, Edison, Victor)

OWENS, RED & HIS GANG = Floyd Mills' Marylanders (Champion)

PALACE GARDENS ORCHESTRA = California Ramblers (Pathé 036260, 036314, 36341, 36467; Perfect 14648)

PALACE TRIO = Rudy Wiedoeft (saxophone), Mario Perry (accordion), J. Russell Robinson (piano) (numerous major and minor labels)

PALM BEACH SERENADERS = California Ramblers (Domino [Canadian] 21328, from Banner masters)

PALMER, DICK (piano) = Zez Confrey (Arto, Bell, Cleartone, Globe and related brands)

PALMER, VI (piano) = Zez Confrey (Banner, Regal)

PALMETTO NIGHT CLUB ORCHESTRA = Baby Aristocrats Band (Champion 15308)

PAMPINI, CARLO (accordian) = Guido Diero (Cameo)

PAN-AMERICAN DANCE ORCHESTRA = Gene Kardos & his Orchestra (Bluebird B-5240, Electradisk 2123, Sunrise S-3323, Victor 24041)

PARK CENTRAL ORCHESTRA = Bert Lown & his Orchestra (Bluebird B-5090, 5091; Electradisk 2006, 2007; Sunrise S-3165, 3166)

PARKS, SEYMOUR (xylophone) = George Hamilton Green (National Music Lovers)

PASTERNACKI'S ORCHESTRA = Original Memphis Five (Mitchell 11359)

PATE, FIDDLIN' IKE (violin) = William B. Houchens (Champion)

PENNSYLVANIA COLLEGIANS = Gene Kardos & his Orchestra (Victor 24084)

PENNSYLVANIA SYNCOPATORS = New Orleans Jazz Band (Emerson 10868)

PERKINS, SLIM (clarinet) = Bob Fuller, usually accompanied by Louis Hooper (piano) and Elmer Snowden (banjo) (Banner, Domino, Regal)

PERRY & HIS STOMP BAND = Henry Johnson's Boys (Black Patti)

PHILHARMONIC STRING QUARTET = Scipione Guidi (1st violin), Arthur Lichstein (2nd violin), Leon E. Barzin (viola), Oswaldo Mazzucchi (cello) (Edison)

PIEDMONT ORCHESTRA = Sam Lanin & his Orchestra (Pathé 036123, Perfect 14303)

PIERCE, ARTHUR (violin) = Jan Rubini (a pseudonym itself?) (Crescent)

PIETRO (accordian) = Pietro Deiro (numerous labels)

PLANTATION SERENADERS = Alex Jackson & his Orchestra (Champion)

PLANTATION TRIO = Van Eps Trio (Victor)

PRINCE, FRANKLIN (organ) = Mark Andrews (Aurora [Canadian], from Victor masters)

PRINCE, SEÑOR C.A. (director) = Charles A. Prince (Columbia)

PROVINSKY, IVOR (violin) = Richard Czerwonky (Famous)

PROVINSKY, VICTOR (violin) = Richard Czerwonky (Banner, Triangle)

QUEEN CITY BLOWERS = Richard Hitter's Blue Knights (Champion)

QUEEN CITY BOYS = Tom Grisselle & his Orchestra (Champion)

RADIO RASCALS = Joe Haymes & his Orchestra (Victor 24007); Gene Kardos & his Orchestra (Bluebird B-5249; Electradisk 1800, 1808; Sunrise S-3332)

RADIOLITES = Benny Goodman & his Orchestra (Columbia 2540-D)

RAMBLERS = California Ramblers (Romeo)

RAMONA (piano) = Ramona Davies (Victor)

RANDALL, DUKE & HIS BOYS = Willie Hightower's Night Hawks (Champion)

RED HEADS = Red Nichols & his Five Pennies/Orchestra (Pathé, Perfect, Melotone and related labels)

RED HOTTERS = Boyd Senter & the Chicago De Luxe Orchestra (Silvertone 3526, 3527)

RED ONION JAZZ BABIES = Johnny Clesi's Areolians (Silvertone 5024 only; on other Gennett and Gennett-derived issues, this name denotes the Louis Armstrong group)

RED-HOT SYNCOPATORS = Original Indiana Five (Bell 445, 456)

RETTER, PROF. FREDERICK (organ) = Mark Andrews (Homochord [British], from Victor masters)

REYNOLDS, DICK & HIS ORCHESTRA = Will Osborne & his Orchestra (World Program Service transcriptions, mid-1930's)

RHYTHM ACES = Jabbo Smith's Rhythm Aces (Brunswick)

RIALTO DANCE ORCHESTRA = California Ramblers (Domino 3439 [*Oh Mabel*]); Sam Lanin & his Orchestra (Banner 1385); New Orleans Jazz Band (Domino 416)

RICHARDS, FRED'S ORCHESTRA = Fred Rich & his Orchestra (Cameo, Domino, probably others)

RICHARDSON, DICK'S ORCHESTRA = Joe Venuti & his New Yorkers (Parlophone [American] PNY-34091, 34092, 34129, 34130)

RING, JUSTIN & HIS OKEH ORCHESTRA = Sam Lanin & his Orchestra (Okeh 40919, 40972). Ring, whose recording career began in the 1890's, was a musical director for Okeh.

ROBERTS, FRANKLYN & HIS ORCHESTRA = Fred Rich & his Orchestra (Associated transcriptions, 1930's)

ROBERTSON, DICK & HIS ORCHESTRA = Bunny Berigan & his Orchestra (Varsity 8098); Eubie Blake & his Orchestra (Varsity 5056, 6017, dubbed from Crown originals)

ROBINSON, THEODORE (organ) = Ralph Waldo Emerson (Challenge)

ROCKAWAY RAMBLERS = California Ramblers (Perfect)

ROCKY MOUNTAIN TRIO = Bob Fuller Trio (Buddy, Gennett)

ROSE, VINCENT & HIS ORCHESTRA = Benny Goodman & his Orchestra (mxs. 15881-15884, on Banner, Melotone, Perfect and related labels); other issues under this name are correct as credited.

ROSELAND DANCE ORCHESTRA = Usually Sam Lanin & his Orchestra (through mid-1925) or Fred Hall's Roseland Orchestra (from late 1925), on numerous minor labels. The following exceptions are known, and there are undoubtedly many others: Fletcher Henderson & his Orchestra (Domino 3445); Original Memphis Five (Regal 9456).

ROSS, DOC & HIS HOTEL RICE ORCHESTRA = Willard Robison & his Orchestra (Pathé 36774, Perfect 14955)

ROSS, HAROLD & HIS SOUTHERNERS = Marion McKay & his Orchestra (Champion)

ROUNDERS = Harry Reser's Orchestra (numerous minor labels)

ROYAL HAWAIIAN GUITARS = Louise & Ferera (Black Swan, from Olympic masters)

RUBENS, KARL (violin) = Leopold Lichtenberg (Oriole)

RUSSELL, BUD & HIS BOYS = Ernie Golden & his Orchestra (Champion)

RUSSELL, TED & HIS ORCHESTRA = Mike Riley, Eddie Farley & their Onyx Club Boys (Champion, from Decca masters)

RUSSELL'S ROVING REVELERS = Ezra Buzzington's Rustic Revelers (Champion)

SALON TRIO = Neapolitan Trio (Aurora [Canadian], from Victor masters)

STUART, HAL & HIS ORCHESTRA = Harry Salter & his Orchestra (World Program Service transcriptions, late 1930's)

SAMUELS, JOSEPH'S ORCHESTRA = California Ramblers (label error on Regal 9439; other issues under this name are correct as credited)

SANFORD'S ORCHESTRA = Paul Sanderson's Orchestra (Oriole)

SANNELLA, ANDY (clarinet) = Wilbur Sweatman (label error on Globe 1402 only; other issues on Grey Gull and related labels are correct as credited)

SANTINI BROTHERS (accordions) = Boudini Brothers (?) (Olympic)

SAVANNAH NIGHT HAWKS = Alphonse Trent & his Orchestra (Vocalion 15641)

SAVANNAH SYNCOPATORS = Connie's Inn Orchestra (Fletcher Henderson) (Brunswick 6176); Jimmie Noone & his Orchestra (Brunswick 7124) ;King Oliver's Dixie Syncopators (Brunswick 3245, 3281, 3361, 3373, 6046 [*Who's Blue?*]); Luis Russell & his Orchestra (Brunswick 6046 [*Honey*])

SAWYER, NED & HIS ORCHESTRA = Todd Rollins & his Orchestra (World Program Service transcriptions, late 1930's)

SAXOPATORS = California Ramblers (Grey Gull 1167)

SCANDALOUS SYNCOPATORS = possibly Louisiana Five (Rust and others attribute this to the Louisiana Five's Alcide Nuñez [clarinet] with unknown others) (Cleartone 3047, Grey Gull and related labels 1065)

SCHUBERT'S METROPOLITAN ORCHESTRA = New Orleans Jazz Band (Carnival/Puretone/Puritan/Triangle 11383, Pennington 1383)

SEVEN BROWN BABIES = a unit of Fletcher Henderson's Orchestra (Ajax)

SEVEN CHAMPIONS = Bailey's Lucky Seven (Champion)

SEVEN LITTLE CLOUDS OF JOY = Andy Kirk & his Twelve Clouds of Joy (Brunswick)

SEVEN LITTLE POLAR BEARS = a unit of Harry Reser's Orchestra (Cameo, Lincoln, Romeo)

SEVEN MISSING LINKS = a unit of Harry Reser's Orchestra (Banner, Pathé, Perfect and related labels)

SEVEN SYNCOPATORS = Piggy Jones' Orchestra (Champion)

SEVEN WILD MEN = a unit of Harry Reser's Orchestra (Harmony and related labels)

SEWARD, HATCH (piano) = Meade Lux Lewis (Broadway)

SHARP, FRED'S DIXIE PLAYERS = Brad Gowan's Rhapsody Makers (Champion)

SHARP, FRED'S ROYAL CUBANS = Brad Gowan's Rhapsody Makers (Champion)

SHAW (piano) = Theodore Shaw (Vaughan 825). Shaw also accompanied a Ku Klux Klan vocal on the reverse side of this issue, and aural evidence suggests that he was responsible for other accompaniments on Gennett-derived Klan labels.

SHAWNE, TED & HIS ORCHESTRA = Louis Armstrong & his Orchestra (Odeon [American] ONY-41276; Parlophone [American] PNY-series)

SHERMAN, CLARENCE'S DANCE ORCHESTRA = California Ramblers (Domino 393)

SHERMAN CLUB ORCHESTRA = Blackbirds of Paradise (Challenge 715)

SHREVEPORT SIZZLERS = Clarence Williams' Jazz Kings (Okeh 8918)

SIEGEL, AL'S ORCHESTRA = Jimmy Wade's Moulin Rouge Orchestra (Paramount 20301 [*You've Got Ways*]; reverse side is an actual Siegel item)

SILENT JOE & HIS BOYS = Jack Stillman & his Orchestra (Champion)

SILVER SLIPPER ORCHESTRA = Dixieland Thumpers (Challenge 806)

SIMPKINS, JOE & HIS RUBE BAND = Ezra Buzzington's Rustic Revelers (Champion)

SIMS, HARRY (guitar) = Charlie Dixon (Oriole)

SIX BLACK DIAMONDS = California Ramblers (Banner 1166, Domino 390); New Orleans Jazz Band (Banner 1428, Oriole 497, Regal 9725). This name was also used on Banner, Regal and related labels for several informal studio groups.

SIX BLACK DOMINOES = California Ramblers (Domino [Canadian] 21003, from Banner masters)

SIX BROWN BROTHERS (saxophones) = Alec, William, Vern, Fred, and Tom Brown, Harry Finkelstein (Victor)

SIX JUMPING JACKS = a unit of Harry Reser's Orchestra (Brunswick)

SKILLET DICK & HIS FRYING PANS = Syd Valentine & his Patent Leather Kids (Champion)

SLIM & HIS HOT BOYS = Slim Lamar & his Southerners (Victor)

SLIM & SLAM = Slim Gaillard (guitar/vibraphone/vocal), Slam Stewart (string bass/vocal) (Vocalion)

SMALL, RALPH (guitar) = Roy Smeck (World Program Service transcriptions, mid-1930's)

SMITH BROTHERS (accordions) = Boudini Brothers (Black Swan, from Olympic masters)

SMITH, DEANE & HIS ORCHESTRA = Frank Leithner & his Orchestra (Oriole), except as noted: Sam Lanin & his Orchestra (Oriole 1731, 1735)

SMITH, FRED'S SOCIETY ORCHESTRA = Green Brothers Novelty Band (Black Swan 2072, 10068, from Olympic masters)

SMITH, HONEY BOY'S BINGHAM BAND = Tampa Red & his Hokum Jug Band (Supertone)

SMITH, SAMMY'S STOMPERS = King Carter & his Royal Orchestra (Clarion, Velvet Tone)

SMOLEV, MARVIN & HIS SYNCOPATORS = Cliff Jackson's Krazy Kats (Grey Gull mxs. 3926-3935, on Grey Gull, Radiex and related labels). Smolev is believed to have been Grey Gull's musical director in the late 1920's; other issues credited to him are probably by the Grey Gull house band (*q.v.*).

SNYDER, CARL & HIS ORCHESTRA = Joe Haymes & his Orchestra (Electradisk 2502)

SOCIETY NIGHT CLUB ORCHESTRA = Bob Haring's Orchestra (Cameo)

SOCIETY SYNCOPATORS = Specht's Jazz Outfit (*q.v.*) (Regal 9341)

SOUTH SHORE MELODY BOYS = Bailey's Lucky Seven (Champion 15062); Art Payne's Orchestra (Champion 15036, 15037)

SOUTHAMPTON SOCIETY ORCHESTRA = California Ramblers (Pathé 036252/Perfect 14433 [*Ah-Ha!*]; Pathé 036276/Perfect 14457); Fletcher Henderson & his Orchestra (Perfect 14395); Six Hottentots (*q.v.*) (Pathé 36643)

SOUTHERN MELODY ARTISTS = Carolina Club Orchestra (Okeh 41216)

SOUTHERN SERENADERS = Luis Russell & his Orchestra (Bluebird B-7367 [*Goin' to Town*]); Clarence Williams' Dixie Washboard Band (Silvertone 2770)

SOUTHERN TRIO = usually a Grey Gull house band (*q.v.*)

SOUTHLAND SIX = Original Memphis Five (Vocalion)

SOUTHLAND SYNCOPATORS = Hal Kemp & his Orchestra (Brunswick 3486); possibly Red & Miff's Stompers (Vocalion)

SPARLING, DICK & HIS ORCHESTRA = Duke Ellington & his Orchestra (Aurora [Canadian], from Brunswick masters)

SPECHT, PAUL'S JAZZ OUTFIT = Georgians (Paramount, Puritan and related labels), issued before this unit from the Specht Orchestra adopted the Georgians name and signed an exclusive Columbia contract in late 1922.

SPECHT'S SOCIETY SYNCOPATORS – see Specht's Jazz Outfit

ST. LOUIS LOW-DOWNS = California Ramblers (Paramount, Puritan)

STANDARD (MILITARY) BAND = Columbia/Prince's Band (Standard, United, probably other Columbia-derived brands)

STEAMBOAT JOE & HIS LAFFIN' CLARINET = possibly Percy Glascoe (identification per Rust) (Black Patti, Champion, Gennett)

STEVENS' QUARTET – Ernest L. Stevens recalled that personnel changed constantly because ''Edison would complain or make unfavorable comments...'' Stevens recalled that one version of the quartet included himself (piano) with Frank Crum (saxophone), Frank Paris (banjo), and Philip Baird (tuba). (Edison)

STEVENS' TRIO – See comments under Stevens' Quartet. The earliest version included Roy Thrall (saxophone), Stevens (banjo), and Mike Aron (guitar). Later members included Frank Crum, Charlie Murray, or Archie Slater (saxophone) and Sam Brown or Chick Paris (banjo). (Edison)

STOKERS OF HADES = Fletcher Henderson & his Orchestra (Columbia)

STRAND ROOF ORCHESTRA = Fletcher Henderson & his Orchestra (Domino 3456)

SUNSET DANCE ORCHESTRA = Bailey's Lucky Seven (Champion)

SUPERIOR JAZZ BAND = Original Memphis Five (Arto, Bell, Globe and related labels)

SUPERTONE DANCE ORCHESTRA = Red Nichols & his Orchestra (Supertone S-2186, S-2191)

SWIFT, SAMMY'S JAZZ BAND = Yerkes' Master Players (Black Swan 2042); other unknown white bands (Black Swan 2000 series, from Olympic masters)

SYNCO JAZZ BAND = Joseph Samuels' Jazz Band (Pathé, Perfect and related labels)

T&T TRIO = Taylor Brothers (Pathé)

TAMPA BLUE JAZZ BAND = Joseph Samuels' Jazz Band (Okeh)

TANNER, LOU & HIS BAND = Ernie Golden & his Orchestra (Champion)

TAYLOR, EMMETT (piano) = Fletcher Henderson (Domino)

TAYLOR TRIO = Alexander Hackel or Alexander Draesin (violin), William E. Berge, Oscar W. Friberg (piano), Albert W. Taylor (cello) (numerous brands). This group also recorded in augmented form as the Hackel-Berge Orchestra (Victor).

TEN BLACK BERRIES = Duke Ellington & his Orchestra (Banner, Cameo, Oriole, Perfect and other American Record Corporation brands); see also Wilson, Duke & his Ten Blackberries.

TEN JACKS OF DIAMONDS = Harry Reser's Orchestra (Banner and related labels)

TENNESSEE HAPPY BOYS = Harry Reser's Orchestra (Oriole 1044)

TENNESSEE MUSIC MEN = Eddie Lang & his Orchestra (Clarion 5461-C, Harmony 1415-H, Velvet Tone 2521-V); Mound City Blue Blowers (Clarion 5389-C, 5392-C, Harmony 1375-H, 1378-H, Velvet Tone 2453-V, 2456-V); Frankie Trumbauer & his Orchestra (mxs. 401811, 404009, 404010, 404433, 404434, on Clarion, Harmony and related labels); Joe Venuti's Blue Four (mxs. 404005, 404006, on Clarion, Harmony and related labels)

TENNESSEE TEN = Original Memphis Five (augmented) (Victor)

TENNESSEE TRAVELERS = Jim Booker (violin), Marion Underwood (banjo), Willie Young (guitar) (Champion)

TEXANS = Sam Lanin & his Orchestra (Okeh 40914)

TEXAS BLUES DESTROYERS = Bubber Miley (cornet) accompanied by Arthur Ray (reed organ) (Ajax, Pathé, Perfect, Vocalion)

TEXAS JASS BAND = Wilbur Sweatman's Original Jazz Band (Operaphone)

THEM BIRMINGHAM NIGHT OWLS = Blackbirds of Paradise (Champion)

THOMAS, GEORGE & HIS MUSIC = Tommy Dandurand & his WLS Barn Dance Gang (Champion)

THOMAS, GRAYSEN (violin) = G.B. Grayson (Champion)

THREE BLACK DIAMONDS = Bob Fuller Trio (Lincoln)

THREE BLUES CHASERS = Bob Fuller Trio (Okeh)

THREE HAPPY DARKIES = Bob Fuller Trio (Silvertone)

THREE HOT ESKIMOES = Bob Fuller Trio (Pathé, Perfect)

THREE JOLLY MINERS = Bob Fuller Trio (Vocalion, Silvertone)

THREE MONKEY CHASERS = Bob Fuller Trio (Harmony, Velvet Tone and related Labels)

TIN PAN PARADERS = Bud Carson & his Collegians (Champion 15890, 15918); Benny Goodman & his Orchestra (Supertone S-2185); this name was also used for an unknown group or groups on Gennett and Champion.

TINSLEY'S WASHBOARD BAND = Clarence Williams' Washboard Band (Bluebird, Victor)

TOLLEFSEN TRIO = Carl H. Tollefsen (violin), Paul Kefer (cello), Mme. Schnabel-Tollefsen (piano) (Edison, Victor)

TOM & JERRY (pianos) = W.E. (Buddy) Burton and Jimmy Blythe (Champion)

TRAVELING MUSKETEERS = Red Flame Kazoo Travelers (Lincoln)

TRAYMORE ORCHESTRA = Duke Ellington & his Orchestra (Vocalion 15556)

TRI-STATE DANCE RAMBLERS = California Ramblers (Champion)

TRICKY TEN = Eddie Peabody & his Orchestra (Oriole 535, 553, 560)

TRIMBLE, BARNEY & HIS OKLAHOMANS = California Ramblers (Diva, Harmony, Velvet Tone)

TRIO DE LUTECE = George Barrere (flute), Paul Kefer (cello), Carlos Salzedo (harp) (Columbia)

TRIXIE'S DOWN HOME SYNCOPATORS = Fletcher Henderson & his Orchestra (vocal by Trixie Smith) (Paramount)

TUCKER, GEORGE & HIS NOVELTY BAND = Lawrence Welk's Novelty Orchestra (Champion)

TURNER, JOE & HIS MEMPHIS MEN = Duke Ellington & his Orchestra (Columbia)

TUXEDO SYNCOPATORS = Cliff Jackson's Krazy Kats (Globe 1839; Madison 951, 5098 only); other issues are usually by the Grey Gull house band (*q.v.*). This name was also used by an unknown group on Pathé in the early 1920's.

TWIN CITIES DANCE ORCHESTRA = Brad Gowan's Rhapsody Makers (Challenge 257)

TWO OF SPADES = Herbert Leonard (harmonica), Harry Mays (banjo/ukulele) (Columbia)

UNDERWOOD, JIMMY & HIS ORCHESTRA = Joe Haymes & his Orchestra (Electradisk 2506)

UNIVERSITY BOYS = Rounders (a Harry Reser group) (all Orioles, except as noted): Harry Reser & his Orchestra (Oriole 1700); Sam Lanin & his Orchestra (Oriole 1446)

UNIVERSITY EIGHT = a unit of the California Ramblers (Lincoln)

UNIVERSITY ORCHESTRA = Sam Lanin & his Orchestra (Champion, Gennett and related labels)

UNIVERSITY SEXTETTE = Varsity Eight (*q.v.*) (Lincoln)

UNIVERSITY SIX = a unit of the California Ramblers (Diva, Harmony, Velvet Tone and related labels)

VAGABONDS = a unit of the California Ramblers (Gennett; Starr [Canadian], from Gennett masters)

VAN EPS BANJO ORCHESTRA -- see Van Eps Quartet

VAN EPS-BANTA DANCE ORCHESTRA -- see Van Eps Quartet

VAN EPS QUARTET -- Instrumentation and personnel vary, but probably includes members of the Van Eps Trio (see next entry).

VAN EPS TRIO -- Originally Fred and William Van Eps (banjos), Felix Arndt (piano); reorganized late 1913 as Fred Van Eps (banjo), Arndt (piano), and various drummers (Eddie King and William H. Reitz are documented on Victor, Howard Kopp on Columbia). Reorganized again late 1916 with Nathan Glantz (saxophone), Van Eps (banjo), Frank Banta (piano). George Gershwin allegedly replaced Banta on occasion in 1916-1920.

VARSITY EIGHT = California Ramblers, or a unit thereof (Cameo)

VARSITY MEN = Carolina Club Orchestra (Broadway 1260, Paramount 20701)

VILLAGE BARN ORCHESTRA, NEW YORK = Gene Kardos & his Orchestra (Victor 24084)

VINCENT, SAM (banjo) = Fred Van Eps (Phoenix [British], from American Columbia masters)

VIRGINIA CREEPERS = Lou Gold & his Orchestra (Pathé 36349)

VIRGINIA POSSUM TAMERS = Paul Miles' Red Fox Chasers (Champion)

VIRGINIANS = a unit of Paul Whiteman's Orchestra, under the direction of Ross Gorman (acoustic recordings); Nathaniel Shilkret's Victor Orchestra (electric recordings) (Victor)

VON TRIPP, FRITZ (violin) = Leopold Lichtenberg (Famous)

WADE'S MOULIN ROUGE ORCHESTRA = Al Siegel & his Orchestra (label error on Embassy/Mitchell/Puritan/Triangle 11363 only)

WADSWORTH, FRANK (saxophone) = F. Wheeler Wadsworth

WADSWORTH, FRED W. (saxophone) = F. Wheeler Wadsworth (minor brands)

WAGER, ROY & HIS ORCHESTRA = Joe Haymes & his Orchestra (Electradisk 2504)

WAILUKA SERENADERS = Frank Plada with unknown Hawaiian instrumental accompaniment (Champion)

WALKER, EDDIE & HIS BAND = Zach Whyte's Chocolate Beau Brummels (Supertone)

WALLACE, FLIP (piano) = Fats Waller (Associated transcriptions, 1930's)

WALLACE, TED & HIS CAMPUS BOYS = California Ramblers (Columbia)

WALLACE, TED & HIS ORCHESTRA = California Ramblers (Columbia, Okeh and related labels)

WALTON, NORMAND (organ) = Edmund Cromwell (Oriole)

WANDERERS = Sam Lanin & his Orchestra (Lincoln 2629)

WARD, BILLY (clarinet) = Buster Bailey (accompanied by Clarence Todd [piano] and Buddy Christian [banjo]) (Oriole)

WARNER, BUD & HIS RED CAPS = Henry Johnson's Boys (Bell 1174)

WARNER, CHUCK & HIS ORCHESTRA = Chick Webb & his Orchestra (World Program Service transcriptions, late 1930's)

WARREN, BERT (clarinet) = Bob Fuller Trio (*q.v.*) (Jewel, Oriole)

WASHBOARD RHYTHM BOYS = Washboard Rhythm Kings (Victor)

WASHBOARD TRIO = Tub Jug Washboard Band (Paramount)

WASHBOARD WONDERS = Jimmy O'Bryant's Washboard Band (Silvertone)

WASHINGTONIANS = Duke Ellington & his Orchestra (Blu-Disc, Cameo, Harmony, and many others)

WATERS, ETHEL'S JAZZ MASTERS = Palace Trio (Black Swan 2074/10070 [*Spread Yo' Stuff*]); Van Eps Quartet (Black Swan 2074/10070 [*Snuggle*]) (all from Olympic masters, and in no way connected with Ethel Waters)

WATSON, CHARLES A. (director) = Charles A. Matson (label error on Gennett)

WATSON'S PULLMAN PORTERS = Henry Johnson's Boys (Gennett)

WEBB, MALCOLM & HIS ORCHESTRA = Hoagy Carmichael & Six Other Fellows (15420 [*One Night in Havana*]); Emil Seidl & his Orchestra (15420 [*Friday Night*])

WEST, THEADOR (clarinet) = possibly Bob Fuller, accompanied by Louis Hooper (piano) and Elmer Snowden (banjo) (Ajax)

WESTERNERS = University Six (*q.v.*) (Harmony 651-H and derivative issues)

WHITE, BOB'S DIXIE TRIO = Jimmy O'Bryant's Washboard Band (Puritan 11400)

WHITE BROTHERS' ORCHESTRA = Original Memphis Five (Rich Tone 7034)

WHITE, HAL'S SYNCOPATORS = Fletcher Henderson & his Orchestra (Domino 3444)

WHITE, TED'S COLLEGIANS = Carolina Club Orchestra (Jewel 5541); pseudonym on Oriole for Carolina Club Orchestra (1503); Willie Creager & his Orchestra (1392 [*Crying Blues*], 1452, 1479,1507, 1509); Ernie Golden & his Orchestra (1392 [*Doin' the Raccoon*]); Hal Kemp & his Orchestra 1503; Sam Lanin & his Orchestra 1477, 1540; Al Lynch & his Orchestra (1046, 1152, 1157, 1203, 1228, 1231); Fred Rich & his Orchestra (1690); Six Hottentots (*q.v.*) (931); Whoopee Makers (*q.v.*) (1544)

WHITEMAN, PAUL & HIS ORCHESTRA = unknown orchestra playing Whiteman Orchestra arrangements under the direction of Ben Selvin (Columbia 1464-D [*Pickin' Cotton*], 1465-D [*What D'Ya Say?*], 1484-D [*If You Don't Love Me*]])

WHITNEY, JACK & HIS NEW YORKERS = Pseudonym on Harmony and related labels for Fred Rich & his Orchestra (Columbia mxs. 100484, 100498); Ben Selvin & his Orchestra (Columbia mxs. 351036, 351055)

WHOOPEE MAKERS = Duke Ellington & his Orchestra (Banner 6548, 32070; Conqueror 7428; Domino 4428; Jewel 6191; Oriole 2191; Pathé 36781, 36787, 37059; Perfect 14962, 14968, 15240, 15418; Regal 10244, Romeo 1556). This name is more frequently associated with a unit from Ben Pollack's Orchestra, on the same labels.

WHYTE, HAL'S SYNCOPATORS = California Ramblers (Domino 429)

WIEDOEFT-WADSWORTH QUARTET = Rudy Wiedoeft, F. Wheeler Wadsworth (saxophones); J. Russell Robinson, Harry Akst (pianos) (Edison, Victor)

WILBER, C. (clarinet) = Wilbur Sweatman (Globe)

WILLIAMS & MOORE (pianos) = W.E. (Buddy) Burton & Jimmy Blythe (Q-R-S)

WILLIAMS, BILL & HIS GANG = Marion McKay & his Orchestra (Champion), except as noted: Ross Gorman's Fire-Eaters (Champion 15226); Jelly James' Fewsicians (Champion 15215, 15216)

WILLIAMS' COTTON CLUB ORCHESTRA = Alex Bartha & his Hotel Traymore Orchestra (Victor 24083); Joe Haymes & his Orchestra (Victor 24083 [*I Would Do Anything*]); Roane's Pennsylvanians (Victor 24039)

WILLIAMS, DUKE & HIS ORCHESTRA = Don Redman & his Orchestra (Vocalion 15892)

WILLIAMS, GEORGE S. (banjo) = Frank C. Stanley (Edison cylinders). Stanley also recorded vocals for Edison under this name.

WILLIAMS, SPEED'S ORCHESTRA = Wingy Mannone & his Orchestra (Superior)

WILMOTT, LEO (banjo) = Fred Van Eps (Grand Pree [Australian], from American Pathé masters)

WILSON, CHICKEN & HINTON, SKEETER = George (Chicken) Wilson (guitar/kazoo) and Jimmy (Skeeter) Hinton (harmonica/washboard) (Paramount, Q-R-S)

WILSON, DUKE & HIS (TEN) BLACKBERRIES = Joe Haymes & his Orchestra (Conqueror 8024, Perfect 15662); Fletcher Henderson & his Orchestra (Oriole 2466, Perfect 15603); Andy Kirk & his Twelve Clouds of Joy (Perfect 15697); Mills' Blue Rhythm Band (Melotone M-12662); Ben Pollack & his Orchestra (multiple issues from American Record Corporation mx. 10422)

WILSON, LEONA & HER DIXIE JAZZ BAND = Original Memphis Five (accompanying vocals by Leona Wilson) (Columbia)

WINTERS, CHICK & HIS ORCHESTRA = Duke Ellington & his Orchestra (Pennington 1437 only). Other issues are correct as credited; Winters was an actual bandleader who recorded for Gennett, Paramount, and related labels.

WIRGES, BILL & HIS ORCHESTRA = Harry Reser's Orchestra (Brunswick, Pathé, Perfect)

WOLVERINE PEPPER POTS = usually a Grey Gull house band (*q.v.*), except for the following: Cliff Jackson's Krazy Kats (Grey Gull 1839)

WOODS, BABE & HIS PALS = Lou Calabrese & his Hot Shots (Champion)

WRIGHT, CLARENCE (piano) = Clarence M. Jones (Harmograph)

WYNN, JACK & HIS DALLAS DANDIES = Johnny Dodds' Black Bottom Stompers (Melotone M-12027, M-12064; Polk P-9034, P-9035); Irving Mills' Hotsy-Totsy Gang (Melotone M-12051, Vocalion 15860); King Oliver & his Dixie Syncopators (Melotone M-12064, Polk P-9034)

YANKEE TEN ORCHESTRA = Buffalodians (Puritan 11469); pseudonym on Oriole for Willie Creager & his Orchestra (798); Devine's Wisconsin Roof Orchestra (Oriole 1207); Lou Gold & his Orchestra (1402, 1420); Sam Lanin & his Orchestra (637, 671, 732 [*She's Still My Baby*]), 754, 910, 934, 955, 959, 991, 1033, 1036, 1037, 1064, 1076); Al Lentz & his Orchestra (732 [*What's the Use of Crying?*], 752, 759, 776); Eddie Peabody & his Orchestra (514); Jack Pettis & his Band (846); Lou Raderman's Orchestra (1127, 1131, 1149, 1184, 1205, 1207 [*There's Something About a Rose*], 1252, 1257, 1258); Fred Rich & his Orchestra (852, 898, 1105); Six Hottentots (*q.v.*) (Oriole 933)

YERKES NOVELTY/SOUTHERN FIVE = possibly Louisiana Five, or a group including its members (Alcide Nuñez [clarinet] almost certainly present, based on aural evidence) (Columbia, Grey Gull, Vocalion and others)

YORK, VINCENT & HIS ORCHESTRA = Victor Young & his Orchestra (World Program Service transcriptions, 1930's)

YOUNG, CLARENCE'S HARMONY SYNCOPATORS = Ollie Powers' Harmony Syncopators (Harmograph)

Appendix I:
Legal Names

*This listing includes birth, legal, or married names of vocal and instrumental performers who recorded in the United States during the period covered by this book. Professional names are listed in **bold type**, followed by actual names.*

ADAMS, SUZANNE = Suzanne Adams Stern (Mrs. Leo Stern)
ALDA, FRANCES = Frances Jean Davies
ALEXANDER, GEORGE = Clifford Alexander Wiley
ARDEN, VICTOR = Louis John Fuiks
ARKANSAS WOODCHOPPER = Luther Ossinbrink
ARLEN, HAROLD = Harold Arluck
ARRAL, BLANCHE = Clara L'Ardenois
AUSTIN, GENE = Gene Lucas

BAILEY, BUSTER = William C. Bailey
BAKLANOFF, GEORGE = Georgy Andreyevitch Bakkis
BARBIROLLI, SIR JOHN = Giovanni Battista
BARBOUR, INEZ = Inez Barbour Hadley (Mrs. Harry Hadley)
BARRYMORE, JOHN = John Blythe
BASIE, COUNT = William Basie
BAYES, NORA = Dora Goldberg (Mrs. Jack Norworth, 1908-1913)
BEIDERBECKE, BIX = Leon Bismarck Beiderbecke
BERLIN, IRVING = Israel Baline
BERNARD, MIKE = Michael Barnett
BERNHARDT, SARAH = Rosine Bernard
BJOERLING, JUSSI = Johan Björling
BLAKE, EUBIE = James Hubert Blake
BLIND BLAKE = Arthur Phelps
BONELLI, RICHARD = Richard Bunn
BORI, LUCREZIA = Lucrecia Borja y Gonzales de Riancho
BRICE, FANNY = Fannie Borach
BRISSON, CARL = Carl Pederson

BROONZY, BIG BILL = William Lee Conely
BRUCE, VIRGINIA = Helen Virginia Briggs
BURNS, GEORGE = Nathan Birnbaum
BURR, HENRY = Harold H. McClaskey
BURT, VERA = Mrs. Saxi Holtsworth

CALVÉ, EMMA = Rosa-Noémie Calvet
CANTOR, EDDIE = Edward Israel Isskowitz (per Rust & Debus), or Isidore
    Itzkowitz (per Hitchcock & Sadie)
CARMICHAEL, HOAGY = Hoaglund Howard Carmichael
CARTER, BO = Armenter Chatmon
CHALIA, ROSALIA = Mme. Rosalia Chalia-Herrera
CHAMLEE, ARCHER -- see next entry
CHAMLEE, MARIO = Archer Cholmondeley
CIAPARELLI, GINA = Gina Ciaparelli Viafora (married name)
CLARK, HELEN = Helen Clark Price (Mrs. Evan Cameron)
COLEMAN, JAY BIRD = Burl C. Coleman
COLONNA, JERRY = Gerard Colonna
COLUMBO, RUSS = Ruggiero de Rudolpho Columbo
CONFREY, ZEZ = Edward Elzear Confrey
CONNOLLY, DOLLY = Dolly Connolly Wenrich (Mrs. Percy Wenrich)
COTA, EL = Lawrence Albert Coates
CRAWFORD, JOAN = Lucille LeSueur
CROSBY, BING = Harry Lillis Crosby
CROSBY, DIXIE LEE = Wilma Winifred Wyatt (Mrs. Bing Crosby)

DAFFAN, TED = Theron Eugene Daffan
DALHART, VERNON = Marion Try Slaughter
DALMORÈS, CHARLES = Henri Alphonse Brin
DAVIS, JIMMIE = James Houston Davis
DE CISNEROS, ELEANORA = Eleanor Broadfoot
DE LEATH, VAUGHN = Lenora Vonderlieth
DEL RIO, DOLORES = Lolita Dolores Asunsolo de Martinez
DESTIN, EMMY = Ema Destinnová
DIETRICH, MARLENE = Maria Magdalene von Losch
DOCKSTADER, LEW = George Alfred Clapp
DOUGLAS, RUSSELL = Lester Reis
DRESSLER, MARIE = Leila Kerber
DUDLEY, S. H. = Samuel Holland Rous
DUPREZ, FRED = Frederick August Duprez
DURBIN, DEANNA = Edna Mae Durbin

FAYE, ALICE = Alice Jeane Leppert (Mrs. Phil Harris)
FIELDS, ARTHUR = Abe Finkelstein
FIELDS, LEW (of WEBER & FIELDS) = Moses Schanfield
FRANKLIN, IRENE = Irene Franklin Green (Mrs. Burton Green)

GARLAND, JUDY = Frances Gumm
GEORGIA TOM = Thomas Andrew Dorsey
GERUN, TOM = Thomas Gerunovitch
GILIBERT, Mme. CHARLES = Gabrielle Lejeune (birth name)
GLUCK, ALMA = Reba Fierson
GOLDEN, BILLY = William B. Shire
GREET, BEN = born Philip Barling; knighted Sir Philip Greet, 1929

HAJOS, MIZZI = Magdalena Hajos
HALL, ARTHUR = Adolph J. Hahl
HALLEY, WILLIAM J. = William Joseph Hanley, Sr.
HARLAN, BYRON G. = George Byron Harlan
HARRIS, MARION = Mary Ellen Harrison
HILL, MURRAY K. = Joseph Tunnicliffe Pope, Jr.
HOMER, LOUISE = Louise Welworth Beatry
HOPPER, DE WOLFE = William D'Wolf
HOWARD, WILLIE = William Levkowitz

IRWIN, MAY = Ada Campbell

JOLSON, AL = Asa Yoelson
JONES, BILLY = William Reese Jones

KANE, HELEN = Helen Schroeder
KING, ROXY = Roxy King-Shaw

LAMBERT, SCRAPPY = Harold Lambert
LAMOUR, DOROTHY = Dorothy Kaumeyer Stanton
LANG, EDDIE = Salvatore Massaro
LAUDER, SIR HARRY = Harold MacLennan
LAWRENCE, GERTRUDE = Gertrude Alexandria Dagmar Lawrence-Klasen
LEGINSKA, ETHEL = Ethel Liggins

LEWIS, TED = Theodore Leopold Friedman
LEONARD, EDDIE = Lemuel Gordon Toney
LOGAN, ELLA = Ella Allan
LOMBARDO, GUY = Gaetano Alberto Lombardo
LORRAINE, LILLIAN = Ealallean de Jacques
LOUISE, HELEN = Helen Louise Ferera (Mrs. Frank Ferera)
LUTHER, FRANK = Francis Luther Crow

MACDONOUGH, HARRY = John Scantlebury Macdonald
MACK, CHARLES (of MORAN & MACK) = Charles E. Sellers
MACON, UNCLE DAVE = David Harrison Macon
MARLOWE, JULIA = Julia Marlowe Sothern (Mrs. E.H. Sothern)
MARTIN, RICCARDO = Hugh Whitefield
MASON, SHIRLEY = Leona Flugrath
MATZENAUER, MARGARETE = Margarethe Preusse-Matzenauer
MAY, EDNA = Edna Pettie
MELBA, NELLIE = Minnie Porter Mitchell
MELCHIOR, LAURITZ = Lebrecht Hommel
MEMPHIS MINNIE = Minnie Douglas
MERMAN, ETHEL = Ethel Agnes Zimmerman
MILES, LIZZIE = Elizabeth Mary Landreaux
MIRANDA, CARMEN = Maria de Carmo Miranda da Cunha
MONTANA, PATSY = Rubye Blevins
MOORE, MONETTE = Monette Moore Erby (Mrs. John Erby)
MORAN, GEORGE (of MORAN & MACK) = George Searcy
MORGAN, CORINNE = Corinne Morgan Welsh (married name)
MORTON, JELLY ROLL — Various accounts list the family surname
   as LaMenthe, LaMothe, or LaMotte. It is definitely known that his first
   and middle names were Ferdinand Joseph.
MURRAY, BILLY = William Thomas Murray
MURRAY, KEN = Don Court

NELSON, ESTHER = Esther Nelson Hart (Mrs. Charles Hart)
NELSON, OZZIE = Oswald George Nelson
NICHOLS, RED = Ernest Loring Nichols
NORDICA, LILLIAN = Lillian Norton
NORWORTH, JACK = John Knauff
NUIBO, FRANCISCO = Augustin Nuibo

OAKIE, JACK = Lewis D. Offield

OAKLAND, WILL = Herman Hinrichs
OAKLEY, OLLY = Joseph Sharpe
OLCOTT, CHAUNCEY = Chancellor John Olcott
ORMANDY, EUGENE = Jenó Blau
OSBORNE, WILL = William Oliphant
OSSMAN, VESS L. = Sylvester Louis Ossman

PARKER, J. DONALD = Horace Ruwe
PATTI, ADELINA = Adela Juana Maria Patti
PAUL, LES = Lester Palfuss
PEERCE, JAN = Jacob Pincus Perelmuth
PERKINS, ALBERTA = Alberta Perkins Fuller (Mrs. Bob Fuller)
PIE PLANT PETE = Claude Moye

QUINN, SNOOZER = Edward Quinn

RAINEY, "MA" = Getrude Pridgett Rainey
RAISA, ROSA = Raisa Burchstein
RAMONA = Ramona Davies
RAYMOND, GENE = Raymond Guion
RAZAF, ANDY = Andrea Paul Razafinkeriefo
REHAN, ADA C. = Ada Crehan
RICHMAN, HARRY = Harold Reichman
RING, JUSTIN = Justus Ringleben
ROBERTS, BOB = Nicolas Roberts
ROBERTS, LUCKEY = Charles Luckeyth Roberts
ROBERTSON, ECK = Alexander Campbell Robertson
ROBYN, WILLIAM = William Rubin
RODGERS, JIMMIE = James Charles Rodgers
ROGERS BROTHERS = Gus & Max Solomon
ROGERS, BUDDY = Charles Rogers
ROGERS, GINGER = Virginia Katherine McMath
ROGERS, WILL = William Penn Adair Rogers
ROSS, BLACK FACE EDDIE = Edward Ross Edinger
ROWLAND, HELEN = Helene R. Daniels (married name)
RUSSELL, LILLIAN = Helen Louise Leonard

SALE, CHIC = Charles Sale
SAMAROFF, OLGA = Luci Hickenlooper (Mrs. Leopold Stokowski)

SCARE CROW = Billy McOwens
SCHENCK, JOE (of VAN & SCHENCK) = Joseph Thuma Schenck
SCHIPA, TITO = Raffaele Attilio Amadeo
SEMBRICH, MARCELLA = Marcella Kochanska
SHARPE-MINOR, C. = Charles Minor
SHAW, OSCAR = Oscar Schwartz
SHUTTA, ETHEL = Ethel Shutta Olsen (Mrs. George Olsen)
SINCLAIR, EDITH = Edith Sinclair Favor (Mrs. Edward M. Favor)
SMITH, WILLIE "THE LION" = William Henry Bonaparte Bertholoff
SPANIER, MUGSY = Francis Joseph Spanier
SPENCER, LEN = Leonard Garfield Spencer
STANLEY, FRANK C. = William Stanley Grinsted
STEWART, CAL = Calvin Edward Stewart
STOKOWSKI, LEOPOLD = Antoni Stanislaw Boleslawowich
STONE, EDDIE = Edward Marblestone
SYLVA, MARGARET = Marguerite Alice Helena Smith

TAMPA RED = Hudson Whittaker
TANNER, GID = James Gideon Tanner
TAYLOR, EVA = Eva Taylor Williams (Mrs. Clarence Williams)
THARPRE, SISTER ROSETTA = Rosetta Nubin
THOMAS, HARRY = Reginald Thomas Broughton
TUCKER, SOPHIE – Some inexplicable confusion surrounds Tucker's real
   name. Hitchcock & Sadie, Kinkle, and numerous other sources list Sonia
   Kalish; Rust & Debus lists Sophia Abuza.

VALENTINO, RUDOLPH = Rodolfo Alonso Rafealo Oierre Filibert
   Guglielmi di Valentina d'Antonguolla
VALLEE, RUDY = Herbert Pryor Vallee
VAN, BILLY B. = William Vandergrift
VAN, GUS (of VAN & SCHENCK) = August Van Glove
VANCE, CLARICE = Clara Ella Buck
VAN DER VEER, NEVADA = Nevada V. Miller (Mrs. Reed Miller)
VELA, LUISA = Mme. Emilio Sagi-Barba
VELEZ, LUPE = Guadelupe Velez de Villalobos

WALKER, POLLY = Heather Eulalie Walker
WALLER, FATS = Thomas Wright Waller
WEBB, CLIFTON = Webb Paremelee Hollenbeck
WEBER, JOE (of WEBER & FIELDS) = Morris Weber

WHITE, JOSH = Joshua Daniel White
WILLIAMS, BERT = Egbert Austin Williams
WILLIAM, FRANCES = Frances Jellineck
WILLS, NAT M. = Edward McGregor
WILSON, LEOLA = Leola B. Pettigrew

YOUNG, BEULAH GAYLORD = Beaulah Harrison (Mrs. Charles Harrison)

ZUCCA, MANA = Augusta Zuckerman

Appendix II: Label Groups

Related labels are grouped below. The occurrence of a pseudonym on one label in any given group does not necessarily indicate its use on related labels, but does increase the likelihood. In some groups, particularly Arto, Harmony, Grey Gull, and Puritan, pseudonym use was fairly consistent on all brands. Within the Banner group, pseudonym use was consistent among certain labels (notably Banner, Domino, and Regal), whereas Oriole and others within the group employed their own set of fictitious names; after the American Record Corporation takeover of Plaza in 1929, pseudonym use declined sharply and became fairly consistent across all brands. In other groups, notably Cameo, Gennett, Paramount, and the RCA budget line, there was little consistency in pseudonym use from label to label. Very early label groups (American Record, Excelsior, Leeds, and Zon-O-Phone) rarely issued pseudonymous material, tending instead to produce anonymous off-brand releases; they are included here for the sake of completeness.

AMERICAN RECORD GROUP
(American Record Company / Hawthorne, Sheble & Prescott) (1904-1907):
American Odeon Record, American Record Company, Busy Bee, Peerless

ARTO GROUP
(The Arto Company) (1920-1923):
Ansonia, Arto, Bell, Crown (black label), Cleartone, Globe, Hytone

BANNER GROUP
(Plaza Music Company / American Record Corporation) (1922-1938):
Banner, Bernardo, Broadway, Challenge, Conqueror, Domino, Homestead, Jewel, Oriole, Regal, Variety; plus Cameo, Pathé, Perfect, Romeo (beginning 1929); plus the Brunswick group (*q.v.*) (beginning 1932)

BRUNSWICK GROUP
(Brunswick Recording Corporation [division of American Record Corporation]) (1931-1938):
Brunswick, Melotone, Polk, Vocalion; plus the Banner group (*q.v.*) (from 1932)

CAMEO GROUP
(Cameo Record Corporation) (1922-1929):
Cameo, Golden Dawn, Harmograph, Lincoln, Mitchell, Muse, Romeo, Tremont, Variety; plus the Pathé group (beginning 1927)

COLUMBIA GROUP
(Columbia Phonograph / Graphophone Company) (c. 1902-1921):
Aretino, Climax, Columbia, Consolidated, Cort, Diamond, D&R (blue label), Golden Crown, Harmony (black label), Harvard, La Belle (blue label), Lakeside, Manhattan, Marconi, Oxford, Peerless, Remick Perfection, Silvertone (single-sided), Silver Tongued, Standard, Thomas, United

CROWN GROUP
(Crown Record Corporation) (1930-1933):
Crown, Gem, Homestead

DANDY GROUP
(Consolidated Record Corporation) (1923-1929):
Clover, Dandy, Emerson (beginning 1924), Emerson Electrasonic, The Electric, Lenox, Marathon, Mitchell, Muse, National, New Emerson, Popular Hit, Wise (*see also* Grey Gull group)

EMERSON GROUP
(Emerson Phonograph Company) (1915-1924):
Emerson, Medallion, Melodisc, Regal, Symphonola (*see also* Dandy group)

EXCELSIOR GROUP
(International Record Company) (1905-1907):
Buckeye, Central, Clico, Eagle (gray label), Excelsior, Faultless Concert, International Record Company, Lyric, Mozart, Nightingale Parlor Grand, Ormsby, Siegel-Cooper, Silver Star, Sir Henri, Square Deal, Vim

FEDERAL GROUP
(Federal Record Corporation) (1917-1925):
Federal, Resona, Silvertone (blue label)

GENNETT GROUP
(Starr Piano Company) (1915-1934):
Buddy, Cardinal, Challenge, Champion, Claxtonola, Connorized, Gennett, Herschel Gold Seal, Herwin, Hitch, KKK, Peerless, Remington, Rich-Tone, Savoy, Starr, Superior, Supertone, Vaughan

GREY GULL GROUP
(Grey Gull Record Company) (1920-1930):
Amco, Bingola, Globe, Grey Gull, Jewel, Madison, Nadsco, New Comfort, Oriole, Phonolamp, Radiex, Sunrise, Supreme, Van Dyke (*note:* Although Grey Gull obtained most of its masters from the Consolidated Record Corporation [Dandy group] from 1924 through mid-1926, both companies used their own sets of pseudonyms.)

HARMONY / CLARION GROUP
(Columbia Phonograph Company budget series) (1925-1932):
Clarion (green label), Diva, Harmony (red label), Publix, Puritone, Metro-Goldwyn-Mayer (black label -S series), Supertone, Velvet Tone

LEEDS GROUP
(Leeds & Catlin) (*c.* 1904-1909):
Concert, D&R (red label), Eagle (full-color label), Imperial, Leeds, National (red label), Nassau, Oxford, Silver Star, Sir Henri, Sun, Symphony, Talk-O-Phone

OLYMPIC GROUP
(Olympic Disc Record Corporation / Fletcher Record Co.) (1920-1924):
La Belle (black label), Majestic, Master Tone, Melody, Olympic, Supertone, Symphony Concert Record (*note:* Although Black Swan frequently drew on Olympic masters, it used its own set of pseduonyms.)

PARAMOUNT GROUP
(New York Recording Laboratories) (1918-1932):
Blue Bird (not the later RCA product), Broadway, Claxtonola, Cook, Embassy, Famous, Harmograph, Herwin, National, Paramount, Puritan (*see also* Puritan group)

PATHÉ / PERFECT GROUP
(Pathé Frères / Pathé Phonograph & Radio Corporation) (1915-1928):
Actuelle, Apollo, Davega, Pathé, Pathé Actuelle, Perfect, Schubert, Starck, Supertone; plus the Cameo group (beginning 1927) and the Banner group (beginning 1929)

PURITAN / TRIANGLE GROUP
(Bridgeport Die & Machine Company) (1921-1925):
Baldwin, Belvedere, Broadway, Carnival, Chautauqua, Hudson, Lyraphone, Master Tone, Mitchell, Music Box, National, Pennington, Puretone, Puritan, Resona, Ross Stores, Triangle (*note:* Although BD&M drew almost exclusively on New York Recording Laboratories [Paramount] masters, it assigned its own pseudonyms, and there is rarely any correlation to NYRL pseudonyms.)

REX GROUP
(Rex Talking Machine Corporation) (1914-1918):
Empire, Imperial, Lyric, McKinley, Mozart, Rex, Rishell

RCA BUDGET GROUP
(Radio Corporation of America) (from 1931):
Bluebird, Electradisk, Montgomery Ward, Sunrise, Timely Tunes

ZON-O-PHONE GROUP
(Universal Talking Machine Company) (1890's-1912):
Busy Bee, Disco Zonofono, Oxford, Universal Zon-O-Phone, Zon-O-Phone

References

AMERICAN RECORD CORPORATION (New York): recording ledgers, 1929-1932 (unpublished)

BAUER, ROBERTO: *New Catalog of Historical Records* (London: Sidgwick & Jackson, 1972)

BAYLEY, E.: *Zonophone Pseudonyms* (*Talking Machine Review* **39**, 4/1976)

BLACKER, GEORGE: *Crescent-Pathé Tie-In* (*Record Research* **102**, 11/1969)

BLACKER, GEORGE: *Parade of Champions* (*Record Research,* serialized beginning with **169/170**, 1/1980)

BROOKS, TIM: *Willie Robyn Discography* (*ARSC Journal* **23/2**, Fall 1992)

BRYAN, MARTIN F. & BRYANT, WILLIAM R.: *Oxford and Silvertone Records, 1911-1918* (St. Johnsbury, VT: New Amberola Phonograph Co., 1975)

COGSWELL, ROBERT: *Discography of Blackface Comedy Dialogues* (Folklore Institute, Indiana University: unpublished doctoral dissertation, 1978)

CONNOR, D. RUSSELL & HICKS, WARREN W.: *BG on the Record* (New Rochelle, NY: Arlington House, 1969)

COTTER, DAVE: *National Music Lovers (New Amberola Graphic,* serialized beginning with **17**, 1972)

DETHLEFSON, RON and WILE, RAYMOND: *Edison Disc Artists and Records, 1910-1929* (Brooklyn, NY: APM Press, 1990)

DIXON, ROBERT & GODRICH, JOHN: *Blues and Gospel Records, 1902-1942* (third edition) (London: Storyville Publications, 1969)

DIXON, ROBERT & GODRICH, JOHN: *Recording the Blues* (New York: Stein & Day, 1970)

HARVITH, JOHN & HARVITH, SUSAN EDWARDS: *Edison, Musicians, and the Phonograph* (Westport, CT: Greenwood Press, 1987)

HITCHCOCK, H. WILEY & SADIE, STANLEY: *New Grove Dictionary of American Music* (London: Macmillan Press, Ltd., 1986)

KIDD, JIM: *Louis Hooper* (*Record Research* **77**, 6/1966)

KINKLE, ROGER D.: *The Complete Encyclopedia of Popular Music and Jazz, 1900-1950* (Westport, CT: Arlington House Publishers, 1974)

KOENIGSBURG, ALLEN: *Edison Cylinder Records, 1889-1912* (Brooklyn, NY: APM Press, 1988)

KRESSLEY, DAVID: *Associated Recorded Program Service* (*Record Research*, serialized beginning with **241/242**, 9-10/1989)

KRESSLEY, DAVID: *Catalog of World Transcriptions* (*Record Research*, serialized beginning with **91**, 8/1968)

KUNSTADT, LEN: *The Labels Behind Black Swan* (*Record Research* **229/230**, 5-6/1987)

PINTA, EMIL R.: *Chronologic Jan Peerce Discography* (Worthington, OH: published by the author, 1987)

PLAZA MUSIC COMPANY (New York): recording ledgers, 1926-1929 (unpublished)

RADIO CORPORATION OF AMERICA (Camden, NJ): recording cards & ledgers, 1929-1933 (unpublished)

ROBERTSON, ALEX: *Rare Canadian Aurora Label* (*Record Research* **219/220**, 1/1986)

ROBERTSON, ALEX & HUMBLE, GEORGE: *Canadian Gennett and Starr-Gennett Numerical* (*Record Research*, serialized beginning with **195/196**, 1-2/1983)

RUST, BRIAN: *American Dance Band Discography, 1917-1942* (New Rochelle, NY: Arlington House Publishers, 1975)

RUST, BRIAN: *Jazz Records A-Z, 1897-1931* (Middlesex, England: published by the author, 1962)

RUST, BRIAN: *Jazz Records, 1897-1942* (New Rochelle, NY: Arlington House Publishers, 1980)

RUST, BRIAN: *Victor Master Book, Vol. II (1925-1936)* (Stanhope, NJ: Walter C. Allen, 1976)

RUST, BRIAN & DEBUS, ALLEN: *The Complete Entertainment Discography* (New York: Da Capo Press, 1986)

STARR PIANO COMPANY (Richmond, IN): recording ledgers, 1925-1930 (unpublished)

SUTTON, ALLAN: *A.K.A.: Pseudonyms on American Records (1900-1932)* (Baltimore: published by the author, 1991)

THOMAS A. EDISON, INC. (Orange, NJ): internal memoranda, recording cards and ledgers, 1912-1929 (unpublished)

VARIETY MAGAZINE: *Variety* Obituaries, 1900-1987 (New York: Garland Publishing, Inc., 1988)

VICTOR TALKING MACHINE COMPANY (Camden, NJ): recording cards and ledgers, 1901-1929 (unpublished)

WALSH, JIM: *A Directory of Pioneer Recording Groups* (*Hobbies Magazine,* 10/62)

WALSH, JIM: *Performers Who Doubled Up* (*Hobbies Magazine*, 5/1944)

WALSH, JIM: *Pioneer Recording Artists Who Used More Than One Name* (*Hobbies Magazine*, 11/62)

WILE, RAYMOND: *Random Notes Concerning Edison Recording Artists* (*New Amberola Graphic* **79**, 1/1992)

Index I:
Vocalists and Vocal Groups
(Cross-Reference by Performer)

This listing is intended as a cross-reference only. Inclusion of a pseudonym here does not necessarily indicate that the performer used that name; refer to the main listing for further information. Performer listings are by professional names; see Appendix for birth, legal, or married names.

Pseudonyms followed by as asterisk (*) appear in the foreign-issue list only. Pseudonyms followed by a section mark (§) appear in both the domestic and foreign lists.

A

AKE, GEORGE -*see*
    Fergus, John
    Johnson, Edward
ALBANE, ANDY
    (*see* CICCONE & ALBANE)
ALCOCK, MERLE - *see*
    Tillotson, Merle
ALEXANDER, GEORGE - *see*
    Clifford, Arthur
ALIX, MAY - *see*
    Alix, May (note)
ALLEN, LIL - *see*
    Hamfoot Ham
ALLEN, MAYBELLE - *see*
    Johnson, Edith
ALLEY, BEN
    (*see* JOHNSON & ALLEY)
ALLINGTON, ED - *see*
    Horton, Robert
AMERICAN QUARTET - *see*
    Murray Quartet
    Premier Quartet
    Premier-American Quartet
ANDERSON, LEROY - *see*
    Red Headed Brier Hopper
ANDERSON, LOUISE - *see*
    Rose, Lucy
ARKANSAS WOODCHOPPER, THE - *see*
    West Virginia Rail Splitter, The
ARMSTRONG, LIL HARDIN
    (*see* TAYLOR & ARMSTRONG)
ARNOLD, KOKOMO - *see*
    Gitfiddle Jim
ASH, SAM - *see*
    Tree, James
AUSTIN, GENE - *see*
    Collins, Bill
AUSTIN, GENE & RENEAU, GEORGE - *see*
    Blue Ridge Duo

AUTRY, GENE - *see*
    Clayton, Bob
    Hardy, John
    Hill, Sam
    Johnson, Gene*
    Long, Tom
    Smith, Jimmie§
AUTRY, GENE & LONG, JIMMIE - *see*
    Long Brothers

B

BACKER, LES - *see*
    Evans, Happy Dick
BAER, FREDERIC - *see*
    Howard, William
BAER, FREDERICK & MOELLER, HENRY - *see*
    Howard & Mitchell
BAILEY & BARNUM - *see*
    Banjo-ker & the Songster
BAKER, CHARLES - *see*
    Wyoming Cowboy
BAKER, ELSIE - *see*
    Brown, Edna
    Watson, Nora
    West, Mabel
BAKER, KATHERINE - *see*
    Tate, Rose
BAKER, WILLIE - *see*
    Steamboat Bill & His Guitar
BALLARD, GEORGE WILTON - *see*
    Wilton, George
BALLARD, GEORGE WILTON & WHEELER,
  WILLIAM - *see*
    Nelson & Gwyne
BALLEW, SMITH - *see*
    Andrews, John
    Bancroft, Ted
    Blue, Bob

BALLEW, SMITH – *cont'd.*
 Blue, Buddy§
 Dale, Teddy
 Fenwyck, Jerry
 Roberts, Charles
 Terry, Arthur*
BARTLETTE, VIOLET - *see*
 Lewis, Ida
BAUR, FRANKLYN - *see*
 Dale, Charles
 Hartley, Lester
 Litchfield, Ben
 Mitchell, Sidney
 Post, Irving
BAXTER, HELEN - *see*
 Coleman, Ellen
 Spencer, Mamie
BENNETT, ELOISE - *see*
 Jackson, Violet
BERNARD, AL - *see*
 Bennett, John
 Clare, Jack
 Clark, Jack
 Moore, Buddy
 Sims, Skeeter
 Uncle Joe
 White, Slim
BERNARD, AL & HARE, ERNEST - *see*
 Clare & Munn
 Jones & White
BERNARD, AL & KAMPLAIN, FRANK - *see*
 Record Boys
BERNARD, AL & ROBINSON, J. RUSSELL- *see*
 Dixie Stars
BESSIGNER, FRANK & WRIGHT, FRANK- *see*
 Burton & Sims
 Burton & Wilson
 Gordon & Glover
 Radio Franks
 Radio Kings
 Tremaine Brothers§
 Two Franks
BIELING, JOHN - *see*
 Biehling
 Livingston
BLOCH, MAX - *see*
 Berini, Stanislau
 Berini, Stassio
 Brefelli, Mario
 Brefelli, Martino
 Martini, Pietro

BOMBURYERO, ERNESTINE - *see*
 Baby Bobbie
BOSWELL, CATHERINE - *see*
 Miller, Daisy
BOWLLY, AL - *see*
 Brady, Art/Arthur
BRADFORD, MARY H. - *see*
 Bradford, Auntie Mary
BRAGG, ARDELLE - *see*
 Blackburn, Mamie
BRICE, FANNIE - *see*
 Bryce, Fannie
BROONZY, BIG BILL
 (*see* SPIVEY & BROONZY)
BROWN, BESSIE - *see*
 Brown, Bessie (note)
 Green, Sadie
 Lee, Caroline
BROWN, KITTY - *see*
 White, Jane
BROWN, LILLYN - *see*
 Baker, Fanny
 Fernandez, Mildred
 Jones, Maude
BROWNE, ALTA & POWELL, BERTHA - *see*
 Floyd, Caroline & May
BRYANT'S JUBILEE QUINTET - *see*
 Southland Jubilee Singers
BULLOCK, CHICK - *see*
 Morton, George
 Snyder, Bobby
BURKHARDT, MAURICE - *see*
 Burton, Maurice*
BURNETT, BARNEY
 (*see also* MILLER & BURNETT); *see*
 Ray, Joey
BURR, HENRY
 (*see also* CAMPBELL & BURR); *see*
 Alexander, Alfred
 Barr, Harry
 Bart, John*
 Gillette, Henry*
 Gillette, Irving
 Haley, Harry
 King, Al
 Knapp, Frank
 Matthew, J.
 McClaskey, Harry
 McClaskey, Shamus
 Rice, Robert
BURR, HENRY & MEYER, JOHN H. - *see*
 McClaskey & Meyers
 Meyers & Gillette

BURTON, W.E. "BUDDY"
(*see also* INDEX II); *see*
  Thomas, Washington

C

CAMPBELL, ALBERT - *see*
  Howard, Frank
  Webster, Frank
CAMPBELL, ALBERT & BURR, HENRY -
see
  Bellwood & Burr*
CAMPBELL, ALBERT & KAUFMAN, JACK -
see
  Collins & Reynolds
  Murphy & Shea§
  Wheeler & Morse
CARHART, RUTH - *see*
  Hart, Ruth
CARSON, MARY - *see*
  Kingston, Kathleen
CHALLIS, BETH - *see*
  Green, Sadie*
CHALMERS, THOMAS - *see*
  Gilbert, Lawrence E.
CHAMLEE, MARIO - *see*
  Rodolfi, Mario
CHAPMAN, EDITH - *see*
  Chappell, Miss
  Goold, Edith C.
CHILDERS, W.C. - *see*
  Wanner, Enos
CHILDERS, W.C. & MRS. - *see*
  Wanner, Enos & Mrs.
CHILDS, VIRGINIA -*see*
  Douglas, Daisy
CHISHOLM, ANNE LEE - *see*
  Snow, Margie
  Walsh, Charlotte
CICCONE, CHICK & ALBANE, ANDY -
see
  Chick & Andy
CLAPP, SUNNY - *see*
  Reese, Claude
CLARK, BUDDY - *see*
  Clayton, Bobby
  Clifford, Bob
CLARK, HELEN - *see*
  Collins, Jane
  Collins, Sallie
  Johnson, Emma
  Lenox, Ruth
  Meredith, May
  Woods, Grace

CLAYBORN, EDWARD W. - *see*
  Guitar Evangelist
CLINTON, ALICE - *see*
  Rush, Lillian
COBB, GENE & GRAY, JACK - *see*
  Honey Gal & Smoke
COLEMAN, JAY BIRD - *see*
  Williams, George "Bullet"
COLE-TALBERT, FLORENCE - *see*
  Bert, Flo§
  Pecelli, Maria
COLLINS, ARTHUR - *see*
  Hawley
COLLINS, SAM - *see*
  Foster, Jim
  Jefferson, George
COLUMBIA (MALE) QUARTET - *see*
  Climax (Male) Quartet
  Consolidated (Male) Quartet
  Harmony (Male) Quartet
  Silvertone Quartet
  Standard (Male) Quartet
COLUMBIA STELLAR QUARTET -*see*
  Stellar (Male) Quartet
COOK, PHIL - *see*
  Cotton & Morpheus
  Phil & His Boyfriend Sam
  Phil & Jerry
  Radio Chef (& His Boyfriend
   Sam)
COOK, PHIL & FLEMING, VICTOR - *see*
  Big Boy & Shorty
  Two Dark Knights
COSTELLO, BILLY - *see*
  Red Pepper Sam§
COTY, BILL - *see*
  Cody, Bill
  Frawley, Tom
  Moore, Webster
  Wood, Robert
COX, BILL - *see*
  Baldwin, Luke
COX, IDA - *see*
  Lewis, Kate
  Powers, Julia
  Powers, Julius
  Smith, Jane
COX, MARIAN EVELYN - *see*
  Crawford, Marian
  Prescott, Carrie
CREAMER & LAYTON - *see*
  Jones & Harrold
CRESCENT TRIO - *see*
  Apollo (Male) Trio

CRESCENT TRIO – *cont'd.*
  Orpheus Trio
CRIPPEN, KATIE - *see*
  White, Ella
CRITERION QUARTET - *see*
  Aeolian Male Quartet
  Champion Quartet
  Music Lovers (Male) Quartet
  Music Lovers Stellar Quartet
  Robinson Quartette
  Roxy Quartet
  Silvertone Quartet
  Stellar (Male) Quartet
  Strand Quartet
CROXTON, FRANK - *see*
  Careau, Franklin

D

DADDY STOVEPIPE & WHISTLING PETE -
see
  Sunny Jim & Whistlin' Joe
DADMUN, ROYAL - *see*
  Crane, Ralph
  Johnson, Charles
  Wallace, Bruce
DALHART, VERNON - *see*
  Ahern, James
  Allen, Mack
  Allen, Mark
  Ballard, Wolfe
  Burton, Billy
  Calhoun, Jeff
  Calhoun, Jess
  Cannon, Jimmy
  Cramer, Al
  Craver, Al
  Cummings, James
  Dalton, Charles
  Dell, Vernon
  Dixon, Martin
  Elliott, Joseph
  Evans, Frank
  Evans, Hal
  Fuller, Jeff
  Fuller, Jep
  Harris, David
  Harris, Harry
  Harris, Henry
  Hayes, Lou
  Kincaid, Joe
  King, Fred
  Little, Tobe
  Massey, Bob

  Massey, Guy
  McLaughlin, George
  Mitchell, Warren
  Moore, Harry A.
  Morris, James
  Morse, Dick
  Mr. X
  Peters, Sam*
  Raymond, Harry
  Scott, Henry
  Smith, Josephus
  Stewart, Cliff
  Stone, Edward
  Stuart, Billy
  Terry, Will
  Turner, Allen
  Turner, Sid
  Tuttle, Frank
  Vernon, Bill
  Vernon, Herbert
  Vernon, Will
  Veteran, Vel
  Watson, Tom
  White, Bob
  White, George
  White, Robert
  Whitlock, Walter
  Williams, Frank
  Woods, George
DALHART, VERNON & ROBISON, CARSON -
see
  Ballard & Samuels
  Calhoun & Andrews
  Cramer Brothers
  Craver & Wells
  Dalhart & Wells
  Dixon & Andrews
  Evans & Clarke
  Jones Brothers*
  Peters & Jones*
DALHART, VERNON; ROBISON, CARSON;
  & HOOD, ADELYN - *see*
  Jewel Trio
  Oriole Trio
  Regal Rascals
DALHART, VERNON & SMALLE, ED - *see*
  Arkansas Trio
  Birmingham Blue Buglers
  Mitchell & White
  Windy City Duo
DARBY, TOM & PITTS, JESSE - *see*
  Georgia Wild Cats
DAVIS, ERNEST - *see*
  Bronson, George

FIELDS, ARTHUR - *see*
  Allen Craig
  Andrews, Jim
  Baker, Donald
  Baldwin, Arthur
  Bernie, D. Bud
  Britt, Addy
  Britten, Ford
  Bronson, George
  Buckley, Eugene
  Calhoun, Jeff
  Clarke, Billy
  Cole, Rex
  Cole, Sam
  Crane, Harry
  Dale, Charles
  Dale, Walter H.
  Dexter, Charles
  Donovan, Hugh
  Edwards, Billy
  Edwrads, Thomas
  Elliott, Joseph
  Evans, Frank
  French, George
  Gent & Wheeler
  Grant, Arthur
  Gray, Henry
  Herold, Francis
  Higgins, Si
  Hilly, Dan
  Hobbs, Herb
  Holton, Larry
  Hunter, James
  Kern, Jimmy
  King, Henry
  Lewis, William
  Lincoln, Mac
  Litchfield, Ben
  Mack, Arthur
  Mander, Ambrose
  Martin, Jack
  Meadows, Arthur
  Mr. X
  Norton, Walter
  O'Brian, Padric
  Randall, Roy
  Richards, Charles
  Ryan, Jimmy
  Seelig, Arthur
  Sloane, John
  Spencer, Samuel
  Stewart, Cliff
  Stone, Fred
  Thomas, Bob
  Trevor, Bert
  Veteran, Vel
  White, Billy
  Wood, Robert
FIELDS, ARTHUR & HALL, FRED - *see*
  Gaunt, Joe & Zeb
  Gunboat Billy & The Sparrow
  Hometowners
  Lumberjacks
  Younger, Eddie & His Mountaineers
FIELDS, ARTHUR & HARRISON,
  CHARLES - *see*
  Christy Brothers
FIELDS, ARTHUR & KAUFMAN, IRVING
  or JACK - *see*
  Two Kaufields
FIELDS, ARTHUR & KAUFMAN, IRVING
  & JACK- *see*
  Three Kaufields
FISK UNIVERSITY JUBILEE QUARTET - *see*
  Southern Four
FITZGERALD, ELLA - *see*
  Fields, Evelyn
FLEMING, VICTOR
  (*see* COOK & FLEMING)
FLETCHER, DAVID & FOSTER, GWEN - *see*
  Carolina Twins
FLETCHER, VICTOR - *see*
  Green, Jack
FLYNN, JIMMY - *see*
  Flynn, Jimmy (note)
FOSTER, GARLEY
  (*see* WALSH & FOSTER)
FOSTER, GWEN
  (*see* FLETCHER & FOSTER)
FOUR HOOLIGANS - *see*
  Valley Inn Quartet
FRANCIS, ADELINE - *see*
  Miss Francis
FRANKEL, HARRY - *see*
  Henderson, Frank
  Singin' Sam
FREER, MARCIA - *see*
  Freer, Margaret A.
FULLER, BLIND BOY - *see*
  Brother George

G

GAILLARD, SLIM & STEWART, SLAM -
  see
  Slim & Slam
GAINES, NEWTON - *see*
  New, Jim

GAINES, ROLAND
    (*see* ECKLER & GAINES)
GARDELLA, TESS - *see*
    Aunt Jemima
GARDNER, BOB
    (*see* McFARLAND & GARDNER)
GARLAND, HATTIE - *see*
    Jackson, Violet
    James, Pauline
    Jordan, Jennie
GARRY, SID - *see*
    Denton, Tom
    Foster, Al
GEORGIA TOM - *see*
    Smokehouse Charley
GENNETT SONGSTERS - *see*
    Four Serenaders
GEORGIA TOM
    (*see also* TAMPA RED); *see*
    Smokehouse Charley
GILLHAM, ART - *see*
    Barrel House Pete
    Thomas, Fred
    Whispering Pianist
GINTER, MARIE - *see*
    Rogers, May
GLENN, WILFRED - *see*
    Green, Marion
GLOVER, MAE - *see*
    Washburn, Alberta
GOLDEN, BILLY & HEINS, BILLY - *see*
    Jones & Crawford
GOWDY, RUBY - *see*
    Anderson, Maybelle
GRAHAM BROTHERS - *see*
    Grant Trio
GRAINGER, PORTER - *see*
    Grey, Harold
GRAUER, BERNIE - *see*
    Roberts, Happy Jack
GRAY, EDDIE - *see*
    Evers, Frank
GRAY, JACK
    (*see* COBB & GRAY)
GRAYSON, G.B. - *see*
    Thomas, Graysen
GRAYSON, G.B. & WHITTER, HENRY - *see*
    Gayle, Norman
    Thomas & Lotty
GRAYSON COUNTY BOYS
    (*see* STONEMAN, ERNEST & GRAYSON
    COUNTY BOYS)
GREEN, DOE DOE & FLOYD, PAUL - *see*
    Two Black Diamonds

GREEN, EDDIE
    (*see* WILSON & GREEN)
GREEN, LEOTHUS ("PORKCHOP") - *see*
    Johnson, Porkchop
GRIFFIN, J. LYNN - *see*
    Mauer, Russell
GROSS, HELEN - *see*
    Clementine Smith

H

HACKETT, CHARLES - *see*
    Dale, Edwin
HAFFORD, HOWARD - *see*
    Douglas, Walter
HAHNE, WEBB - *see*
    Ukulele Bailey
HAJOS, MIZZI - *see*
    Mitzi
HALL, ARTHUR - *see*
    Burton, Howard
    Craig, Al
    Hahl, Adolph J.
    Howard, Frank
    Lewis, Howard
    Maynard, James
    Nichols, Frank
    Perry, George
    Stewart, Cliff
HALL, ARTHUR & RYAN, JOHN - *see*
    Gilbert & Nelson
    Radio Boys
HALL, FRED
    (*see* FIELDS & HALL)
HALL, WENDELL - *see*
    Radio Red
HANSHAW, ANNETTE - *see*
    Bingham, Ethel*
    Dare, Dot
    Ellis, Gay
    Lee, Marion*
    Miss Annette
    Sandford, Leila*
    Shaw, Janet
    Stewart, Bessie
    Young, Patsy
HARE, ERNEST (*see also* BERNARD & HARE;
    JONES & HARE); *see*
    Blake, Harry
    Burton, Sammy
    Confidential Charlie
    Cox, Wallace
    Daniels, Wallace
    Donovan, Hugh

HARE, ERNEST – *cont'd.*
  Grant, Arthur
  Harris, David
  Jones, Henry
  Judson, Robert
  Leon, Albert
  Leslie, Walter
  Mann, Frank
  Marron, John
  Mr. Hare
  Phillips, Curt
  Radio Joe
  Roberts, Roy
  Spencer, Ernie
  Thomas, Bob
  Thomas, John
  Turner, Hobo Jack
  Uncle Ernest
  Uncle Ernie
  Walters, Nat
HARLAN, BYRON G. - *see*
  Holland, Byron
  Lincoln, Chester
  Pippins, Cyrus
  Stebbins, Cy
  Terry, Bert
  Treadway, Deacon
HARMONIZERS - *see*
  Amphion Quartet
  County Harmonizers
  Great White Way Quartet
HARRIS, ALFONCY & BETHENEA - *see*
  Harris & Harris
HARRIS, ELTON SPIVEY - *see*
  Za Zu Girl
HARRIS, EVANGELIST R.H. &
 PENTECOSTAL SISTERS - *see*
  Rev. George H. Sims & Congregation
HARRIS, SAM
  (*see* UNDERWOOD & HARRIS)
HARRISON, CHARLES - *see*
  Black, Herbert
  Burton, Billy
  Curtis, Harry
  Donivetti, Hugo
  Donovan, Hugh§
  Elliott, Joseph
  Everett, Frank
  Gordon, Westell
  Gould
  Harris, David
  Hilton, Charles
  Miller, Kenneth
  Moore, Harry A.

  Rundall, William
  Rundle, William
  Shannon, Thomas
  Sullivan, Walter
  Terrill, Norman
HARRISON, CHARLES & HOLLINSHEAD,
 REDFERNE - *see*
  Kendall & Kelly
HARROD, JAMES - *see*
  Wilson, George
HART, CHARLES (*see also* MEYER & HART)
 see
  Curtis, Harry
  Dalton, Charles
  Elliott, Joseph
  Jordan, Henry
  Jordan, James
  Stone, Edward
  Turner, Allen
  Warren, Charles
  Wells, Lorenzo
  Wilson, Arthur
HART, CHARLES & SHAW, ELLIOTT - *see*
  Black, Herbert
  Harris & Smith
  Jamieson & Turner
  Jordan Brothers
  Morris & Elliott
HARVEY, MORTON - *see*
  Moreley, Herbert
  Rogers, Gene
HARVEY, ROY - *see*
  Runnels, George
HARVEY, ROY & HOKE, BOB - *see*
  Runnels & Hall
HASKINS, MATTHEW - *see*
  O'Brien, Pat
HASKINS, MATTHEW & MARY - *see*
  O'Brien, Pat & Mary
HAYDN (HAYDEN) QUARTET - *see*
  American Quartet
  Edison (Male) Quartet
  Victor Minstrels
HEGAMIN, LUCILLE - *see*
  Baker, Fanny
HEMUS, PERCY - *see*
  Fredericks, William
  Gordon, Charles
  Roe, Turner
  Wells, Lorenzo
HENDERSON, ALMA - *see*
  Rotter, Alma*
HENDERSON, BERTHA - *see*
  Mann, Estelle

JONES, ALBERTA - *see*
  Sanders, Bessie
JONES, BILLY - *see*
  Blake, Harry
  Burton, Sammy
  De Rex, Billy§
  Gargolo, Ugeso
  Hall, Freddy
  Harold, Eugene
  Harris, David
  Johnson, William
  Jones, Mr.
  Jones, Reese
  Jones, W. Reese
  Jones, Willy
  Lyons, Billy
  Morris, William
  O'Malley, Dennis
  Rees, William
  Reese, William
  Roberts, Victor
  Smith, Bertram
  Uncle Billy
  Vernon, Walter
  West, Billy
  West, William
  White, Joe
  Williams, Carlton
JONES, BILLY & HARE, ERNEST -*see*
  Black & White
  Blake & Judson
  Bluebird Trio
  Clarke & Thomas
  Gale & Fisher
  Happiness Boys
  Harmony Broadcasters
  Harrow & Edwards
  James & Marron
  Lewis & Scott
  Lyons & Heilman
  Radio Kings
  Romeo Boys
  Spencer & Harris
  Thomas & West
  Topnotchers
  West & Thomas
JONES, JACK
  (*see* MILLS & JONES)
JONES, MAGGIE - *see*
  Barnes, Fae

       K
KAISER, MARIE - *see*
  De Kaiser, Marie

  De Kyzer, Marie
  Kyzer, Marie
KALEY, CHARLES - *see*
  Baxter, Clyde
  Keene, Charles
KAMPLAIN, FRANK
  (*see also* BERNARD & KAMPLAIN); *see*
  Hazelton, Joe
KAUFMAN, IRVING (*see also* FIELDS,
  KAUFMAN & KAUFMAN); *see*
  Andrews, Jack
  Andrews, Jim
  Andrews, John
  Baker, Donald
  Bancroft, Ted
  Beaver, George
  Beaver, Harry
  Beaver, Henry
  Bronson, George
  Brown, Arthur
  Burnette, Dick
  Burton, Sammy
  Carroll, Bob
  Charles, Harold
  Christy, Frank
  Clark, Billy
  Clarke, Billy
  Combs, Irving
  Confidential Charlie
  Coombs, Irving
  Cortes, Lester
  Craig, Allen
  Crane, George
  Dale, Charles
  Day, Billy
  De Wees, George
  Dickson, Charles
  Dixon, Charles
  Dowe, John
  Duffy, Tom
  Edwards, Irving
  Edwards, Tom
  Epstein, George
  Flynn, Jimmy
  Ford, Eddy
  Frawley, Tom
  Harper, Billy
  Harris, David
  Harris, Frank
  Holt, Arthur*
  Irving, Henry
  Irving, John
  Killeen, Pete
  Loew, Jack

Morrow, George
Nelson, Charles
Nevill, Tom*
Parsons, (Happy) Jim
Roberts, Ed
Russell, Al
Shea, Jack
Taylor, Noel
Topping, Harry*
Veteran, Vel
Ward, Sleepy
Watt, Brian*
Winters, Horace
Young, Marvin
KAUFMAN, IRVING & JACK - *see*
　Christy Brothers
　Dooley & Shea
　Irvings & Jackson
　Irvings Brother
KAUFMAN, JACK
　(*see also* CAMPBELL & KAUFMAN;
　FIELDS & KAUFMAN); *see*
　Carroll, Jack*
　Couert, Ray
　Clark, Roy
　Dalton, Jack
　Green, Bert
　Holmes, Dick
　Loew, Jack
　MacFarland, Bob
　Mark, Freddie
　Martin, Happy
　Mitchell, Sidney
　Patti, Orville
　Post, Irving
　Smith, Harry
　Weary Willie
　White, Jerry
KAY, DOLLY - *see*
　Cross, Henrietta
　Hiller, Josephine
KEEFE, MATT - *see*
　Uncle Josh
KEESEE, HOWARD - *see*
　Marlow, Andy
KENNEDY, WILLIAM A. - *see*
　Bonner, William
KERNS, GRACE - *see*
　Clarke, Catherine
　Clarke, Jane
KIMBROUGH, LOTTE - *see*
　Beaman, Lottie
　Johnson, Martha
　Kimbrough, Lena

KINCAID, BRADLEY - *see*
　Hughey, Dan
KIRKEBY, ED - *see*
　Lloyd, Ed
　Loyd, Eddy
　Wallace, Ted
KLINE, OLIVE - *see*
　Green, Alice
KURTZ & CULLY - *see*
　Salt & Pepper

L

LA, MAR PETE - *see*
　Le Maire, Pete
LAIRD, CHARLES - *see*
　Braslau, Marcel
LAMBERT, HAROLD "SCRAPPY" - *see*
　Blue, Buddy
　Brown, William
　Bruce, A.L.*
　Campbell, George*
　Clarke, Harold
　Fenwyck, Jerry
　Frawley, Tom
　Green, Jimmy
　Haines, Ralph
　Hale, Chester§
　Holton, Larry
　Hughes, Phil
　King, Martin
　Lance, Roland
　Lang, Harold
　Lewis, Rodman
　Lord, Jack
　Lorin, Burt
　Moore, Webster
　Nelson, Gerald
　Noble, Howard
　Radio Eddie
　Roberts, John
　Russell, Roy
　Wood, Robert
LAMBERT, HAROLD "SCRAPPY" &
　HILLPOT, BILL - *see*
　Holt & Singer
　Holton & Cross
　Smith Brothers (Trade & Mark)
LA VIZZO, THELMA - *see*
　Hargens, Trilby
　Nance, Mabel
LAWSON, HAPPY - *see*
　Graham, Lucky
LAYMAN, ZORA - *see*
　Zora

LEE, BUDDY - *see*
   Wilson, Lucky (& His Uke)
LEE, ELIZA CHRISTMAS - *see*
   Jones, Saddie
   Miss Lee
LEE, MANDY - *see*
   Brown, Lindy
   Lee, Mandy (note)§
   Smith, Julia
LENNOX, ELIZABETH - *see*
   Earle, Emily
   Ferrell, Louise
   Terrall, Louise
   Terrell, Louise
LEWIS, BERT - *see*
   Smith, Barney
LINTHECOME, JOE - *see*
   Red Onion Joe & His Uke
LONG, HOWARD
   (*see* McCARN & LONG)
LONG, JIMMIE
   (*see* AUTRY & LONG)
LOOKOUT MOUNTAIN BOYS - *see*
   Great Gap Entertainers
LUTHER, FRANK - *see*
   Adams, Joe
   Bell, Eddie
   Billings, Bud
   Birmingham Bud & His Uke
   Blanchard, Dan
   Calhoun, Jeff
   Carson, Cal
   Cook, Tom
   Daniels, Walter
   Dixon, Martin
   Jackson, Happy
   Luther, Francis
   Thompson, Bud
   Wiggins, Pete
LUTHER, FRANK & ROBISON, CARSON - *see*
   Adams & Clark
   Billings Brothers
   Billings, Bud & Joe§
   Black Brothers§
   Calhoun & Leavitt
   Carson, Cal & Gid
   Chester & Rollins*
   Jimson Brothers
   Luther & Faber
   Luther Brothers
   Southerners
   Turney Brothers
   Weary Willie
   Williams Brothers

M

MacDONALD QUARTET - *see*
   Goodman Sacred Singers
MACDONOUGH, HARRY - *see*
   MacDonald, Harry
   Raymond, Ralph
MACK, ALURA - *see*
   Ross, Lucy
MACY, GERALD UNDERHILL - *see*
   Macy, Jerry
   Underhill, Jerry
MACY, GERALD UNDERHILL & SMALLE,
ED - *see*
   Elliott & Spencer
   Howard & Doran
   Melody Twins
   Radio Aces
   Radio Imps
   Ted & Ned
MARSH, LUCY ISABELLE - *see*
   Howard, Anna
MARSHALL, BILL - *see*
   Young, Jack
MARTIN, ASA
   (*see also* ROBERTS & MARTIN); *see*
   Coat, Jesse
MARTIN, SARA - *see*
   Johnson, Margaret*
   Roberts, Sally
MARVIN, FRANKIE - *see*
   Ball, Ray
   Cowboy Rogers
   Dalton, Walter (& his Guitar)
   Lazy Larry
   Texas Ranger
   Wallace, Frankie (& His Guitar/Uke)
   Warfield, Lewis
   Warner, Yodlin' Jimmy
   Weary Willie
   West, Jack
   White, George
   Wright, Jim & His Guitar*
   Wright, Joe & His Guitar*
MARVIN, JOHNNY - *see*
   Duke & His Uke
   Duke, Henry (& His Uke)
   Duke, Honey (& His Uke)
   Lane, Jack & His Uke
   MacDonald & Broones
   May, Jimmy
   Price, Jimmy
   Robbins & Uke
MATTHEWS, MAE - *see*
   Harris, Maxine

MILLER, EMMETT & CHILES, CHARLES - *see*
  Sam & Bill*
MILLER, FLOURNOY & LYLES, AUBREY - *see*
  Jones & Moore
MILLER, LILLIAN - *see*
  Harris, Helen
  Mills, Lillian
  Thomas, Bessie
MILLER, REED - *see*
  Bronson, George
  Clements, George
  Lenox, George
  Pinckney, Harry
  Reed, James
MILLER, REED & ROGERS, LANE - *see*
  Burrell & Bronson
  Lenox & Johnson
MILLER, SODARISA - *see*
  Collins, Vie
  Ward, Amy
MILLS BROTHERS - *see*
  Southern Singers
MILLS, IRVING - *see*
  Goodwin, Goody
MILLS, MAUDE - *see*
  Crane, Mary
MILLS, MAUDE & JONES, JACK - *see*
  Frankie & Jones
MOELLER, HENRY (*see also* BAER &
  MOELLER; MEYER & MOELLER); *see*
  Fairbanks, Henry
  Goddard, Charles
  Myrick, Russell
  Roberts, Stickney & Grisselle
  Sawyer, Charles
MONROE COUNTY BOTTLE TIPPERS - *see*
  Boys from Wildcat Hollow
MOODY, JULIA - *see*
  Mills, Violet
  Vaughan, Edith
MOONEY, JOE & DAN - *see*
  Desmond Duo*
  Harmony Twins*
  Melotone Boys§
  Sunshine Boys§
MOORE, MONETTE - *see*
  Hayes, Ethel
  Potter, Nettie
  Smith, Susie
  White, Grace
MORAND, HERB - *see*
  Hamfoot Ham

MORGAN, CORINNE - *see*
  Clarke, Ethel*
  Welsh, Corinne Morgan
MORGAN, DICK - *see*
  Morgan, Icky
MOSS, TEDDY - *see*
  Platt, James
MUNN, PAUL
  (*see also* REA & MUNN); *see*
  Oliver, Paul
  Smith, Oliver
MURPHY, LAMBERT - *see*
  Dixon, Raymond
MURRAY, BILLY - *see*
  Hughes, Dan
  Pitkin, Cy
  Weary Willie Trio
MURRAY, BILLY & VAN BRUNT,
  WALTER - *see*
  Saunders & White

N

NATIONAL MALE QUARTET - *see*
  Oriole Male Quartet
NAZARENE CONGREGATIONAL
CHURCH CHOIR OF BROOKLYN, NEW
YORK - *see*
  Nazarene Choir
NELSON, EDDIE - *see*
  Howard, Albert
NELSON, ESTHER - *see*
  Nielson, Jane
NELSON, OZZIE - *see*
  Andrews, Barney
  Briggs, Arnold
  Burton, Dick
NORFOLK JAZZ/JUBILEE QUARTET - *see*
  Georgia Sacred Singers
NORWORTH, JACK - *see*
  Norton, Jack

O

O'CONNOR, WILLIAM - *see*
  Hauser, Robert
OHLHEIM, HELEN - *see*
  Patterson, Florence
ORPHEUS QUARTET - *see*
  Victor Male Quartet
OSBORNE, WILL - *see*
  Reynolds, Dick
OSCAR, JOHN
  (*see* THEARD & OSCAR)

P

PACE JUBILEE SINGERS - *see*
  Dixie Jubilee Singers
PARKER, CHUBBY - *see*
  Jackson, Smilin' Tubby
PARKER, J. DONALD - *see*
  Happy Jack
  Parker, Jack
PARKER, JACK; DONALDSON, WILL; &
 DEWEY, PHIL - *see*
  Melody Three
  Men About Town
PATRICOLA, ISABELLA - *see*
  Miss Patricola
  Peters, Sadie*
PATTON, CHARLEY - *see*
  Hadley, Elder J.J.
  Masked Marvel
PEERCE, JAN - *see*
  Joyce, Randolph
  Pearl, Jack
  Pearl, Pinkie / Pinky
  Robinson, Paul
PEERLESS ENTERTAINERS - *see*
  Big Four Quartet
PEERLESS QUARTET - *see*
  Columbia (Male) Quartet
  Consolidated (Male) Quartet
  Harmony (Male) Quartet
  Invincible Four
  Lakeshore Club Quartet
  Minstrels
  Peerless Minstrels
  Quartet
  Silvertone Quartet
  Standard (Male) Quartet
  U.S. Minstrels
  Victor Minstrel Company
  Victor Vaudeville Company
PERKINS, ALBERTA - *see*
  Jones, Louella
PHILLIPS, JOSEPH A. - *see*
  Kent, Franklin
  Lawrence, Harry
  Lewis, Justice
  Phillips, Joe
  Strong, Arthur
PICCO, MILLO - *see*
  Bruno, Antonio
PICKARD FAMILY - *see*
  Pleasant Family
PIERCE, BOB - *see*
  Old King Cole
  Old Man Sunshine

PIE PLANT PETE - *see*
  Asparagus Joe
PITTS, JESSE
  (*see* DARBY & PITTS)
POLLACK, BEN - *see*
  Bracken, Jimmy
  Gale, Eddie
PORTER, STEVE - *see*
  Reeve, Floyd
POTEET, BLYTHE
  (*see* McGEE & POTEET)
POWELL, BERTHA
  (*see* BROWNE & POWELL)
POWELL, EUGENE - *see*
  Sonny Boy Nelson
POWELL, MATILDA - *see*
  Mississippi Matilda
POWERS, OLLIE - *see*
  Sims, Howard
PREER, EVELYN - *see*
  Franks, Sinclair*
  Jarvis, Hotsy
  Kaufman, Irving*
  Radio Red*
PRITCHARD, B.L. ("SUNSHINE") - *see*
  Moonshine Dave
PUCKETT, HOLLAND - *see*
  David Miller
  Watson, Harvey
PUCKETT, RILEY - *see*
  Wilson, Fred

Q

QUINN, DAN W. - *see*
  Williams, Frank

R

RAINEY, GERTRUDE "MA" - *see*
  Patterson, Lila
  Smith, Anne
RAMBLER MINSTREL COMPANY - *see*
  Colonial Quartet
  Minstrels
  Victor Minstrels
RAZAF, ANDY - *see*
  Smith, Dan
REA, VIRGINIA - *see*
  Palmer, Olive
REA, VIRGINIA & MUNN, FRANK - *see*
  Palmer & Oliver
REBER, HARRY - *see*
  Murray, Dick

REEVES, GOEBEL - *see*
   Texas Drifter
RENEAU, GEORGE
   (*see* AUSTIN & RENEAU)
REVELERS - *see*
   Acme Male Quartet
   Cathedral Male Quartet
   Gaeity Musical Chorus
   Merrymakers
   Shannon Four
   Singing Sophomores
   Victor Salon Group
RICE, GLADYS - *see*
   Bergere, Bettina
   Grant, Rachel
   Marsden, Victoria
RICE, HOKE - *see*
   Landon, Lee
RINES, JOE - *see*
   Ryan, John
ROBERTS, BOB - *see*
   Roberts, Robert
ROBERTS, DOC - *see*
   Burke, Fiddlin' Jim
   Elmer & Judd
   Jorday, Billy
ROBERTS, DOC & MARTIN, ASA - *see*
   Burke & Coat
ROBERTSON, DICK - *see*
   Carroll, Roy
   Dickson, Bob
   Dix, Bobby
   Dixon, Bob
   Fenwyck, Jerry
   Hughes, Phil
   Leighton, Chester
   Roberts, Ben
   Wood, Robert
ROBISON, CARSON (*see also* DALHART &
ROBISON; LUTHER & ROBISON;
ROBISON TRIO); *see*
   Billings, Joe
   Carson, Cal
   Clark, James
   Evans, Frank
   Evans, Franklin
   Faber, Ed
   Jones, Harry*
   Leavitt, Bob
   Robison, C.J.
   Samuels, Claude
   Tuttle, Frank
ROBISON, (CARSON) TRIO - *see*
   Black Brothers

ROBISON, WILLARD - *see*
   Howe, Paul
ROBYN, WILLIAM - *see*
   Allison, James*
   Bolton, Jamie*
   Brown, Tom
   Clarke, Walter*
   Conroy, Frank
   Conroy, Fred
   Crane, Thornely
   Ender, Jack
   Forsythe, Reg*
   Foster, Al§
   Francis, William
   Franklin, Fred
   Gravelle, Buddy
   Haines, Ralph
   Hamilton, Edward
   Hamilton, Ray
   Henderson, Larry*
   Henry, Lawrence*
   Hillman, Bob*
   Johnston, Al*
   Lambert, Harold*
   Lee, ALbert*
   Mack, Bobby
   Norton, Walter
   O'Shea, Allen*
   O'Shea, John*
   Playman, Edmund*
   Powell, Roy
   Ray, Walter
   Remick, Walter*
   Richards, Edgar*
   Richards, Walter
   Rickman, Eddie*
   Roberts, Billy*
   Robin, Wyllie*
   Robinow, William
   Robinson, William
   Robyn, ("Wee") Willie§
   Robyn, Wyllie*
   Ruban, George
   Rubin, Cantor William
   Rubinoff, William
   Scarpioff, William
   Scott, Henry
   Shaw, Eddie
   Smith, Harry
   Spear, John§
   Stanley, William
   Thomas, Brian*
   Turner, Ray*
   Waters, Frankie

SPENCER, LEN - *see*
  Allen, Gary
SPER, FRANCIS - *see*
  Smith, Wini
SPIVEY, ADDIE "SWEET PEASE" - *see*
  Sweet Peas
SPIVEY, VICTORIA & BROONZY, BIG
 BILL - *see*
  Harris, Magnolia & Smith, Howlin'
STACKS, TOM - *see*
  Howard, Tom
  Thomas, Harry
  Frawley, Tom
STAMPS, FRANK'S ALL STAR QUARTET -
see
  Piedmont Melody Boys
STANLEY, AILEEN - *see*
  Jones, Mamie
  Nielson, Varna
  Warner, Florence
STANLEY, FRANK C. - *see*
  Grinsted, William S.
  Parker, H.C.*
  Williams, George S.
STAPLETON BROTHERS - *see*
  Three 'Baccer Tags
STERLING TRIO - *see*
  Apollo Vocal Trio
  Miami Valley Trio
STEVENSON, ELISE - *see*
  Stevenson, Alice C.
  Wood, Elsie
STEWART, CAL - *see*
  Jones, Duncan
  Uncle Josh
STEWART, PRISCILLA - *see*
  Stewart, Mae
STEWART, SLAM
  (*see* GAILLARD & STEWART)
STOKES, FRANK & SANE, DAN - *see*
  Beale Street Sheiks
STONEMAN, ERNEST - *see*
  Harris, Sim
  Hawkins, Uncle Ben
  Seaney, Uncle Jim
STONEMAN, ERNEST & GRAYSON
 COUNTY BOYS - *see*
  Hawkins, Uncle Ben & His Boys
STONEMAN, WILLIE - *see*
  Hunt, Dave
STRAINE, MARY - *see*
  Harris, Pearl
SUBLETT, JOHN
  (*see* WASHINGTON & SUBLETT)

SWEET BROTHERS - *see*
  Clark Brothers
SWEET, HERBERT - *see*
  Clark, John
SYKES, ROOSEVELT - *see*
  Kelly, Willie
SYLVESTER, HANNAH - *see*
  Scott, Genevia

T

TAGGART, BLIND JOE - *see*
  Blind Amos
TAMPA RED & GEORGIA TOM - *see*
  Honey Boy Smith & Southern Jack
TAYLOR, EVA - *see*
  Gibbons, Irene
  Henderson, Catherine
  Williams, Irene
TAYLOR, EVA & ARMSTRONG, LIL
 HARDIN - *see*
  The Riffers
TENNILLE, FRANK - *see*
  Randall, Clark
THEARD, SAM & OSCAR, JOHN - *see*
  Sam & Oscar
THOMAS. F.T. - *see*
  Ruthers, George "Hambone"
  Thomas, Bud
THOMAS, JOHN CHARLES - *see*
  Martini, Enrico
THOMPSON, ERNEST - *see*
  Johnson, Ernest
  Tompkins, Jed
TIFFANY, MARIE - *see*
  Barrett, Betty
TODD, CLARENCE
  (*see also* HUNTER & TODD); *see*
  Green, Frank
  Howard, Frank
  Shufflin' Sam
TOOMEY, WELBY - *see*
  Jennings, Herb
TRACEY, CORA - *see*
  Prescott, Carrie
TUCKERMAN, EARL & HINDERMEYER,
 HARVEY - *see*
  Gold Dust Twins
TUNNELL, GEORGE - *see*
  Bon Bon
TWEEDY BROTHERS - *see*
  Jennings Brothers
  Three Tweedy Boys

U

UNDERWOOD, MARION & HARRIS, SAM -
see
    Clinch Valley Boys

V

VALESCO, DELORES - *see*
    Beason, Kitty
    Garland, Dorothy
VAN BRUNT, WALTER
    (*see also* MURRAY & VAN BRUNT); *see*
    Burns, John
    Clemon, James
    Ely, Carl
    Finnegan, John
    Harris, David
    McHugh, Martin
    O'Brien, John
    Scanlan, Walter
    Shannon, Thomas
VICCARINO, REGINA - *see*
    Donnelli, Josepha
VINSCON, WALTER - *see*
    Walter Jacobs

W

WAKEFIELD, HENRIETTA - *see*
    Vernon, Mary
    Volevi, Marie
WALLACE, SIPPIE - *see*
    Thomas, Sippie
WALSH, DOCK & FOSTER, GARLEY - *see*
    Pine Mountain Boys
WARNER, THOMAS - *see*
    Jones, Wallace
WASHINGTON, BUCK & SUBLETT, JOHN -
see
    Buck & Bubbles§
WASHINGTON, ELIZABETH (LIZZIE) - *see*
    Reed, Sadie
WATEROUS, HERBERT - *see*
    Thompson, Conrad
WATERS, ETHEL - *see*
    Jones, Mamie
WATSON, GEORGE P. - *see*
    Hubbard, George
WEIDERHOLD, ALBERT - *see*
    Stuart, Herbert
WELDON, WILL - *see*
    Casey Bill

WELLING, FRANK
    (*see also* McGHEE & WELLING); *see*
    Young, Clarence
WELLS, JOHN BARNES - *see*
    Barnes, William
WELSH, NOLAN - *see*
    Welch, Barrel House
WERRENRATH, REINALD - *see*
    Hamilton, Edward
WESTON, WILLIE - *see*
    Kendall, Edward
WHEELER, ELIZABETH - *see*
    Kenyon, Jane
WHEELER, FREDERICK J.
    (*see also* YOUNG & WHEELER); *see*
    Harrison, James
WHEELER, WILLIAM
    (*see also*   BALLARD & WHEELER); *see*
    Brunn, Ewart
WHIDBY, LULU - *see*
    White, E.
WHISTLING PETE
    (*see* DADDY STOVEPIPE & WHISTLING
    PETE)
WHITE, GEORGIA - *see*
    White, George
WHITE, JERRY - *see*
    Beckner, Frederick
    Litchfield, Ben
    White, Jerry (note)
WHITE, JOSEPH M. - *see*
    Burke, Terrance*
    Silver-Masked Tenor
WHITTER, HENRY
    (*see also* GRAYSON & WHITTER); *see*
    Lotty, Will
WILKINS, ROBERT - *see*
    Wilkins, Tim
WILLIAMS, EVAN - *see*
    Evans, Harry
    Evans, William T.§
WILLIAMS, IRENE - *see*
    Audrey, Irene
WILLIAMS, TRIXIE & BROWN, WILL - *see*
    Brown, Lil & Will
WILSON, BILLIE - *see*
    Cole, Lucy
WILSON, BILLIE & GREEN, EDDIE - *see*
    Mack & Mitchell
WILSON, LENA - *see*
    Colman, Nancy*
WILSON, LEOLA B. & WILSON, KID
    WESLEY - *see*
    Hunter & Jenkins

WINSCH, LOUIS - *see*
    Burnside, George
    Jackson, Charles
    Keap, Oscar
    Lewis, Justice
    Oakland, Charles
    Prescott, George
    Remington, Joe
    Williams, Harry
WINTERS, KATIE - *see*
    Spears, Blossom
WOODLAWN QUARTET OF WOODLAWN,
 ALABAMA - *see*
    Hamlin Quartette
WOOLF, WALTER - *see*
    Winters, Horace
WRIGHT, FRANK
    (*see* BESSINGER & WRIGHT)

WSAI MAIDS OF MELODY - *see*
    Judson Sisters

Y

YATES, BLIND RICHARD - *see*
    Anderson, Jelly Roll
    Richards, Uncle Charlie
YOUNG, BEAULAH GAYLORD - *see*
    Ames, Molly
    Vaughn, Caroline
YOUNG, JOHN - *see*
    Anthony, Harry
    Young, Jack
YOUNG, JOHN & WHEELER,FREDERICK J.
    see
    Anthony & Harrison

Index II:
Instrumental Soloists and Groups
(Cross-Reference by Performer)

This listing is intended as a cross-reference only. Inclusion of a pseudonym here does not necessarily indicate that the performer or group used that name; refer to the main listing for further information.

A

ADLER TRIO - *see*
  National Trio
ALTSCHULER, BERNARD - *see*
  Lane, Audrey
ANDERSON, WALTER & HIS GOLDEN
  PHEASANT HOODLUMS - *see*
  Northwest Melody Boys
ANDREWS, MARK - *see*
  Prince, Franklin
  Retter, Prof. Frederick
ARDEN, VICTOR (& HIS ORCHESTRA)
  (*see also* WADSWORTH & ARDEN); *see*
  Armstrong, Ben's Orchestra
ARMSTRONG, LOUIS & HIS
  ORCHESTRA-*see*
  Shawne, Ted & his Orchestra
AUSTIN, LOVIE (& HER BLUES
  SERENADERS) - *see*
  Bobby's Revelers
  Hall, Goldie (& her Blues Serenaders)
  Hot Dogs
AVERY, CHARLES - *see*
  Barnes, Billie

B

BABY ARISTOCRATS BAND - *see*
  Palmetto Night Club Orchestra
BACON, FRED J. - *see*
  Anderson, Ernie
BAILEY, BUSTER - *see*
  Ward, Billy
BAILEY'S DIXIE DUDES - *see*
  Alabama Creole Band
  Kentucky Blowers
BAILEY'S LUCKY SEVEN - *see*
  Cardinal Dance Orchestra
  Jazz Harmonizers

  Seven Champions
  South Shore Melody Boys
  Sunset Dance Orchestra
BALLEW, SMITH & HIS ORCHESTRA - *see*
  Auburn, Frank & his Music/Orchestra
  Bell, Kyrle & his Orchestra
  Curran, Joe & his Orchestra
  Deauville Syncopators
  Keating, Lloyd & his Music/Orchestra
  Lem, Harold & his Orchestra
  Mason, Albert & his Orchestra
BALTZELL, JOHN - *see*
  Barton, John
  Jones, Hiram
BANKS, BILLY & HIS ORCHESTRA - *see*
  Harlem Hot Shots
BANTA, FRANK - *see*
  Andrews, Jimmy
BARNET, CHARLIE & HIS ORCHESTRA - *see*
  California Ramblers
BARTHA, ALEX & HIS HOTEL
  TRAYMORE ORCHESTRA - *see*
  Williams' Cotton Club Orchestra
BASIE, COUNT'S QUINTET - *see*
  Jones-Smith, Incorporated
BECHET, SIDNEY - *see*
  King Pops
BEIDERBECKE, BIX & HIS GANG - *see*
  New Orleans Lucky Seven
BERIGAN, BUNNY & HIS ORCHESTRA -
  see
  Causer, Bob & his Cornellians/Orchestra
  Robertson, Dick & his Orchestra
BIRDHEAD, BLUES - *see*
  Harmonica Tim
BLACKBIRDS OF PARADISE - *see*
  James, Corky & his Blackbirds
  Sherman Club Orchestra
  Them Birmingham Night Owls

BLAKE, EUBIE (& HIS ORCHESTRA) - *see*
   Black, Robert
   Blake, Ruby
   Blake's Jazzone Orchestra
   Martin, Ben & his Orchestra
   Robertson, Dick & his Orchestra
BLYTHE, JIMMY& HIS RAGAMUFFINS /
 SINFUL FIVE (*see* also BURTON & BLYTHE);
 see
   Birmingham Bluetette
   Night Owls
BOOKER, CHARLES' JAZZ BAND - *see*
   Dixie Jazz Band
BOUDINI, DAN & PHIL - *see*
   Boudini Brothers
   Brown & Edwards
   Santini Brothers
   Smith Brothers
BROWN, HENRY - *see*
   Charles, Henry
BROWN, SAMMY - *see*
   Lillard, Preston
BUFFALODIANS - *see*
   Connors, Lou's Collegians
   Yankee Ten Orchestra
BULLOCK, CHICK & HIS LEVEE
 LOUNGERS - *see*
   Causer, Bob & his Cornellians/Orchestra
BUNCH, FRANK & HIS FUZZY WUZZIES - *see*
   Alabama Fuzzy Wuzzies
   Jackson, Little Joe & his Boys
   New Orleans Strutters
BURTON, W.E. (BUDDY) & BLYTHE,
 JIMMY - *see*
   Tom & Jerry
   Williams & Moore
BURTON, W. E. (BUDDY) & HUDSON, BOB -
 see
   Black Diamond Twins
BURTON, W.E. (BUDDY) & NORMAND,
 MARCUS - *see*
   Alabama Jim & George
   Louisiana Joe & Slim
BUZZINGTON'S RUSTIC REVELERS - *see*
   Russell's Roving Revelers
   Simpkins, Joe & his Rube Band

C

CALABRESE, LOU & HIS HOT SHOTS -
 see
   Woods, Babe & his Pals
CALIFORNIA RAMBLERS - *see*
   Alamac Hotel Orchestra

Baltimore Society Orchestra
Big City Six Orchestra
Broadway Melody Makers
California Vagabonds
Californian Ramblers
Chiclet Orchestra
Collins, Roy & his Orchestra
Coreyphonic Orchestra
Cotton Blossoms Orchestra
Dixie Boys
Dixie Jazz Band
Dixie Players
Edwards, Wally & his Orchestra
Emerson Dance Orchestra
Empire Dance Orchestra
Evans, Billy's Happy Five
Five Birmingham Babies
Golden Gate Orchestra
Goofus Five
Gorman's Sundowners
Grimes, Gordon & his Orchestra
Harmograph Dance Orchestra
Harmonians
Hickory Knoll Pavillion Kings
Little Ramblers
Missouri Jazz Band
Muse Novelty Sextet
Musical Comrades
National Music Lovers (Dance) Orchestra
New York Syncopators
Oriole Dance Orchestra
Palace Gardens Orchestra
Palm Beach Serenaders
Ramblers
Rialto Dance Orchestra
Rockaway Ramblers
Samuels, Joseph's Orchestra
Saxopators
Sherman, Clarence's Dance Orchestra
Six Black Diamonds
Six Black Dominoes
Southampton Society Orchestra
St. Louis Low-Downs
Trimble, Barney & his Oklahomans
Tri-State Dance Ramblers
University Eight
University Sextette
University Six
Vagabonds
Varsity Eight
Wallace, Ted & his Campus Boys/
 Orchestra
Westerners
Whyte, Hal's Syncopators

CALLOWAY, BLANCHE & HER JOY BOYS -
see
 Armstrong, Fred & his Syncopators
CALLOWAY, CAB & HIS ORCHESTRA - *see*
 Galloway, Bob & his Orchestra
CAMEO DANCE ORCHESTRA - *see*
 Harmograph Dance Orchestra
CANDIDO, CANDY & HEIMAL, OTTO - *see*
 Candy & Coco
CANDULLO, JOE & HIS (EVERGLADES)
 ORCHESTRA - *see*
 Alamo Garden Jazzers
 Dixie Jazz Band
 Hot Henry's Lucky Seven
 Jones, Bobby & his New Yorkers
CARMICHAEL, HOAGY & SIX OTHER
 FELLOWS - *see*
 Webb, Malcolm & his Orchestra
CAROLINA CLUB ORCHESTRA - *see*
 Carolina Collegians
 Clevelanders
 Elite Orchestra
 Varsity Men
 White, Ted's Collegians
CARR, JIMMY & HIS ORCHESTRA - *see*
 Hill Top Inn Orchestra
CARSON, BUD & HIS COLLEGIANS - *see*
 Tin Pan Paraders
CASA LOMA ORCHESTRA - *see*
 Laska, Hal & his Orchestra
CAWLEY, JACK'S OKLAHOMA RIDGE
 RUNNERS - *see*
 Buster & Jack
CLAPP, SUNNY & HIS BAND O'
 SUNSHINE - *see*
 Green, Sonny & his Orchestra
CLESI, JOHNNY'S AREOLIANS - *see*
 Hill Top Inn Orchestra
 Red Onion Jazz Babies
CLIFFORD'S LOUISVILLE JUG BAND - *see*
 Martin, Sara's Jug Band
 Old Southern Jug Band
CLINTON, LARRY & HIS ORCHESTRA - *see*
 Carson, Lenny & his Orchestra
CLUB MAURICE ORCHESTRA - *see*
 Baltimore Blues Orchestra
COATES, LAWRENCE ALBERT - *see*
 Cota, El
COLUMBIA BAND - *see*
 Band
 Banda Española
 D&R (Military) Band
 Manhattan Band
 Standard (Military) Band

CONFREY, ZEZ - *see*
 O'Keefe, Jimmy
 Palmer, Dick
 Palmer, Vi
COTTON PICKERS - *see*
 Johnson's Jazz Band
CREAGER, WILLIE & HIS ORCHESTRA /
 RHYTHM ACES - *see*
 Champion Melody Boys
 Collins, Roy & his Orchestra
 Dixie Jazz Band
 Georgia Collegians
 Green, Bob's (Dance) Orchestra
 Hill Top Inn Orchestra
 James, Billy & his Orchestra
 Missouri Jazz Band
 White, Ted's Collegians
 Yankee Ten Orchestra
CROMWELL, EDMUND - *see*
 Le Sieur, Leo
 Loring, Stanley
 Ludwig, Norbert
 Walton, Normand
CROSBY, BOB & HIS ORCHESTRA - *see*
 Collins, Brad & his Orchestra
CZERWONKY, RICHARD - *see*
 Chenski, Ivan
 Provinsky, Ivor
 Provinsky, Victor

D

DANDURAND, TOMMY & HIS (WLS BARN
 DANCE) GANG - *see*
 Thomas, George & his Music
DAVENPORT, CHARLES (COW COW) - *see*
 Bat "The Humming Bird"
 Georgia Grinder
 Hamilton, George
DAVIES, RAMONA - *see*
 Ramona
DEIRO, GUIDO - *see*
 Pampini, Carlo
DEIRO, PIETRO - *see*
 Pietro
DEVINE'S WISCONSIN ROOF ORCHESTRA-
 see
 Green, Bob's (Dance) Orchestra
 Miami Society Orchestra
 Missouri Jazz Band
 Yankee Ten Orchestra
DIXIELAND THUMPERS - *see*
 Silver Slipper Orchestra

DIXON, CHARLIE - *see*
  Ames, Melville
  Sims, Harry
DODDS, JOHNNY'S BLACK BOTTOM
 STOMPERS - *see*
  Wynn, Jack & his Dallas Dandies
DORSEY BROTHERS' ORCHESTRA - *see*
  Daly Brothers' Orchestra
  Manley Brothers' Orchestra
DUBIN'S DEMONS - *see*
  Dixie Jazz Band
DUERSON, HERVE - *see*
  Barbecue Pete

E

ELLINGTON, DUKE & HIS (COTTON
 CLUB)/(FAMOUS) ORCHESTRA -
 see
  Brown, Frank & his Tooters
  Chicago Footwarmers
  Dixie Jazz Band
  Georgia Syncopators
  Greer, Sonny & his Memphis Men
  Harlem Footwarmers
  Harlem Hot Chocolates
  Harlem Music Masters
  Jackson, Earl & his Musical Champions
  Johnson, Lonnie's Harlem Footwarmers
  Jungle Band
  Louisiana Rhythm Makers
  Memphis Hot Shots
  Mills' Ten Blackberries
  New York Syncopators
  Sparling, Dick & his Orchestra
  Ten Black Berries
  Traymore Orchestra
  Turner, Joe & his Memphis Men
  Washingtonians
  Whoopee Makers
  Winters, Chick & his Orchestra
EMERSON, RALPH WALDO - *see*
  Robinson, Theodore

F

FARLEY, EDDIE (*see* RILEY & FARLEY &
 THEIR ONYX CLUB BOYS)
FENTON, CARL & HIS ORCHESTRA - *see*
  Burton, Dick & his Orchestra
FERERA & FRANCHINI - *see*
  Honolulu Trio
FERERA, FRANCHINI & GREENUS - *see*
  Honolulu Trio

FERERA & PAALUHI - *see*
  Hawaiian Serenaders
FERERA, FRANK - *see*
  Ferera, Frank (note)
FERERA, FRANK'S HAWAIIANS - *see*
  Hawaiian Serenaders
FERRARO, JAMES
  (*see* NAWAHI & FERRARO)
FIELDS, ARTHUR & THE NOODLERS - *see*
  Dixie Jazz Band
FIVE BIRMINGHAM BABIES - *see*
  Dixie Jazz Band
FIVE BROWN BROTHERS - *see*
  Brown Brothers Saxophone Quintet
FLANAGAN BROTHERS - *see*
  County Cork Trio
FRANCHINI'S SOUTH SEA SERENADERS -
 see
  Gray, Don & his Collegians
FULLER, BOB (TRIO) - *see*
  Jackson, Slim Trio
  National Music Lovers Syncopators
  Perkins, Slim
  Rocky Mountain Trio
  Three Black Diamonds
  Three Blues Chasers
  Three Happy Darkies
  Three Hot Eskimoes
  Three Jolly Miners
  Three Monkey Chasers
  Warren, Bert
  West, Theador
FULLER, EARL'S NEW YORK ORCHESTRA
 see
  Haynes' Harlem Syncopators

G

GAILLARD, SLIM & STEWART, SLAM - *see*
  Slim & Slam
GEORGE, HORACE & SNOWDEN, Q.
 ROSCOE - *see*
  George & Roscoe
GEORGIANS - *see*
  Specht, Paul's Jazz Outfit
  Specht's Society Syncopators
GILLHAM, ART - *see*
  Barrelhouse Pete
GLASCOE, PERCY - *see*
  Steamboat Joe & his Laffin' Clarinet
GOERING, AL'S COLLEGIANS - *see*
  Baltimore Society Orchestra
GOLD, LOU & HIS ORCHESTRA - *see*
  Baltimore Society Orchestra

Hollywood Dance Orchestra
Lucky Strike Dance Orchestra
Missouri Jazz Band
NML Dance Orchestra
Oriole Dance Orchestra
Virginia Creepers
Yankee Ten Orchestra
GOLDEN, ERNIE & HIS ORCHESTRA - *see*
Davidson, Jack & his Orchestra
Goodwin, Earl & his Orchestra
Russell, Bud & his Boys
Tanner, Lou & his Band
White, Ted's Collegians
GOLDMAN, EDWIN FRANKO'S BAND - *see*
Gorman, Elwood's (Military) Band
GOODMAN, BENNY (& HIS ORCHESTRA) -
see
Dodge, Bill's Orchestra
Jackson, (Shoeless) John
Kahn, Art & his Orchestra
Radiolites
Rose, Vincent & his Orchestra
Tin Pan Paraders
GORMAN'S FIRE-EATERS - *see*
Williams, Bill & his Gang
GOWAN, BRAD'S RHAPSODY MAKERS -
see
Sharp, Fred's Dixie Players
Sharp, Fred's Royal Cubans
Twin Cities Dance Orchestra
GRAINGER, PORTER - *see*
Gray, Harold
Nelson, Clarence
GRAY'S OKLAHOMA COWBOY BAND -
see
McGinty's Oklahoma Cowboy Band
GRAYSON, G.B. - *see*
Thomas, Graysen
GREEN BROTHERS NOVELTY BAND - *see*
Laurel Dance Orchestra
Smith, Fred's Society Orchestra Band
GREEN, GEORGE HAMILTON - *see*
Hamilton, George
Parks, Seymour
GREEN, LEOTHUS (PORKCHOP) - *see*
Johnson, Porkchop
GREY GULL HOUSE BAND - *see*
Artistic Trio
Astoria Dance Players
Atlanta Merrymakers
Atlanta Syncopators
Bay State Broadcasters
Cotton Pickers Orchestra
Dixie Rag Pickers

Dixie Trio
High Society Seven
Hub Syncopators
Jazzopators
Joy Dispensers
Kansas City Blue Boys
Levee Syncopators
Memphis Jazzers
Mosiello, Mike & his Radio Stars
New Orleans Pepsters
Novelty Blue Boys
Smolev, Marvin & his Syncopators
Southern Trio
Tuxedo Syncopators
Wolverine Pepper Pots
GRISSELLE, TOM & HIS ORCHESTRA - *see*
Queen City Boys
GROSSO, ELMER & HIS ORCHESTRA - *see*
Champion Dance Kings

H

HAID, BILL'S CUBS - *see*
Oriole Dance Band
HALL, FRED & HIS ORCHESTRA - *see*
Crane, Mark's Orchestra
Curran, Joe & his Orchestra
Dixie Jazz Band
Hometowners
Manhattan Musicians
NML Dance Orchestra
Roseland Dance Orchestra
HAMP, JOHNNY & HIS ORCHESTRA - *see*
Graub, Carl & his Orchestra
HARING, BOB & HIS ORCHESTRA - *see*
Dale's Dance Orchestra
Manhattan Musicians
Master Melody Makers
Society Night Club Orchestra
HAYES, NAP & PRATER, MATTHEW - *see*
Blue Boys
Johnson Boys
HAYMES, JOE & HIS ORCHESTRA - *see*
Clark, Dick & his Orchestra
Dooley, Phil & his Orchestra
Doty, Mike & his Orchestra
Everett, Eliot & his Orchestra
Harlem Hot Shots
Heins, Joe & his Orchestra
Mad Hatters
Radio Rascals
Snyder, Carl & his Orchestra
Underwood, Jimmy & his Orchestra
Wager, Roy & his Orchestra

HAYMES, JOE & HIS ORCHESTRA – *cont'd.*
  Williams' Cotton Club Orchestra
  Wilson, Duke & his Ten Blackberries
HENDERSON, FLETCHER - *see*
  Hill, Sam
  Taylor, Emmett
HENDERSON, FLETCHER & HIS
 ORCHESTRA - *see*
  Badgers
  Baltimore Bell Hops
  Broadway Melody Makers
  California Melodie Syncopators
  Carolinians
  Carr, Sreve's Rhythm Aces
  Club AlabamOrchestra
  Connie's Inn Orchestra
  Daly, Frank's Bell Record Orchestra
  Dixie Jazz Band
  Dixie Stompers
  Frisco Syncopators
  Fry's Million Dollar Pier Orchestra
  Gendron, Henri's Strand Roof Orchestra
  Harmograph Dance Orchestra
  Henderson's Wonder Boys
  High Society Seven
  Hill, Sam & his Orchestra
  Jack's Fast-Steppin' Bell Hops
  James, Billy & his Orchestra
  Lennox Dance Orchestra
  Louisiana Stompers
  Manhattan Musicians
  Master Melody Makers
  Miami Jazz Band
  Missouri Jazz Band
  National Music Lovers Dance Orchestra
  Roseland Dance Orchestra
  Savannah Syncopators
  Seven Brown Babies
  Southampton Society Orchestra
  Stokers of Hades
  Strand Roof Orchestra
  Trixie's Down Home Syncopators
  White, Hal's Syncopators
  Wilson, Duke & his (Ten) Blackberries
HENDRICKSON, HENNY'S LOUISVILLE
 SERENADERS - *see*
  Harlem Hot Shots
HIGHTOWER, WILLIE'S NIGHT HAWKS -
see
  Randall, Duke & his Boys
HIMBER, RICHARD & HIS ORCHESTRA - *see*
  Bradford, Larry's Orchestra
HINTON, JIMMY (SKEETER)
 (*see* WILSON & HINTON)

HITCH'S HAPPY HARMONISTS - *see*
  Cross Town Ramblers
  Memphis Melody Boys
HITTER, RICAHRD'S BLUE NIGHTS - *see*
  Queen City Blowers
HOTSEY TOTSEY BOYS - *see*
  National Music Lovers Dance Orchestra
HOUCHENS, WILLIAM B. - *see*
  Hawkins, Uncle Billy
  Pate, Fiddlin' Ike
HUDSON, BOB
  (*see* BURTON & HUDSON)
HUNTER, JIMMY & HIS ORCHESTRA - *see*
  Causer, Bob & his Cornellians/Orchestra
HURDY-GURDY SOLOS - *see*
  Signor Grinderino
HURTADO'S ROYAL MARIMBA BAND - *see*
  Marimba Players

I

INDIANA SYNCOPATORS - *see*
  Broadway Melody Masters
  Jazz Maters

J

JACKSON, ALEX & HIS (PLANTATION)
 ORCHESTRA - *see*
  Plantation Serenaders
JACKSON, CLIFF'S KRAZY KATS - *see*
  Smolev, Marvin & his Syncopators
  Tuxedo Syncopators
  Wolverine Pepper Pots
JACKSON, PRESTON & HIS UPTOWN
 BAND - *see*
  Golden Melody Men
JAMES, JELLY & HIS FEWSICIANS - *see*
  Memphis Daddy & his Boys
  Williams, Bill & his Gang
JENTES, HARRY - *see*
  Iantes, Harry
JOHNSON, HENRY'S BOYS - *see*
  Jones, Ginger Hank
  Perry & his Stomp Band
  Warner, Bud & his Red Caps
  Watson's Pullman Porters
JOHNSON, JAMES P. - *see*
  Johnson, Jimmie
JOHNSON, JIMMIE'S JAZZ BOYS - *see*
  Arto Blue Flame Syncopators
JOHNSON, JOHNNY & HIS ORCHESTRA -
see
  Musical Comrades

JONES, CLARENCE M. - *see*
  Wright, Clarence
JONES, ISHAM'S ORCHESTRA - *see*
  Hale, Jimmy's Orchestra
JONES' PARAMOUNT CHARLESTON
  FOUR - *see*
  Birmingham Bluetette
JONES, PIGGY'S ORCHESTRA - *see*
  Seven Syncopators
JORDAN, JOE'S TEN SHARPS & FLATS-
see
  Dixie Jazz Band

K

KALAMA MAUI ISLAND TRIO - *see*
  Leihele Trio
KARDOS, GENE & HIS ORCHESTRA - *see*
  Blaine, Rex & his Orchestra
  Calloway, Jean & his Orchestra
  Causer, Bob & his Cornellians/Orchestra
  Dickson's Harlem Orchestra
  Everett, Eliot & his Orchestra
  Gene & his Glorians
  Gloria Palace Orchestra
  Green, Harry's Rhythm Boys
  New Yorkers
  Pan-American Dance Orchestra
  Pennsylvania Collegians
  Radio Rascals
  Village Barn Orchestra, New York
KEMP, HAL & HIS ORCHESTRA - *see*
  Keene, Hall & his Orchestra
  Southland Syncopators
  White, Ted's Collegians
KIMMEL, JOHN - *see*
  Kelly, Edward
  Kimmble, John
  Kimmel, Joseph
  McConnell, Edward
KING BRADY'S CLARINET BAND - *see*
  Joe's Hot Babies
  Michall, Ernest (& his New Orleans
    Boys)
KING CARTER & HIS ROYAL ORCHESTRA -
see
  Smith, Sammy's Stompers
KING MUTT & HIS TENNESSEE
  THUMPERS - *see*
  Jackson, Frisky Foot & his Thumpers
  Johnson, Graveyard & his Gang
KING NAWAHI'S HAWAIIANS - *see*
  King's Hawaiians

KIRK, ANDY & HIS TWELVE CLOUDS OF
  JOY - *see*
  Seven Little Clouds of Joy
  Wilson, Duke & his (Ten) Blackberries
KIRKEBY, ED - *see*
  Lloyd, Ed
  Loyd, Ed
  Wallace, Ted
KRESS, CARL - *see*
  Kendall, Clyde
KRUEGER, BENNIE'S ORCHESTRA - *see*
  Baltimore Blues Orchestra
  Henderson's Dance Orchestra
  Laurel Dance Orchestra

L

LAMAR, SLIM & HIS SOUTHERNERS - *see*
  Slim & his Hot Boys
LANG, EDDIE (& HIS ORCHESTRA) - *see*
  Dunn, Blind Willie
  Tennessee Music Men
LANGE, HENRY TRIO - *see*
  Andrews Instrumental Trio
LANI'S HAWAIIANS - *see*
  Hawaiian Serenaders
LANIN, SAM & HIS FAMOUS PLAYERS /
  (ROSELAND) ORCHESTRA - *see*
  Auburn, Frank & his Music/Orchestra
  Baltimore Blues Orchestra
  Baltimore Society Orchestra
  Collins, Roy & his Orchestra
  Connor, Lou's Collegians
  Deauville Syncopators
  Dixie Daisies
  Dixie Jazz Band
  Edwards, David & his Boys
  First National Jazz Boys
  Green, Bob's (Dance) Orchestra
  Henderson's Dance Orchestra
  Hollywood Dance Orchestra
  Hughes, Phil & his High Hatters
  Imperial Dance Orchestra
  Ipana Troubadours
  James, Billy & his Orchestra
  Keating, Lloyd & his Music/Orchestra
  Laurel Dance Orchestra
  Leighton, Chester & his Orchestra/
    Sophomores
  Levee Loungers
  Lucky Strike Dance Orchestra
  Manhattan Musicians
  Mason, Albert & his Orchestra

LANIN, SAM – *cont'd.*
　Master Melody Makers
　Miami Society Orchestra
　Missouri Jazz Band
　Moore, Webster & his High Hatters
　Morris, Joe & his (Specialty) Orchestra
　New York Syncopators
　Oriole Dance Orchestra
　Oriole Varsity Ten
　Piedmont Orchestra
　Rialto Dance Orchestra
　Ring, Justin & his Okeh Orchestra
　Roseland Dance Orchestra
　Smith, Deane & his Orchestra
　University Boys
　University Orchestra
　Wanderers
　White, Ted's Collegians
　Yankee Ten Orchestra
LEI, FRANCIS & SMITH, CHESTER - *see*
　Kilaura & Hanelei
　Lei's Royal Hawaiians
LEI'S ROYAL HAWAIIANS - *see*
　Kilaura & Hanelei
　Kulani Trio
LEITHNER, FRANK & HIS ORCHESTRA -
see
　Smith, Deane & his Orchestra
LENTZ, AL & HIS ORCHESTRA - *see*
　Dixie Jazz Band
　Green, Bob's (Dance) Orchestra
　Yankee Ten Orchestra
LEONARD, HERBERT & MAYS, HARRY -
see
　Two of Spades
LEWIS, EDDIE'S TROPICAL
　SERENADERS - *see*
　Four Hawaiians
　Four Troubadours
LEWIS, MEADE LUX - *see*
　Seward, Hatch
LEWIS, NOAH'S JUG BAND - *see*
　Carolina Peanut Boys
LICHTENBERG, LEOPOLD - *see*
　Bouruchoff, Hans
　Rubens, Karl
　Von Tripp, Fritz
LOMBARDO, GUY'S ROYAL CANADIANS
see
　Hill Top Inn Orchestra
LONGO TRIO - *see*
　National Trio
LOOKOUT MOUNTAIN BOYS - *see*
　Great Gap Entertainers

LOUISE & FERERA - *see*
　Royal Hawaiian Guitars
LOUISIANA FIVE - *see*
　Scandalous Syncopators
　Yerkes' Novelty Five
　Yerkes' Southern Five
LOWN, BERT & HIS ORCHESTRA - *see*
　King Cole & his Music Weavers
　Park Central Orchestra
LUSK, MILAN - *see*
　Martin, Gustavus
LYNCH, AL & HIS ORCHESTRA - *see*
　Imperial Dance Orchestra
　James, Billy & his Orchestra
　Lynn, Al & his Orchestra
　Majestic Dance Orchestra
　White, Ted's Collegians

M

MANNONE, WINGY & HIS ORCHESTRA -
see
　Barbecue Joe & his Hot Dogs
　Williams, Speed's Orchestra
MANSFIELD, ANDY & HIS BAND - *see*
　Cotton Pickers
MARTIN, ALFRED & COOKSEY, ROBERT -
see
　Martin & Roberts
MATSON, CHARLES A. - *see*
　Watson, Charles A.
MAYS, HARRY
　(*see* LEONARD & MAYES)
McCLENNON, GEORGE - *see*
　Harlem Trio
McCOY, CLYDE & HIS ORCHESTRA
　Clyde, Billy & his Orchestra
McKAY, MARION & HIS ORCHESTRA - *see*
　Ross, Harold & his Southerners
　Williams, Bill & his Gang
McKENZIE, RED'S CANDY KIDS - *see*
　Dancing Stevedores
McKINNEY'S COTTON PICKERS - *see*
　Chocolate Dandies
　Little Aces
McMICHEN, CLAYTON - *see*
　Nichols, Bob
McPHAIL, LINDSAY - *see*
　Brown, George
MELROSE, FRANK (& HIS KANSAS CITY
　FOOTWARMERS) - *see*
　Broadway Rastus
　Harry's Reckless Five
　Kansas City Frank

ORIGINAL MEMPHIS FIVE - *cont'd.*
   Henderson's Dance Orchestra
   Hollywood Syncopators
   Jazz-Bo's Carolina Serenaders
   Kentucky Serenaders
   Ladd's Black Aces
   Lanin, Sam & his Roseland Orchestra
   Lanin's Southern Serenaders
   Majestic Dance Orchestra
   Missouri Jazz Hounds
   National Music Lovers Dance Orchestra
   New Orleans Five
   Original Dixieland Jazz Band
   Original Tampa Five
   Pasternacki's Orchestra
   Red-Hot Syncopators
   Roseland Dance Orchestra
   Southland Six
   Superior Jazz Band
   Tennessee Ten
   White Brothers' Orchestra
   Wilson, Leona & his Dixie Jazz Band
OSBORNE, WILL & HIS ORCHESTRA - *see*
   Reynolds, Dick & his Orchestra

P

PALACE TRIO - *see*
   Haynes' Harlem Syncopators
   Waters, Ethel's Jazz Masters
PARAMOUNT PICKERS - *see*
   Broadway Pickers
   Herwin Hot Shots
PAYNE, ART'S ORCHESTRA - *see*
   South Shore Melody Boys
PEABODY, EDDIE & HIS BAND - *see*
   Continental Dance Orchestra
   National Music Lovers Dance
    Orchestra
   Tricky Ten
   Yankee Ten Orchestra
PERKINS, RED'S DIXIE RAMBLERS - *see*
   Browne, Sam & his Orchestra
PETERSON, WALTER C. - *see*
   Burkhardt, Abner
PETTIS, JACK & HIS BAND - *see*
   Badgers
   Binny, Jack & his Orchestra
   Dixie Jazz Band
   Master Melody Makers
   Yankee Ten Orchestra
PLADA, FRANK - *see*
   Wailuka Serenaders

POLLACK, BEN & HIS ORCHESTRA - *see*
   Badgers
   Bennett, Phil & his Orchestra
   The Dean & his Kids
   Whoopee Makers
   Wilson, Duke & his (Ten) Blackberries
POLLOCK, HARRY'S BLUE DIAMONDS/
CLUB MAURICE DIAMONDS - *see*
   Alabama Red Jackets
   Alabama Serenaders
   Indiana Hotel Broadcasters
POWERS, OLLIE'S HARMONY
SYNCOPATORS - *see*
   Young, Clarence's Harmony Syncopators
PRATER, MATTHEW
   (*see* HAYES & PRATER)
PREER, ANDY & THE COTTON CLUB
ORCHESTRA -*see*
   Dixie Boys
PRINCE, CHARLES A. - *see*
   Adams, Charles
   Prince, Señor C.A.
PRINCE'S BAND - *see*
   Banda Española
   Columbia Band
   King's Military Band
   Manhattan Band
   Standard (Military) Band
PRINCETON TRIANGLE BAND - *see*
   Equinox Orchestra of Princeton, NJ
PURVIS, JACK & HIS ORCHESTRA - *see*
   Ayres, John's Orchestra

R

RADERMAN, LOU'S ORCHESTRA - *see*
   Yankee Ten Orchestra
RAY, ARTHUR
   (*see* MILEY & RAY)
RED & MIFF'S STOMPERS - *see*
   Six Hottentots
   Southland Syncopators
RED FLAME KAZOO TRAVELERS - *see*
   Traveling Musketeers
REDMAN, DON & HIS ORCHESTRA - *see*
   Causer, Bob & his Corenllians/Orchestra
   Harlan, Earl & his Orchestra
   Williams, Duke & his Orchestra
REEVES, REUBEN & HIS RIVER BOYS - *see*
   Hollywood Shufflers
RESER, HARRY'S ORCHESTRA - *see*
   Bluebirds
   Clevelanders
   Dixie Jazz Band

SELVIN, BEN & HIS ORCHESTRA – *cont'd.*
  Leighton, Chester & his Orchestra/
    Sophomores
  London, Sid & his Orchestra
  Marlow, Rudy & his Orchestra
  Whiteman, Paul & his Orchestra
  Whitney, Jack & his New Yorkers
SENTER, BOYD & CHICAGO DE LUXE
  ORCHESTRA - *see*
  Red Hotters
SHAW, JOEL & HIS ORCHESTRA - *see*
  Harlem Wildcats
SHAW, THEODORE - *see*
  Shaw
SHILKRET, NAT'S VICTOR ORCHESTRA -
  see
  Virginians
SIEGEL, AL & HIS ORCHESTRA - *see*
  Broadway Melody Makers
  Wade's Moulin Rouge Orchestra
SISSLE, NOBLE & HIS ORCHESTRA - *see*
  Missouri Jazz Band
SISSLE, NOBLE & HIS SIZZLING
  SYNCOPATORS - *see*
  Brown, Willie & his Sizzling Syncopators
SIX BLACK DIAMONDS - *see*
  Dixie Jazz Band
SIX HOTTENTOTS (RED & MIFF'S
  STOMPERS) - *see*
  Dixie Jazz Band
  NML Dance Orchestra
  Southampton Society Orchestra
  White, Ted's Collegians
  Yankee Ten Orchestra
SMECK, ROY - *see*
  Alabama Joe
  Hawaiian Serenaders
  Small, Ralph
SMITH, CHESTER
  (*see* LEI & SMITH)
SMITH, JABBO'S RHYTHM ACES - *see*
  Four Aces & the Joker
  Rhythm Aces
SNOOKS & HIS MEMPHIS RAMBLERS -
  see
  Friedman, Ben's Paramount Hotel
    Orchestra
SNOWDEN, Q. ROSCOE
  (*see* GEORGE & SNOWDEN)
SOUTH SEA ISLANDERS - *see*
  Hawaiian Serenaders
STANLEY, FRANK C. - *see*
  Grinsted, William Stanley
  Williams, George S.

STATE STREET RAMBLERS - *see*
  Blue Jay Boys
  Blythe's Blue Boys
  Chicago Stompers
  Jeffries, Speed & his Night Owls
STEVENS, ERNEST L. - *see*
  Falkenburg, Franz
  Osborne, Harry
STEWART, SAMMY'S ORCHESTRA - *see*
  Golden Gate Orchestra
STEWART, SLAM
  (*see* GAILLARD & STEWART)
STILLMAN, JACK & HIS (ORIOLE)
  ORCHESTRA - *see*
  Maynard, Sid & his Orchestra
  O'Neil, Jack's Orchestra
  Silent Joe & his Boys
STRAIGHT, CHARLIE & HIS ORCHESTRA
  see
  Frisco Syncopators
  Harmograph Dance Orchestra
SWETAMAN, WILBUR - *see*
  Johnson, Ed
  Sannella, Andy
  Wilber, C.
SWEATMAN, WILBUR'S ORIGINAL JAZZ
  BAND - *see*
  Texas Jass Band
SYLVESTER, JOHNNY & HIS ORCHESTRA -
  see
  Hollywood Dance Orchestra
  Jones, Billy & his Orchestra
  Jones, Bobby & his New Yorkers
  Memphis Melody Players

T

TAMPA RED & HIS HOKUM JUG BAND - *see*
  Smith, Honey Boy's Bingham Band
TAYLOR BROTHERS - *see*
  T&T Trio
TEAGARDEN, JACK & HIS ORCHESTRA - *see*
  Carroll, Roy & his (Sands Point)
    Orchestra
  Cloverdale Country Club Orchestra
  Imperial Dance Orchestra
  Keyes, Frank & his Orchestra
  Majestic Dance Orchestra
TEMPO KING & HIS KINGS OF TEMPO -
  see
  Chicago Rhythm Kings
TENNESSEE TEN - *see*
  Jack's Fast-Steppin' Bell Hops

WILLIAMS, JOHN & HIS MEMPHIS
  STOMPERS - *see*
    Helms, Bud & his Band
WILSON, GEORGE & HINTON, JIMMY - *see*
    Wilson, Chicken & Hinton, Skeeter
WOLVERINES - *see*
    Jazz Harmonists

Y

YERKES' MASTER PLAYERS - *see*
    Brown, Joe's Alabama Band

Swift, Sammy's Jazz Band
YOUNG, VICTOR & HIS ORCHESTRA -
  see
    York, Vincent & his Orchestra

Z

ZEEMAN, BARNEY'S KENTUCKIANS -
  see
    Jack's Fast-Steppin' Bell Hops
ZUCCA, MANA - *see*
    Kiriloff, Efrem

About the Compiler

ALLAN SUTTON is an independent researcher.